BEST DOG HIKES
COLORADO

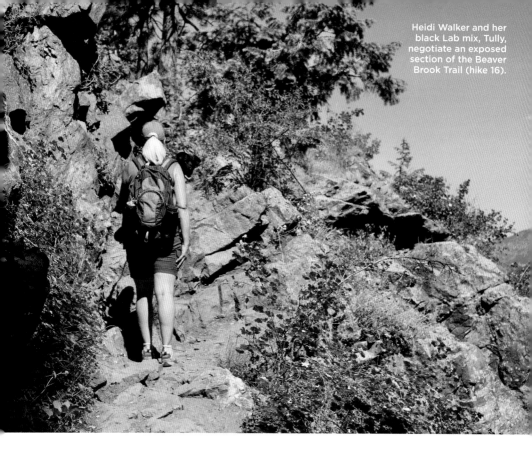

Heidi Walker and her black Lab mix, Tully, negotiate an exposed section of the Beaver Brook Trail (hike 16).

BEST DOG HIKES COLORADO

SECOND EDITION

Emma Walker

FALCONGUIDES

GUILFORD, CONNECTICUT

For my parents, Tim and Heidi

FALCONGUIDES®

An imprint of The Rowman & Littlefield Publishing Group, Inc.
4501 Forbes Blvd., Ste. 200
Lanham, MD 20706
www.rowman.com

Falcon and FalconGuides are registered trademarks and Make Adventure Your Story is a trademark of The Rowman & Littlefield Publishing Group, Inc.

Distributed by NATIONAL BOOK NETWORK

Copyright © 2019 The Rowman & Littlefield Publishing Group, Inc.

Photos by the author unless otherwise noted
Maps by Melissa Baker

British Library Cataloguing in Publication Information available

Library of Congress Cataloging-in-Publication Data available

ISBN 978-1-4930-4129-9 (paperback)

ISBN 978-1-4930-4130-5 (ebook)

∞™ The paper used in this publication meets the minimum requirements of American National Standard for Information Sciences—Permanence of Paper for Printed Library Materials, ANSI/NISO Z39.48-1992.

Printed in the United States of America

CONTENTS

Overview

MEET YOUR GUIDE

EMMA WALKER grew up on the Colorado Front Range, where she hiked with a series of loyal family pups (mostly Labradors) throughout her childhood. She earned a degree in English from the University of Colorado at Boulder, then moved to Anchorage, Alaska, in search of adventure. While she was there, she also earned a master's degree in outdoor and environmental education. Emma is a Wilderness First Responder and Leave No Trace Master Educator, and has worked as a whitewater raft guide, avalanche educator, and camp counselor. She's also a freelance travel and adventure writer whose work has been published in *Outside*, *Trail Runner*, and *Powder*. Emma lives with her husband and their loyal dog, Bodhi, in Boise, Idaho, where she hits the trails whenever she can to hike, bike, and ski. She is perpetually in training for an ultramarathon or a big ski trip, and while she isn't particularly fast, she loves nothing more than spending a day outside.

Map Legend

═══〔70〕═══ Interstate Highway	Continental Divide National Scenic Trail
═══〔34〕═══ US Highway	Bridge
═══〔72〕═══ State Highway	Campground
═〔FR 2361〕═ County/Forest Road	Capital
═══════ Local Road	Cavern/Cave/Natural Bridge
= = = = = = Unpaved Road	Radio Tower
= = = = = = Jeep Trail	Gate
┝━┿━┿━┿━┥ Railroad Tracks	Horse Trail
━━━━━ Paved Trail	Mountain Peak/Summit
━ ━ ━ ━ ━ Featured Trail	Parking
‐ ‐ ‐ ‐ ‐ ‐ Trail	Pass
·················· Off-Trail Hike	Picnic Area
—·—·—·— Continental Divide	Point of Interest/Structure
‐ ‐ · ‐ ‐ · ‐ State Line	Ranger District Office
Body of Water	Restroom
Marsh/Swamp	Spring
River/Creek	Town
Intermittent Streams	Trailhead
National Park/National Forest	Tunnel
National Monument/ Wilderness Area	Water
Local/State Park/Wildlife Refuge	Waterfall
Miscellaneous Fill	Viewpoint/Overlook
	Visitor/Information Center
	Wheelchair Accessible

INTRODUCTION

In my early twenties, I had an energetic black Labrador mix, Lucky. He was probably about a year old when I got him. I didn't quite trust him off leash for the first few months—he'd disappear for longer than I was comfortable with, and though he always came back, I was uneasy about what he was getting into out of my sight. Eventually, as we got to know each other better, Lucky stuck a little closer to me when we hiked.

This was a dog who loved hiking so much he'd lope big, joyous circles around me, often barking incessantly when I stopped to take a break. He simply couldn't contain his excitement. I often told friends Lucky probably covered twice as much mileage as I did on any given hike. One day I stuck a GPS unit in his doggie backpack as we set off from the trailhead, and lo, when we made it back to the car, I'd covered six miles; Lucky had run nearly ten.

"A tired dog is a good dog," according to my mother. She used to say it about the yellow Labs we had throughout my childhood, who tended to destroy newspapers and couches when left to their own devices without being walked first. This was true of Lucky, too. He was on his best behavior after a long hike, and the more elevation we covered, the better.

Lucky isn't around anymore, but I've still got a canine hiking companion. My cattle dog mix (we've christened his "breed" the West Texas Dirt Dog: a perpetually grubby, floppy-eared, medium-sized mix bred for maximum snuggling), Bodhi, is his best self when he's been well exercised. This sometimes means getting up early for a pre-work jog or, failing that, a walk around the block. In a pinch, he'll make do with a half-hour of fetch at the dog park. But what he really wants to do is hike.

There's something special about hiking with a dog. When Bodhi and I hike—whether we're doing our usual neighborhood jaunt (Nightbird Gulch in Golden) for the dozenth time, or walking through the woods somewhere new altogether, he physically acts out everything I'm feeling. He stops to take in smells. He watches chirping birds, cools his paws in every stream, lifts his chin and closes his eyes when we're hit by a pleasant breeze. The whole time, his tail is wagging. Bodhi feels the same way I do about exploring Colorado's forests and mountains: It feels good to be outside.

When I watch him pounce on a grasshopper or race circles around me, I always think the same thing. *What did we do to deserve dogs?*

I'm not sure, but one way to repay the favor—for our beloved pets so enrich our lives—is to take them along on our adventures. The Centennial State is the perfect place to do it: Something like 35 percent of land in Colorado is public land. We have thousands of miles of trails, many of them dog-friendly; there's no shortage of opportunities to hit the trail with your pooch. I hope this book will help you and your dog get out there.

WHAT'S DIFFERENT ABOUT HIKING WITH YOUR DOG?

When you head out for a hike, you likely begin by packing a backpack. That's one of the first things new hikers are instructed to do: pack what we call the ten essentials. The idea is that what's in your pack varies depending on what you're doing and how long you're planning to be out, but there are some crucial items you should *always* have with you. Conventional wisdom holds that on every hike, your backpack should include: navigation (map and compass and/or GPS), a headlamp and extra batteries, sun protection, a first-aid kit, a knife, a way to start a fire, a shelter (this could simply be a layer warm enough to sustain you overnight, even if it's a bit uncomfortable), and extra food, water, and clothing.

Hitting the trail with your dog requires some additional preparation. You'll need to add a few items to your ten essentials (more on that in a moment), but you'll also need to do some additional research: Are dogs allowed at your intended destination? Do they need to be on a leash? Of course, dog regulations vary depending on where you're headed, but here are a few rules of thumb to get you started.

GENERAL OVERVIEW OF REGULATIONS

More often than not, you can find out whether dogs are allowed at a given destination by running a quick Internet search for the land manager's website. In the western United States, the vast majority of land you'll be hiking on is public land; some of it is federally owned and operated, while other tracts are run by the state or local counties, and even cities.

FEDERAL LAND

Federal land includes public land operated by the National Park Service (NPS), including national parks and national monuments, the USDA Forest Service (USFS), and the Bureau of Land Management (BLM). All three agencies operate land in Colorado.

In general, US national parks do not permit dogs on trails. In some parks, dogs may be allowed in campgrounds and parking lots on a six-foot leash—but that's it. With that in mind, don't bring Fido to Rocky Mountain National Park, Colorado National Monument, or Black Canyon of the Gunnison National Park and expect to take him for a hike.[1]

Land operated by the USFS and BLM, in general, allows dogs. You may occasionally encounter areas or parts of trails that are closed seasonally for, say, elk calving or raptor nesting, but things are a little less closely regulated in national forests and on BLM land. If you're required to leash your dog, the land manager's website or a sign at the trailhead typically notes that regulation. Wherever you bring your dog, of course, you should always plan to pick up after them.

---

1   Great Sand Dunes National Park and Preserve is an exception to this rule. Dogs are allowed in the Preserve section of the park, but not in most backcountry areas. Visit www.nps.gov/grsa/planyourvisit/pets .htm for more-detailed information.

STATE, COUNTY, AND CITY LAND

There are forty-one state parks open to the public in Colorado, and all are operated by Colorado Parks and Wildlife (CPW). Dogs are allowed in most of those parks;[2] where dogs are allowed, they must be kept on a six-foot leash. Some parks have designated dog off-leash areas, including Cherry Creek State Park, which is a great place to work on off-leash training with your dog (see page 29) and Chatfield State Park. The dog off-leash areas in both parks require a daily fee on top of your park entrance fee—you can purchase an annual pass or pay on a daily basis at the entrance station. Keep your paper off-leash permit with you; it's likely a ranger will ask you for it, and they're not shy about ticketing visitors without permits.

County and city open space parks are where things get a little murkier, since regulations very widely—and, of course, since there are dozens of cities and counties that operate open space in Colorado. In Boulder, for example, you'll need a Boulder County–specific Voice and Sight Tag that indicates you and your dog have passed a test and he's under voice control.[3] Just one county to the south, in Jefferson County, dogs must be kept on a ten-foot or shorter leash on all open space trails, and owners are subject to a fine if they're cited.

Your best bet, for non-federally or state-owned and -operated land, is to check the land manager's website or give them a quick call to ask about dog regulations. Where dogs are allowed, do your part to keep it that way by letting only well-behaved, non-aggressive dogs off leash and packing out your pup's waste.

LAND ACKNOWLEDGMENT

Many of the hikes in this book are on land that I'm referring to as "public land." While that is true in the sense that it is now open for recreation to the American public, I want to respectfully acknowledge that these hikes take place on the traditional lands of several indigenous nations, including the Apache, Arapaho, Cheyenne, Comanche, Kiowa, Navajo, Pueblo, Shoshone, and Ute People, who have stewarded this land throughout the generations. For more information on the specific people whose ancestral land your hike is on, you can visit https://native-land.ca/.

WHAT YOU'LL NEED TO BRING

If an extra person were tagging along on your hike, your party would need to bring enough extra snacks, water, and layers to sustain them. The same goes for your dog. You won't necessarily need to replicate the ten essentials—your dog doesn't need a headlamp, for example, though you might consider attaching a light to his collar so you can keep

---

2   Dogs are not allowed in several Colorado state parks, including Roxborough State Park. Regulations vary by park—some have wildlife refuge areas; others allow dogs only on certain designated trails—so be sure to check the park's individual website or call park management before you show up expecting to hike with your dog.

3   The Voice and Sight Tag program began in 2006, and dogs who are enrolled may be off leash (and, as the name of the program indicates, within their owner's line of sight and under voice control, meaning they'll come back when called) on certain designated trails. Where indicated, dogs must remain on leash. Regardless of their Voice and Sight status, all dogs are prohibited from the following open space areas in Boulder County: Caribou Ranch, Dodd Reservoir, Hall Ranch, and Heil Valley Ranch. For more information on taking part in the Voice and Sight Tag program, visit https://bouldercolorado.gov/osmp/voice-and-sight.

track of him, should you find yourself on the trail at night—but you'll definitely need to modify or add to your usual packing list, to a certain extent.

FOR DAY HIKING

Your daypack already includes the ten essentials for you, and you can make slight adjustments to the ten essentials to accommodate your dog in case of an emergency, too. Some things will remain the same: Unless your dog is a genius, they won't need their own map and compass (although I definitely recommend replicating Lucky's and my GPS experiment, if only for the sake of amusement), knife, or fire-starting equipment. Still, there are some adjustments to make:

- **First Aid.** Bring along enough medical supplies to apply first aid in case of a doggie emergency. If you tend to carry a fairly robust first-aid kit (the preassembled ones you'll find at any outdoor gear store are a good bet), that might be enough. Consider throwing in an extra ACE bandage, which comes in handy for applying pressure to bleeding wounds (and keeping them clean) when your patient isn't going to hold a bandage in place.

- **Food.** If you're just headed out for a day hike, consider bringing along a few dog treats you know your dog will eat. Dogs burn calories just like humans do, and it won't hurt to toss them a snack when you stop for a break.

- **Water.** Dogs can get dehydrated, too. Do some research before your hike to determine whether there's water available along the trail. If there's not, you'll definitely need to bring along plenty of extra water for your pooch—I have a one-liter water bottle specifically reserved for slobbery dogs to drink out of. (If your dog thinks he's people, like mine does, he may drink directly from a water bottle. Otherwise, you'll need to bring along something for him to drink out of. Most outdoor gear stores sell lightweight, collapsible bowls for this very purpose.)

    If there is water along the trail, you have a choice to make. Most people don't drink directly from water sources in the wilderness without purifying it. There are numerous options out there for purifying your water: You can filter it, use a UV light, add purification tablets or iodine, or do it the old-fashioned way and bring it to a rolling boil over a camp stove. Experienced hikers all have their preferred method, and it's a frequent topic of debate; each method has its merits and its deficiencies.

    In any case, even if water *looks* clear, it's likely filled with all kinds of contaminants—you never know if an animal has died upstream (more commonly a concern in desert regions, especially on open cattle ranges), what predators have been defecating in the water, or, of particular concern with Colorado's mining-heavy history, what heavy metal residue might be lurking in even the cleanest-looking mountain stream.

    If there are no obvious contaminants, some folks choose to let their dogs drink directly from water sources along the trail. This is convenient because it means not having to carry additional water, which adds significant weight to your pack. It does, however, mean you run the risk of having your pup contract giardia or some other gastrointestinal disease—it's not a guarantee, but certainly a consideration.

- **Layers.** Whether your dog will be warm enough, should you find yourselves caught in a sudden storm or spending the night out, depends greatly on your dog.

That's what fur is for, right? If you've got a husky mix or other long-haired dog, that's probably true. A lot of shorter-haired breeds, though, don't thermoregulate as well in extreme temperatures. This is a matter of knowing your dog: If you've noticed them getting the shivers in colder temperatures, consider bringing along a doggie jacket if you're heading into the high alpine or on a longer hike.

FOR BACKPACKING

Most of what you'll need to bring on a backpacking trip with a canine plus-one is the same as what you'd bring for a day hike. The primary difference is the additional food and shelter you'll need to provide, and how you'll carry those items to your campsite.

- **Food.** If you'll be spending the night out, you'll need to bring along your dog's usual evening and morning meals. One thing that makes this easier is that unlike the fancy freeze-dried meals popular with backpackers, you won't need to do any additional planning for your dog's backpacking dinners and breakfasts: The usual kibble will do just fine. Like you, your dog has likely burned significantly more calories than on a typical day, so consider bringing along some extra food to help replenish that lost energy. This isn't an exact science, but if you're not sure how much extra food your dog needs, consult with your vet to figure out an appropriate ratio.

- **Sleep system.** One complicating factor of backpacking with a dog is where they'll sleep. If you've got a small- or medium-sized pooch (and if, like me, you're not a particularly light sleeper), you can likely get away with squeezing them into your own sleeping bag. The added benefit here is that your dog acts as a little furnace, keeping you warm even on chilly high-altitude nights.

    If your dog is bigger—or if, reasonably, you're not willing to share your sleeping bag—you'll need to figure out another system. Some folks bring along dog-specific sleeping bags, though for my money, an old synthetic puffy jacket works just as well and is significantly less expensive. (I specify synthetic because a down jacket will make a gigantic mess when your pup inevitably claws a hole in it.) Consider testing out your sleep system on a shorter, lower-consequence trip (maybe somewhere at lower elevation, where you're less likely to shiver through a miserable night if your system isn't yet up to par) before you head out for a challenging multiday trip.

- **Dog backpacks.** It's appealing to saddle your dog with a backpack to carry his own supplies. Not only does it cut weight from your own pack (and look cute), the extra weight might wear out an energetic dog a little faster—at least, that was always my plan with Lucky the black Lab. Before you load up a backpack for your dog, though, consider whether it's in their best interest.

    The conventional wisdom is that dogs shouldn't be made to carry more than a quarter to a third of their own body weight, and for some dogs, even that's a stretch. How much weight your dog can carry, and whether they should carry any weight at all, depends on their fitness, the terrain you'll be covering, and the environmental factors of your hike (e.g., will it be especially hot or cold?).

    If you do choose to have your dog carry their own food, collapsible bowl, and other supplies, make sure you're weighting the backpack evenly. Most dog backpacks are set up like saddlebags, so the dog is carrying half the weight on either side, rather than centered directly on the spine. If you weight one side more heavily than the other (just like in your own backpack), it'll not only be uncomfortable, but can actually get caught up on branches along the way and cause rubbing or even sores.

PREPARING YOUR DOG TO HIT THE TRAIL

Hiking is more fun when you're in great shape. You can hike farther and faster, and you'll spend more mental energy on enjoying your surroundings than on feeling exhausted. So it is for dogs. We often think of our canine companions as being endlessly energetic, but they, too, have varying levels of fitness.

You can get your pooch ready for hiking season by spending the winter and spring months doing some basic conditioning, both for mental and physical fitness.

DOG-SPECIFIC LEAVE NO TRACE AND ETIQUETTE

If you've spent some time on the trail, you've likely heard of the concept of Leave No Trace (LNT). In essence, LNT means minimizing one's impact on the natural world and on other users when traveling in wilderness areas. There are seven LNT principles: Plan Ahead and Prepare, Travel and Camp on Durable Surfaces, Dispose of Waste Properly, Leave What You Find, Minimize Campfire Impacts, Respect Wildlife, and Be Considerate of Other Visitors.

The Leave No Trace Center for Outdoor Ethics has published extensively about the application of LNT principles for dogs (visit lnt.org for more information). I can't say it any better than they already have, but there are a few principles in particular that merit special attention.

DISPOSING OF WASTE

This is such a hot topic—and, unfortunately, such a source of conflict—between dog owners and other trail users that it would be easy to make picking up dog waste a whole section of this book. I'm not going to do that (who wants to spend that much time talking about poop?). Instead, I'm going to boil it all down to one big idea: Pick up after your dog!

There is, occasionally, some nuance to the disposal of dog waste. If you're on a day hike, there's really no excuse not to pick up after your dog. Many trailheads now provide bags specifically for dog waste pickup, but you should come equipped with your own (preferably one or two more than you think you need) so you don't come up short if that's not the case.

If you've hiked more than a handful of miles on your local trails, you've likely noticed something I consider a pet peeve (no pun intended): neon-colored bags, filled with dog poop, sitting on the side of the trail. Probably most people who leave these bags there really do intend to pick them up later, but unfortunately, that doesn't always happen. People forget altogether, or they're tired, or they don't remember the spot where they stashed their bag and walk right by it on the way back to the trailhead. And then there's a bright blue or green bag full of dog waste sitting on the trail until some other good citizen decides to pick it up and throw it away.

I get it. It smells bad! It's no fun to smell your dog's poo throughout your hike, though some would argue that's part of the cost of bringing one's dog on a hike—and that other hikers, who are not the owners of your dog, shouldn't have to look at or smell it, either. There are some workarounds for this. Bring along a plastic grocery bag or even an extra dog poo–specific bag to double-bag the doo, which can help contain the smell and keep it from leaking if you stick it in an outside pocket on your backpack. Many pet stores and outdoor gear stores also sell handy, leak-proof nylon pouches, which you can stick bagged poo in. They work surprisingly well, and you can reuse them. In short: Picking up after your dog is not an option.

Of course, this gets more complicated when you're on an overnight or multiday trip. Study the regulations for waste management in the area where you'll be traveling: What are humans supposed to do with their waste? Bury it? Pack it out? Make your dog waste plan accordingly. You won't go wrong if you're willing to pack out your dog's poop. If, on the other hand, you're bringing along a trowel to bury your own waste, keep an eye out when your dog's doing the deed so you can bury theirs, too.

RESPECT WILDLIFE

You can explain to humans why they shouldn't harass wildlife, but that doesn't stop everybody from approaching bison and bears and moose to take selfies. Dogs, on the other hand, have limited ability to understand language and a much stronger prey drive than we do, so it's even tougher to keep them from chasing critters.

This is largely a matter of knowing your dog. Sure, most dogs are interested in squirrels and rabbits and deer. We can't hold that against them; it's in their nature. But if they tend to chase those critters, and particularly if they have a habit of venturing far off trail in order to chase them, you'll need to make some changes. Dogs who chase wildlife are not only in danger of being hurt themselves—the terrain out of your sight could include cliffs to fall off, or the creature they're chasing may retaliate; more on this on page xxi— they're also disrupting the natural ecosystem.

Even if your dog doesn't manage to catch up to that elk or deer they're after, those animals need every calorie they've got on board in order to survive. Wasting a lot of energy on running away from Fido can have dire consequences for wildlife and, at certain times of the year, can even be fatal.

With that in mind, consider whether your dog is a good candidate to be off leash, even if there's no regulation prohibiting you from doing so. If they're not quite there yet, you may very well be able to get those prey instincts under control with diligent training. If not, you and your dog can certainly still enjoy your hikes on leash.

CONSIDER OTHER VISITORS

Most of the aforementioned reasons to keep your dog from harassing wildlife apply to other trail users, too. If you're on a multiuse trail, ensure that your dog doesn't chase mountain bikers or equestrians. Even if you're headed somewhere that's hiker-only, remember that (hard as it may be to believe for those of us who adore dogs) not everyone is comfortable around dogs. You may know your pooch to be a friendly, lovable fellow, but some folks are afraid of dogs or, understandably, simply don't want to be jumped on by a strange dog.

Remember, too, that folks with dogs who are nervous or aggressive may choose (responsibly!) to keep their dogs on a leash. If your pooch is off leash and comes bounding up to a dog who doesn't play well with others, it's a recipe for disaster—and in this scenario, you're in the wrong.

The big picture here is that dogs should only be allowed off leash if they're under voice command. See page xix for resources on training your dog.

GET YOUR PUP TRAIL-READY

Dogs need physical conditioning to be trail-ready, just like humans do; that means slowly working your way up in terms of mileage and difficulty, and, if you're using a backpack, gradually adding weight over time. That's all fairly straightforward, and you can find dog-conditioning plans written by experts in dog physiology online by running a quick search. There are, however, a number of other things to consider as you get ready to hit the trail with your dog:

- **Dewclaws.** Dogs are born with dewclaws (a fifth digit) on their front legs, and some dogs have dewclaws on their back legs, too. Some folks have their dogs dewclaws removed, since they're more likely to tear, especially at the nail. If it's not done during early puppyhood, though, this is painful and more likely to cause complications. If your adult dog is the owner of a set of dewclaws, your best bet is to keep the nail fairly short.

- **Nails.** Since dogs don't wear sturdy hiking boots or shoes with traction, like humans do, they rely on their claws. Keep these fairly short to avoid tearing, but not so short that your pup has no traction on slippery surfaces. Some dogs are active enough that their nails are worn down naturally, but if your dog's nails aren't ground down on their own, you'll need to get them trimmed. If you're not comfortable doing this yourself, check with your vet or head to a kennel or groomer, most of whom offer this service fairly inexpensively and can do it quickly and painlessly.

- **Feet.** Like the calluses on human hands and feet, the pads of your dog's paws get fairly tough over years of walking on various surfaces. Still, if you're hiking on especially rough terrain, your dog's paws may get worn down or tender. Keep an eye out for limping; if you check the culprit paw and don't find anything caught between the pads, this may be the problem. If you think this may be a problem for your dog, consider carrying a set of dog booties in your first-aid kit. These don't have to be the expensive specialty kind, though those are certainly nice to have, if your dog will tolerate them. You can pick up a fairly inexpensive set from a dog-mushing retailer online; this is what Iditarod mushers use for their dogs, and they work great in a pinch.

- **Vaccinations.** Before you hit the trail, make sure your dog is up to date on all their vaccinations. In Colorado you'll want to make sure your dog is vaccinated against rabies and Distemper/Parvo/Bordetella (DA2PPV), both of which are three-year vaccines. Many Colorado veterinarians also advise dog owners to get on a monthly preventative heartworm supplement, which comes in the form of a meat-flavored tablet most dogs find irresistible.

- **Grooming.** If your pooch has long hair, you'll be happier later if you keep it well trimmed, especially in the spring and fall shoulder seasons, which tend to be muddy in Colorado. This is true in the winter, too, when balls of snow and ice often form on long fur and between the toes. If balled-up snow and ice in the paws tends to be a problem for your pooch, consider trying out Musher's Secret, which helps prevent uncomfortable ice buildup.

TRAINING RESOURCES

Your dog needs some training to be the best pooch they can be. Some dogs are certainly easier to train than others—some of this is based on breed characteristics, and some if it is simply that, like humans, dogs each have their own personalities.

I'm not an expert in dog training. I've typically trained my dogs simply by repetition and positive reinforcement: I take them hiking all the time, and, especially when they're young, I carry treats to reward them for coming back when I call them. So far, that's worked fairly well for me, though I realize not every dog is so cooperative.

The Cherry Creek State Park Dog Off-Leash Area (hike 6) is a great spot to start working with your dog off leash. If you're looking for more-specific resources, consider stopping by your local pet shop or shelter, many of which have relationships with local trainers with good reputations.

As far as written resources, the *Whole Dog Journal* has a thorough breakdown of what goes into good off-leash training, including some specific drills to try with your dog.[4] *Outside Online* has also published a more-hiking-specific primer on training dogs to be off leash.[5]

HAZARDS ON THE TRAIL

As with most things worth doing, there are some risks to hiking with dogs. They include a lot of the same risks humans take when we go out on the trail, with the added complication that dogs can't explain to us how they're feeling or what's wrong. With that in mind, you'll need to keep an eye out for a few key potential dog hazards, including some that are specific to Colorado.

FLORA

Poison ivy is less common in Colorado than in many parts of the country (if you've hiked much in the southeastern United States, you'll be pleasantly surprised how much less frequently you run into it in the Centennial State). Still, it's around, and you should be able to recognize it and keep your pooch away from it. The plant has a distinctive three-leaved shape (poison oak is similar, but with shiny leaves) and grows low to the ground. The oil from the plant can get trapped in your dog's fur, causing you to react when you touch him; if your dog has short hair, poison ivy may cause a reaction on particularly hairless areas, like their belly and armpits. If you find that one or both of you is having a reaction, topical cortisone cream will provide some relief.

There are also some poisonous plants that may make your dog sick. Most dogs are pretty discriminating when it comes to eating plants, so it's not necessarily a likelihood you'll catch your dog munching on rhododendrons or Japanese yew. If your dog does start acting strangely and you suspect poisoning, though, make a note of what they've eaten and head back to the trailhead, where you can call poison control and figure out your next steps.

---

4   www.whole-dog-journal.com/issues/5_3/features/Building-Off-Leash-Reliability_5440-1.html.
5   www.outsideonline.com/2201211/how-train-your-dog-walk-leash.

FAUNA

We've already discussed at length why it's important to keep your dog under voice control so it doesn't harass wildlife. That's true both for predator-type animals and those that fall into the prey end of the food chain. As a general rule, if there have been recent sightings of a predator in the area, it's smart to keep your dog on a leash. There are also some specific considerations to keep in mind for the various critters you might run into on the trail.

PREDATORS

Most predators in Colorado are even less interested in running into us than we are in encountering them. If you do run into any charismatic megafauna, though, there are a few rules of thumb that may help keep the situation from escalating. Do your best to keep your dog close to you, preferably on a leash; if they run away, they'll appear to be prey, and if they attack, the odds are not in their favor.

- **Bears.** As a general rule, black bears (we don't have grizzlies or brown bears in Colorado) are quite afraid of humans, and as long as you're being smart about not leaving food or other smelly items (toiletries like toothpaste, for example) out overnight, you'll likely avoid bears altogether. If you do run into a black bear, talk to it in a loud, calm voice and back away slowly. Black bears often bluff when they charge (which they're likeliest to do if you surprise them, so make some noise when you hike in bear country), so stand your ground. Fight back if you're attacked.

- **Mountain lions.** Big cats are among the most formidable predators in Colorado, and they're a compelling reason to keep your dog on a leash, particularly if you happen to be hiking in an area they're known to frequent or where they've been sighted recently. Again, stand your ground. Make yourself as big as possible, and make plenty of noise—yell loudly and confidently; if you're lucky, your dog will join you in barking. Don't turn your back on the cat, and if it begins to advance, feel free to throw rocks or whatever else you can reach for in its direction. If you're attacked, fight back.

- **Snakes.** There are plenty of snakes in Colorado, and many species are harmless. Their slinky movements are often very interesting to dogs, so if you're hiking somewhere known for rattlesnakes (North Table Mountain in Golden is a good example; I've rarely hiked there during the summer months and not seen a rattler), keep your dog on a leash. It's exceedingly rare that adult humans die from rattlesnake bites, but it takes less venom to kill a dog than it does a human. The antivenin is terribly expensive (think thousands of dollars), and that's if you make it to a vet in time. Your best bet is prevention. Don't let your dog go off trail if you're hiking in rattlesnake country, and keep a keen ear out for that telltale rattle.

INSECTS

- **Mosquitoes.** Mosquitoes make the top of the list because they have a knack for ruining any trip where they show up. They're irritating, and can also carry diseases that can be dangerous to dogs, including West Nile virus and heartworm. Applying DEET isn't an ideal solution, since dogs lick themselves to stay clean and can get sick from ingesting those chemicals. You can use more-natural remedies, including organic eucalyptus solutions, to keep mosquitoes at bay. I've also been known to put a fleece on my dog to keep bugs away when the mosquitoes were especially thick.

- **Ticks.** Ticks are less common in Colorado's super-dry climate than in many parts of the country, but they do still exist. Since they carry Rocky Mountain spotted fever and Lyme disease, you should make a habit of checking your dog for ticks whenever you've been hiking anywhere wet or heavily wooded.

    Look for ticks in cracks and crevices: behind and under your dog's ears, around the neck, near the eyes, under the tail, and so forth. If you find one before it's latched on, that's great, since things get a little trickier once they've got their mouthparts attached to their host.

    It can be tough to get your dog to hold still long enough to safely remove a tick, so if you've got a companion (or a handful of tempting treats), you'll likely have an easier time. The key is not to leave the tick's head in place, so use tweezers to grasp the tick as close to the skin as possible. Give one steady pull to remove the tick, and then wash your hands and the spot you just removed the tick from. If you've had to remove a latched-on tick, check in with your vet as soon as you get home. In that case, try to get a photo of the tick before getting rid of its remains so you can show the vet.

PREY

- **Elk and deer.** On a scale from "fight" to "flight," these ungulates fall just about as close as possible to the flight end of things: If they're chased, they are going to run. This is bad for the wildlife (as mentioned earlier, stressors like this can have big consequences for wildlife), but there are potential dangers for your dog, too. Unfortunately, many dogs have been injured or killed by taking big falls while chasing wildlife, so that's a good reason to leash your dog if you see critters out and about. And while elk and deer are often docile, there are occasional exceptions. During the fall elk rut (mating season), bull elk can become quite aggressive, and those big antlers can cause serious damage.

- **Moose.** These giants hardly belong in the prey category; they're enormous and can easily trample a dog. (They also have razor-sharp hooves and knee joints that allow them to kick in four different directions.) Moose are often aggressive, so keep your distance and leash your dog if you spot one, particularly if they're accompanied by a calf.

- **Goats.** Mountain goats aren't native to Colorado, but they're here nonetheless. You'll find them in high alpine areas, particularly above tree line. Unfortunately, many mountain goats in Colorado are habituated, and they can be fairly bold about approaching humans—and less likely to flee from dogs. They've been known to charge and even gore dogs, so keep your distance and keep your pooch close if you spot them.

- **Sheep.** Many bighorn sheep populations in Colorado are vulnerable, and a stressful interaction with an overly enthusiastic dog is the last thing they need. Those giant horns are also attached to a very thick skull, used for literally butting heads with other sheep. Keep dogs away so they're not victims of an angry head-butting.

ENVIRONMENTAL HAZARDS

Think about how you plan ahead for a hike: If you think you will be especially hot or cold, apply those principles to your dog. For the most part, they're capable of thermo-regulating—their fur and panting mechanisms can generally keep them at a comfortable temperature. When the mercury really starts to rise or fall, though, there are precautions you can take to keep your pup comfortable.

HEAT

It's easy to dismiss Colorado's summer temperatures—it's a dry heat, after all—but despite the lack of humidity, it's possible to suffer from heat exhaustion and heat stroke, particu-larly when there's no shade, as is often the case on the Eastern Plains and in the high des-ert of western Colorado. Reduce your dog's risk of suffering from heat-related illness by starting your hike early (this has the added benefit of getting you back to the car before those reliable afternoon thunderstorms roll in). You should also plan to carry plenty of water and give your dog frequent opportunities to drink it. If you come across a stream or pond, give your pup the chance to wade in and cool off. If you've got some extra water, you can also dump a little on your dog's head and back to help keep them cool.

COLD

Dogs can get frostbite just like people, and are particularly vulnerable on their ears, paws, and other extremities. If you'll be hiking on snow or ice, carry some booties or Musher's Secret, which gives you a backup plan if your dog's paws are chafed on the snow or keep collecting balls of ice.

If your dog is of the short-haired variety, consider investing in a jacket; several manu-facturers make specialized dog jackets. If you're going to buy one expensive, specialized item for your dog, make it this one; a jacket that fits well can keep your dog so much happier even when it's miserably cold and wet out.

Most of the hikes in this book are best done in the spring through fall, not in the winter, when they're under feet of snow. Still, depending on when you go, you may encounter occasional patches of deep snow. In this case, encourage your pup to walk in your tracks, which makes it much easier for them to make progress without flotation.

Cold weather also means the advent of hunting season in many parts of Colorado. That means your dog could be mistaken for a game animal, so if you're hiking in the fall, consider outfitting your dog with an orange vest to make it clear that they're not game.

EXPOSURE

"Exposure" is hiker- and climber-speak for the risk of falling, essentially. If you're hik-ing along an exposed ridgeline, for example, you might look to either side and see sheer drop-offs. If the risk (or consequence) of falling is especially high, the exposure is more significant. Of course, people have different tolerances for exposure: Some are fine with it, while others freeze up when they're around it, or avoid it altogether. Dogs are the same way: Some will trot right along, while others become terrified and refuse to keep moving.

You won't find serious exposure on many of the hikes in this book, since it doesn't mix well with dogs; why put your dog in that situation if you don't need to? Should you find yourself facing the possibility of exposure, know your dog. Make sure you have a backup plan in case your dog isn't thrilled about the exposure. More than one pup has gotten stuck and had to be rescued from notoriously exposed hikes like the Sawtooth Traverse between Mount Bierstadt and Mount Evans.

Avoid becoming part of this statistic by working up to exposure slowly and avoiding coaxing your dog to do anything they're clearly uncomfortable with.

A WORD ABOUT THE FOURTEENERS

Colorado is home to more than 50 peaks over 14,000 feet above sea level, or Fourteeners, as they're affectionately called. Many of the Fourteeners are Class 1 or 2 hikes, meaning they're on a well-marked trail the whole way. These peaks—especially those of the nontechnical variety—are enormously popular among Coloradans, and for good reason: It's a great way to challenge yourself, test your fitness, and see how your body performs at high altitude.

Understandably, lots of folks bring their dogs with them to hike the Fourteeners. You'll find one Fourteener hike included in this book, but that's it. Why? For the most part, Fourteener hikes aren't inherently especially dog-friendly, and this book is focused on hikes that are great for dogs. Your pup may be able to do the hike, but a number of factors make them less than ideal for lots of dogs:

- **They're crowded.** The standard route on a Fourteener might see hundreds of ascents on a given summer weekend, while a peak just a few miles away might see just a handful. Unless your dog is the sort who just walks along right next to you, it can wear thin to constantly have to rein them in, especially on a narrow trail.

- **They're at high altitude.** Despite extensive research, there's no hard-and-fast rule as to what causes altitude sickness in people; you might be fine on one Fourteener ascent and come down with a terrible headache and nausea on the next one, and researchers aren't sure why. Dogs certainly can't tell you when they've got a headache, but keep an eye on them in case they're acting oddly as a result of the lack of oxygen.

- **Much of the hike will be above tree line.** When you're hiking up to more than 14,000 feet above sea level, much of your day will be spent above tree line, meaning you won't be sheltered from sun, wind, precipitation, or lightning. It's one thing to put yourself in that position, but unfortunately, dogs have been killed by lightning strikes on Colorado Fourteeners in the past. It's just another reason to get an early start and keep a close eye on the weather.

- **There's a greater possibility of exposure.** Not all Fourteeners have a great deal of exposure, but many standard routes (even the less-technical ones) feature sheer drop-offs, narrow trails, and trails marked only by cairns (stacks of rocks), meaning there's a chance of getting off trail and ending up somewhere you can't retreat from. Having a four-legged friend along only complicates this scenario, and many dogs are squeamish about exposure.

- **Scree and loose dirt are tough for dogs on a leash—and the humans on the other end.** Due to their high-altitude nature, many Fourteener trails have long sections of scree, or loose dirt and small rocks on a steep-angled section of the trail. If your dog is capable of being well-behaved off leash, this may not present much of a challenge, but if your guy is on a leash, it can be tough to avoid dragging each other downhill and losing your balance as you both try to maintain your footing (especially if your dog tends to pull).

That's not to say you shouldn't take your dog with you to hike a Fourteener! If you know your dog—and are comfortable with the risk you're taking on by bringing them along, just as you would be with any other hike—then suit up, get an early start, and get out there. (Bodhi has accompanied me on nearly a dozen Fourteener hikes, and has always been a happy camper.) It does mean, though, that there are some additional concerns to take into account on a high-altitude hike.

HOW TO USE THIS GUIDE

The 52 featured hikes in this guide offer a sample of Colorado's beautiful and varied terrain and its fascinating geology, flora and fauna, and human history. Hikes range from easy to strenuous, but your dog can go with you on every hike in this book, either on leash or under voice control.

Please realize that trail locations and conditions, roads, and signage are subject to change over time. Trail mileage is as much an art as a science, even for land managers. Times change and so do trail conditions. Remember to check with the appropriate land management agency for current fees, regulations, and trail information before heading out, and then have a great hike!

DOGS UNDER CONTROL

Under Canine compatibility in the hike specs, the words "Dogs must be under control" mean dogs can be off leash but must be under immediate voice control. If you cannot control your dog by voice command, regulations typically require the dog be leashed. According to the Colorado Division of Wildlife, harassment of wildlife (even chasing squirrels) by dogs and humans is illegal in Colorado.

LEVELS OF DIFFICULTY

This hike rating system was developed from several sources and personal experience. These difficulty levels are meant as guidelines; the trails may prove easier or harder depending on ability and physical fitness. Hikes are rated by having one or more of the noted characteristics.

Easy—4 miles or less total trip distance in one day; elevation gain less than 600 feet; paved or smooth-surfaced dirt trail; less than a 6 percent grade average

Moderate—Up to 8 miles total trip distance in one day; elevation gain of 600 to 1,200 feet; a 6 to 8 percent grade average

Difficult—Up to 12 miles total trip distance in one day; elevation gain of 1,200 to 2,500 feet; an 8 to 10 percent grade average

Most difficult—Up to 16 miles total trip distance in one day; elevation gain of 2,500 to 3,500 feet; trail not well defined in places; a 10 to 15 percent grade average

Strenuous—Mainly reserved for peak climbs or canyon descents; greater than 15 percent grade average

EASTERN PLAINS

Colorado's **EASTERN PLAINS** are largely ignored by much of the hiking community. But if you're writing off the Great Plains region of Colorado, you're missing out on nearly half the state! It's true, the plains aren't teeming with majestic peaks, like much of the western part of the state, but eastern Colorado is beautiful in its own way: Where else but in the West do you see wide-open spaces and big skies like this? (It's also no slouch in terms of elevation; the lowest point in the state, near the Nebraska border, still sits at 3,337 feet above sea level.)

The Eastern Plains do harbor more private land than much of the rest of the state, where the US Forest Service and Bureau of Land Management administrate much of the real estate. But there's still plenty of hiking to do out east. A word to the wise: Unlike many popular mountain hikes, where you'll have trouble finding a spot to park your car on a busy summer weekend, you may very well still find solitude on the trails of the plains region.

Facing page: Dinosaur Trackway in Picketwire Canyon (hike 2)

1 HOMESTEAD TRAIL

WHY GO?

The Homestead and Arch Rock Trails travel across a variety of landforms and through human history. Rock art dating from 2,000 years ago to the modern era is pecked and painted onto canyon walls. An equinox carving exists in a crack on a canyon wall. Remains of homesteads from the late 1800s and early 1900s dot the landscape. Hells Half Acre, a rock arch, numerous little canyons, springs, a forlorn windmill, windblown plains, prairie flowers, and juniper trees are just some of the sights you'll see as you hike this loop. Watch for great horned owls!

THE RUNDOWN

Start: From the Picture Canyon Picnic Area
Distance: 8.5-mile loop (9.5 miles if you include three spur trails)
Approximate hiking time: 3 to 5 hours
Difficulty: Moderate due to length
Elevation gain: 570 feet (280 feet, plus another 290 feet in undulations)
Seasons: Best in spring and fall. Summer can be very hot, and winter can bring blizzards and snow.
Trail surface: Dirt trail, forest roads, shortgrass prairie

Other trail users: Equestrians, mountain bikers, motorists (in a few places), hunters (in season)
Canine compatibility: Dogs must be on leash. Water is scarce along the trail, so bring your own.
Fees and permits: None
Maps: USGS Campo SW and Tubs Springs
Trail contacts: Comanche National Grassland, Carrizo Unit, Springfield; (719) 523-6591; www.fs.usda.gov/psicc
Other: There's no garbage service available here—pack it out!

FINDING THE TRAILHEAD

From the junction of US 287/385 and US 160 in Springfield, drive south on US 287/385 for 16.4 miles to just south of mile marker 13. Turn right onto Baca CR M. The road is wide and well-graded dirt, but it can have washboards. The rest of the drive to the trailhead in the Picture Canyon Picnic Area is on maintained dirt roads. Drive 9 miles west to BCR 18 and turn left (south). Drive another 7.9 miles to the entrance to Picture Canyon Picnic Area and turn right onto FR 2361. The road splits in 0.6 mile; take the left branch. The picnic area is another 1.4 miles south. **GPS:** N37 00.73' / W102 44.66'

THE HIKE

Most people think of eastern Colorado as a flat, uninspiring expanse, but the southeastern corner bordering Oklahoma is full of interesting canyons, rock formations, wildlife, reptiles, birds, and human history.

There's evidence of people dwelling in Picture Canyon as far back as 2,000 years ago. The canyons provided their inhabitants with abundant wildlife and shelter from the elements, and supported wet bottomlands and running streams and springs, which made life in the canyons even more attractive. The first inhabitants were hunter-gatherers. By AD

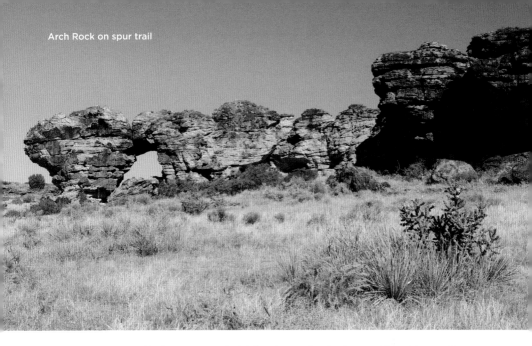
Arch Rock on spur trail

1000, farming enabled a more-settled lifestyle. In Crack Cave within Picture Canyon, ancient residents carved lines onto the wall. Experts surmise the markings may have been used to help with crop planting and harvesting, or to indicate ceremonies. During spring and fall equinox, the sun's rays illuminate these lines at sunrise. Because of vandalism, a locked gate now prevents the casual visitor from entering the cave, but festivals held in spring and fall allow a limited number of people to see the sunrise illumination.

On a side spur just under half a mile from the trailhead, numerous petroglyphs and pictographs are displayed on the canyon wall. A sea that covered much of Colorado back in Cretaceous times (about 100 million years ago) deposited these sandstone cliffs. Depictions of horses indicate that some of the artwork was done as recently as 500 years ago. Sadly, in more-recent times, visitors have carved or painted initials and drawings over preexisting artwork. It's sometimes hard to tell what is old and what is new. In one large opening, look for parallel lines carved in the rock. Some people believe these lines to be related to *ohgam* writing, an alphabet used in the British Isles from about AD 0 to 500. Some of the drawings have been interpreted as compasses and sundials, as well as equinox indicators.

The Antiquities Act of 1906 and the Archaeological Resources Act of 1979 protect rock art and homestead ruins. Please respect the rock art by not touching it. Others arriving after you want to see original, not scarred, rock art. Touching rock art with hands, chalk, or even paper can hasten deterioration; plus, it can interfere with new archaeological dating techniques.

The Jicarilla Apache are known to have inhabited this area since the early 1600s, and the Comanche arrived around 1700. In 1541 the conquistador Coronado claimed this land for Spain during his search for the legendary cities of gold. By 1846 the United States had declared ownership of the region. Cattle barons grazed their herds on the endless grasslands in the 1870s and 1880s. Homesteaders arrived between 1890 and 1926 in search of a new life. But making a living was tough in the arid climate. A continuous water supply was of utmost importance, and visitors today can still see the remains of rock houses close to the springs at Crack Cave and Cave Spring.

Unfamiliar with the dry climate, settlers practiced ranching and farming methods they had brought from wetter homelands. Overgrazing and plowing methods combined to damage the fragile land. Several drought years, in conjunction with the normally windy weather, blew away the topsoil in the Dust Bowl of the 1930s. By 1938 farmers and ranchers were broke and begged the federal government for relief. A federal land purchase program was created, and between 1938 and 1942 the government bought thousands of farms, totaling 11.3 million acres of land. The USDA Forest Service was assigned to manage 5.5 million of these acres, and in 1960, 4 million acres were designated a national grasslands, where restoration efforts continue today. The US Forest Service currently manages 200 grazing allotments in Comanche National Grassland.

The prairies also attract diverse wildlife, including approximately 275 species of birds, 40 of reptiles, 9 of amphibians, 11 of fish, and 60 of different mammals, including bear, mountain lion, bobcat, coyote, deer, and antelope. (**Caution:** Watch for rattlesnakes in the grass, rock crevices, and ruins. Keep your dog on leash in these areas.)

Although the trail is decently marked, this hike is often an exercise in *Where's the next trail marker?* Occasionally markers have fallen over or are farther apart. Trail markers consist of juniper logs with white paint on top, rock cairns, and carsonite posts (like highway reflector posts, but brown). Some trail sections follow forest roads. Three spurs are included in the hike description: one to rock art, one to homestead ruins and Crack Cave (closed), and the other to a rock arch and rock molar.

MILES AND DIRECTIONS

0.0 Start at the trail register box by the Picture Canyon Picnic Area after checking out the big interpretive sign with the trail map and three smaller signs.

The Homestead Trail quickly joins a nonmotorized two-track road—turn left. Elevation: 4,300 feet.

0.4 A faint trail heads left near a sign about protecting Indian pictures and carvings. (*Side trip:* You can turn left here to see the rock art on the canyon walls. It's about 0.4 mile out and back. Return the way you came and turn left onto the road to continue on the Homestead Trail.)

0.6 Arrive at a trail and road junction. The road goes left and the Homestead Trail makes a very sharp right onto a singletrack trail. Take the Homestead Trail, following the wooden posts with white tops. GPS: N37 00.40' / W102 45.01' (*Side trip:* You can continue on the two-track road slightly to the right to the base of the cliff, where you'll see house ruins and Crack Cave [closed]. This spur is about 0.3 mile out and back.)

0.8 Arrive at a check dam and the HOMESTEAD TRAIL AND ARCH ROCK TRAIL sign with a left arrow. Turn left and walk across the check dam, continuing to curve left to the next post. Turn right and walk up the trail. Some juniper trees almost cover the trail, and it crisscrosses a little dry creek several times. Keep following the wooden posts.

1.1 The trail forks. The right fork is a hiker bypass trail and offers an interesting glimpse of Hells Half Acre. The Homestead Trail goes left and is better marked. Turn left onto this trail, which soon makes a left turn to climb up out of the canyon. Continue following wooden posts. (*Note:* Watch out for yucca plants—members of the lily family—as their pointy leaves tend to hurt if you bump into them.)

1.3 Reach the ridgetop. The trail tread disappears, so follow the white-topped posts. GPS: N37 00.55' / W102 45.39'

1.7 Cross a doubletrack trail just before the next wooden post. At the post a sign indicates the horse trail goes right and the hiker bypass goes left. GPS: N37 00.85' / W102 45.61'. Turn left and follow the cairns down into a little slickrock canyon, following more cairns and the rock-lined trail. (*Note:* Toward the bottom, if there's water in a pond, look for little frogs. You'll also see Indian marbles on the nearby rocks.)

1.9 Arrive at the junction where the Homestead Trail and Arch Rock Trail split. Turn left onto the Homestead Trail. (*Side trip:* It's worth the 0.25-mile out-and-back hike on the Arch Rock Trail [the right fork] to see the arch and molar [as in tooth] rock.)

2.8 The trail intersects a road (FR 2361.E). Turn left and walk down the road.

3.25 An old rock house is on the right. An OKLAHOMA STATE LINE sign is on the left.

3.5 Cave Spring is on your right. (*Note:* Although the water comes from a spring, the Forest Service suggests treating it as a safety precaution.) Continue walking down the road, which turns into a singletrack soon after Cave Spring. The trail heads through a wonderful cottonwood grove, then across a lush grassy area.

3.9 Arrive at the ruins of an old homestead. Look for the wooden post at the top of the slickrock. The trail goes up the slickrock.

4.75 Arrive at a broken windmill. The trail turns right. The trail tread disappears. Follow the white-topped trail posts.

5.25 The trail leads to a post at the canyon edge. GPS: N37 01.06' / W102 46.80'. Look for rock cairns as the trail drops down into the next canyon. Walk a little right, follow the water line down the slickrock, and then turn a little left. You'll see some big cairns. Follow them down to the canyon bottom.

5.4 Arrive at a dirt road (FR 2361.L) and turn right, walking on the road, which is the Homestead Trail.

0   Kilometer   1

0   Mile   1

N

To Campo

18

D

COMANCHE
NATIONAL
GRASSLAND

Homestead Trail

FR 2361

Windmill

Arch Rock Trail

HOLT CANYON

Arch Rock

Homestead Trail

HELLS
HALF
ACRE

Homestead Trail

CANYON

Homestead Trail

Check Dam

Crack Cave
House Ruins

Rock Art

House Ruins

Cave
Spring   House
Ruins

PICTURE

COLORADO
OKLAHOMA

5.7 The road forks. Take the left fork (FR 2361.E).

5.8 The road forks. Take the right fork (FR 2361.E).

6.25 The Homestead Trail turns right off FR 2361.E at a sign. Follow the trail right, up a little canyon of sorts and past some interesting rock formations. Continue following wooden posts. As you reach the high area, head to the post on the right. The trail curves right here as the tread disappears.

6.8 Reach the junction of Arch Rock and Homestead Trails. GPS: N37 01.28' / W102 45.67'. Go straight (southeast); do not turn right. Continue on Arch Rock (also Homestead) Trail, ignoring any doubletrack trails.

7.3 Turn left up an open area, following the posts. GPS: N37 01.17' / W102 45.21'. Once up on the ridge, turn right, and walk along the high area for a while, heading generally southeast.

8.0 At the post the trail starts heading downhill to FR 2361 (the road to the picnic area). Follow the cairns down a little slickrock area.

8.2 Reach FR 2361. Turn right and walk down the dirt road.

8.5 Arrive back at the trailhead.

2 PICKETWIRE CANYONLANDS

WHY GO?
Picketwire Canyonlands is a trip back in time. You'll visit early homesteads and a mission, and even see evidence of dinosaurs. It is a beautiful rimrock canyon with junipers, cacti, grasses, cottonwoods, and the Purgatoire River. Once down in the wide canyon, the hike is mostly gentle, with a few hills. Intricately carved headstones in an old cemetery, and dinosaur tracks from 150 million years ago, are the highlights of this hike. The dinosaur track site is the largest documented in North America.

THE RUNDOWN

Start: From the Withers Canyon Trailhead
Distance: 10.8 miles out and back
Approximate hiking time: 5.5 to 7 hours
Difficulty: Strenuous due to distance
Elevation gain/loss: 150-foot gain / 415-foot loss, including undulations
Seasons: Best in spring and fall
Trail surface: Dirt road, mainly doubletrack, sometimes rocky, with one steep section
Other trail users: Equestrians, mountain bikers, hunters (in season), 4WDs during tours
Canine compatibility: Dogs must be on leash
Fees and permits: None
Maps: USGS Riley Canyon and Beaty Canyon; USDA Forest Service Comanche National Grassland

Trail contacts: Comanche National Grassland, La Junta; (719) 384-2181; www.fs.usda.gov/psicc
Other: No camping allowed in the canyon. Primitive camping is allowed on top of the canyon near Withers Canyon Trailhead. A vault toilet, pullouts, and fire grates are available year-round. Camping is also available at Picketwire Corrals, along with a vault toilet. Visiting equestrians may use the corrals for their horses. Only day use is allowed in the canyon itself, and a dusk-to-dawn closure order is in effect. Bring water. If you want to cross the river to explore more of the dinosaur track site, bring old shoes with you. Be careful crossing, because the tracks create drops in the streambed.

FINDING THE TRAILHEAD
From La Junta, drive south on CO 109 for 13.6 miles (past mile marker 43) to FR 2200, with a sign to Vogel and Picketwire Canyons. Turn right onto FR 2200 and drive about 8 miles to Otero CR 25, also with a sign for Picketwire Canyonlands. Turn left and continue for 6 miles to FR 2185. Turn left at Picketwire Corrals. FR 2185 is to the left of the vault toilet. Drive 3.3 miles to Withers Canyon Trailhead and park. **GPS:** N37 39.59' / W103 34.22'

THE HIKE
Comanche National Grassland was established in 1960 and remains one of the exclamation points of Colorado's Eastern Plains region. The US Forest Service has managed some 435,000 acres of Comanche National Grassland since it was charged with rehabilitating the area in 1954. The government bailed out Dust Bowl victims whose property had been rendered virtually worthless by poor farming techniques and overgrazing;

thanks to revegetation efforts and the protection of natural grasses—still ongoing—the grassland today serves as both a wildlife habitat and a playground for human recreation. Conservation and control methods have also allowed for the reintroduction of livestock grazing.

Humans have lived in the Purgatoire Valley for perhaps as long as 10,000 years. Experts place rock art in the canyonlands between 375 and 4,500 years old. Spanish explorers first came to the area in the 1500s, when the Purgatoire Valley was verdant and full of wildlife. Legend has it that a group of early Spanish military explorers met their deaths in the Purgatoire Valley. It's not clear how they died, but in any case, they're thought to have died before having their last rites administered, and so the river that courses through the canyon was named El Rio de las Animas Perdidas en Purgatorio (the River of Lost Souls in Purgatory). French trappers who wandered into the canyon during the eighteenth century shortened the name to Purgatoire. Settlers struggled with the French pronunciation, and the river became known as Picketwire. (By the way, Purgatoire is

IF YOU MEET A RATTLESNAKE

Rattlesnakes tend to avoid humans. They will strike if surprised, threatened, or hassled, so be extra alert with your dog. Watch where you step or where you put your hands on rocks or ledges. If it's really hot, snakes rest in shaded areas. In spring and fall they try to warm up in sunny areas. If you see or hear a rattlesnake, *freeze!* Make sure your dog is under control or on leash. That may be hard to do, but rattlesnakes strike at motion and heat. Stand still and look for the snake. Be quiet until the snake calms down, uncoils, and slithers away. Follow the 30/30 Rule: If you see a rattlesnake, back at least 30 feet away and wait 30 seconds for it to slither away. Back away slowly, and bring your dog with you.

pronounced "purgatory" in these parts; in Colorado we have a knack for mispronouncing place names.)

Jicarilla Apache hunted and farmed the area for about a century, between 1620 and 1720, after which the Comanche took control. French traders and trappers arrived prior to 1800 and hunted the plentiful beaver down to very low levels. Without a healthy beaver population to build and maintain dams, the pools and marshes of the Purgatoire River disappeared. Today you see a small river meandering along a broad valley between rimrock walls.

Leave the parking area by the bulletin board, pass through a wide opening in a fence, sign the trail register, and descend to a pipe gate. Be sure to close any gates behind you once you've passed through. From the gate the trail drops steeply through the rimrock layer of Withers Canyon, losing 250 feet in the next 0.25 mile. Right after the trail joins another doubletrack road in Purgatoire Canyon, ruins of an old homestead appear on the right. The trail goes up and over a few side ridges, bringing you close to the cliffs. Farther upstream, remains of adobe walls rise from the ground just past the RIVER WATER sign. (You'd be smart to treat any river water before drinking it.)

Just a little farther down the trail are the remains of the Dolores Mission, with its small cemetery. In 1871 Damacio Lopez led twelve families here, where they remained for two generations. The little headstones are intricately carved with a variety of symbols (like hearts) and inscribed with dates between 1896 and 1900. They are fragile and several are broken, so avoid touching them. A vehicle turnaround for guided tours is located here. A smoother dirt road takes you to the dinosaur track site another 1.6 miles upstream.

Envision yourself here 150 million years ago. Imagine a large lake of about 6 miles in diameter, set in a semiarid region. Algae, snails, minute crustaceans, fish, and horsetail

Purgatoire River and trail

Picketwire Canyonlands

plants live in and along the lake. Watch as a group of brontosaurs walk along the shore, side by side. Come another time, as brontosaurs and two-legged dinosaurs use the area heavily, trampling anything underfoot. Visit yet another time to see three-toed carnivorous dinosaurs, perhaps allosaurus, walk near the lake. Today interpretive signs explain the fossil footprints.

By the river the three-toed footprints jump out at you. Compare your foot size with theirs. Depending on the river flows, tracks can sometimes be filled with mud. The brontosaur tracks lie on the south side of the river. They extend for 0.25 mile and contain about one hundred different trackways with 1,300 visible footprints. Dinosaur science has not progressed enough to verify which dinosaurs created the tracks; however, current speculation includes members of the brontosaur order (large terrestrial plant eaters) such as brachiosaurid, camarasaurid, and diplodocid families, and the theropod order (terrestrial carnivores) such as allosaurus. Take care while you're here—help to preserve the tracks for future generations. If you wander off trail, remember the US Army's Pinyon Canyon Maneuver Site is just north of Picketwire Canyonlands and is off-limits, besides being dangerous.

MILES AND DIRECTIONS

0.0 Start at the Withers Canyon Trailhead. Elevation: 4,630 feet.

0.05 Arrive at the trail register. Turn left onto Picketwire Trail.

0.2 Reach a pipe gate and walk around it.

0.9 Reach the intersection with a nonmotorized dirt road (doubletrack) in Purgatoire Canyon and turn right. GPS: N37 39.73' / W103 33.70'

1.1 Reach the remains of an old homestead.

3.5 Reach the remains of old adobe buildings.

3.8 Reach the Dolores Mission ruins and cemetery.

5.1 The road forks. Take the left road branch to reach the vault toilet and the trail to the dinosaur track site. Turn left.

5.4 Stop and read the interpretive signs before looking for tracks along the riverbank (both sides). Elevation: 4,360 feet. GPS: N37 37.05' / W103 35.78'. Return the way you came.

10.8 Arrive back at the trailhead.

3 DAWSON BUTTE RANCH OPEN SPACE

WHY GO?

The loop trail in Dawson Butte Ranch Open Space winds gently through ponderosa pine and Gambel oak (oakbrush) forest and across several meadows on the south side of Dawson Butte. Occasionally you get glimpses of the tops of Pikes Peak and Devils Head, along with the ridge of the Rampart Range to the west. This open space features separate bridle trails complete with over sixty horse jumps. The area is excellent wildlife habitat with a good diversity of birds. With a picnic table almost halfway around the loop, this trail provides for a leisurely hike.

THE RUNDOWN

Start: From the Dawson Butte Ranch Trailhead on the north side of the parking lot

Distance: 5.0-mile loop

Approximate hiking time: 1.5 to 2.5 hours

Difficulty: Moderate due to distance

Elevation gain: 320 feet (including undulations)

Seasons: Best Apr through Nov—you can cross-country ski or snowshoe when there's enough snow

Trail surface: Natural surface trail

Other trail users: Equestrians and mountain bikers

Canine compatibility: Dogs must be on leash

Fees and permits: None

Maps: USGS Dawson Butte; Douglas County Open Space Dawson Butte Ranch Trail map at www.douglas .co.us/openspace/Dawson_Butte_ Ranch.html

Trail contacts: Douglas County Open Space, 100 Third St., Castle Rock; (303) 663-7495; www.dcoutdoors.org

FINDING THE TRAILHEAD

From Castle Rock, head south on I-25 to exit 181, Plum Creek. At the traffic light, go straight ahead on the Frontage Road. Drive south 5.3 miles to Tomah Road. Turn right (west) onto Tomah Road, cross the railroad tracks (coal trains may take a long time to clear the crossing), and drive 1.6 miles to the Dawson Butte Ranch entrance on the right. A portable toilet and picnic tables are located by the parking lot. Bring your own water, as none is available along the trail. There is no access or trail to the top of Dawson Butte, both to protect wildlife and because part of the top is private property. Please stay on established trails. **GPS:** N39 17.70' / W104 55.23'

THE HIKE

In June 1820 Major Stephen H. Long set out from the area around Council Bluffs, Iowa, with a group of nineteen men under orders from the Secretary of War to explore the Platte River and its tributaries. His expedition included a naturalist, a landscape painter, a zoologist, and a physician with a background in geology and botany. The expedition's physician, Dr. James, kept a detailed diary of the trip, in which he described vegetation, climate, fauna, geology, and geography. On July 10 the group arrived at and described

Dawson Butte framed by ponderosa pine

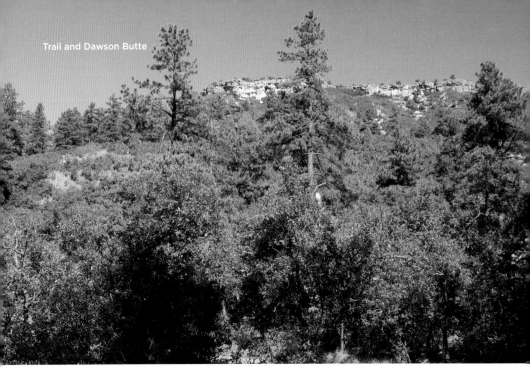

Dawson Butte; three day later, Dr. James and two others started to ascend Pikes Peak. (They summited in the late afternoon on July 14.)

Some forty years later, Thomas Dawson established squatters' rights on the area below the butte that now bears his name. He became the first postmaster at nearby Bear Canyon.

Dawson's name also became attached to the sandstone formation that makes up a good portion of the buttes and cliffs east of the foothills in Douglas County. About 70 million years ago, the Rocky Mountains started slowly rising, and Pikes Peak, a huge block of granite, emerged. While the mountains rose, erosion wore them down, creating large alluvial fans at their bases. No buttes existed back in those early times. Instead, dinosaurs like triceratops, as well as crocodiles and turtles, roamed what is now the plains. In the temperate climate fig trees, palms, magnolias, willows, and maples grew instead of today's ponderosa pines. The coarse eroded granite from Pikes Peak became the 55-million-year-old white-and-buff rock (mostly quartz and feldspar) called "Dawson Arkose." Petrified wood is the most common fossil found in this formation. Some layers erode very easily, leaving behind the many buttes along I-25, such as Castle Rock and Dawson Butte, as well as hoodoos (rock columns weathered into interesting shapes). The caps on the buttes are held together by a harder, iron-containing rock layer that covered the looser rocks, pebbles, and sand. Imagine this area 50 million years ago when no buttes existed—only a high plain at the base of the mountains.

Today Gambel oak (oakbrush) and ponderosa pines have replaced palms and magnolias. Oakbrush produces small acorns, about 1 inch long. Native Americans shelled the nuts and soaked them in water to release the bitter tannic acid. Then they ground the nuts into acorn meal that became bread, mush, and pancakes. Deer enjoy browsing oakbrush, while birds and bears eat the acorns. Oakbrush only grows roughly south of Morrison (CO 74) on the eastern slope of the Colorado Rockies, but on the western slope it grows in most locations between 5,500 to 10,000 feet.

Ponderosa pines live in dry, warm places between 5,500 and 9,000 feet elevation. Trees can grow 150 feet tall and 3 to 4 feet in diameter. Bigger trees may live 300 to 500 years. Their needles are long and grow in packets of two or three. Some people say the bark smells like butterscotch. The bark of a mature ponderosa is fairly thick and fire-resistant. However, if the fire reaches the tree's crown, then the tree will burn. Douglas County thinned the ponderosa forest in 2009 to provide more space between the trees to suppress potential wildfires.

The Chapman Young family owned the Dawson Butte Ranch between 1950 and 2004. Douglas County purchased 828 acres of land from the family between 2004 and 2007, with help from Great Outdoors Colorado, the Douglas County Open Space fund, and some private donations. The land is protected by a conservation easement, meaning it cannot be developed or subdivided. Douglas Land Conservancy holds the conservation easement, while Douglas County owns the land. A little piece of private property exists in the middle of this open space area, so please respect the property owners' rights. The Youngs designed and created many horse paths and jumps on their property. The county selected sixty of the jumps and kept them for local equestrians to enjoy with their horses.

Douglas County was especially interested in the Dawson Butte Ranch because of the good wildlife habitat. The land also supports a diversity of birds. Some that come to nest at Dawson Butte Ranch include prairie falcons, ovenbirds, western tanagers, and black-headed grosbeaks. The Audubon Society sponsors a Christmas bird count over about a three-week period starting in mid-December each year, and Dawson Butte Ranch Open Space is one of their locations. Results are used to study the status of wintering bird populations across North America and to create strategies for habitat protection and resolution of any environmental threats.

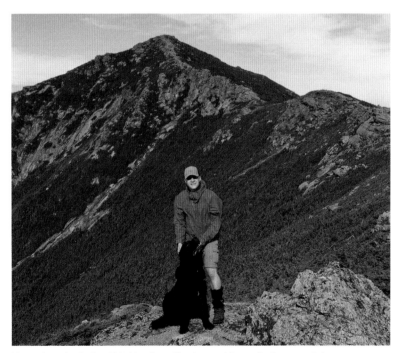

Many dogs, including this Newfoundland, are at home in the mountains.

Dawson Butte Ranch Open Space

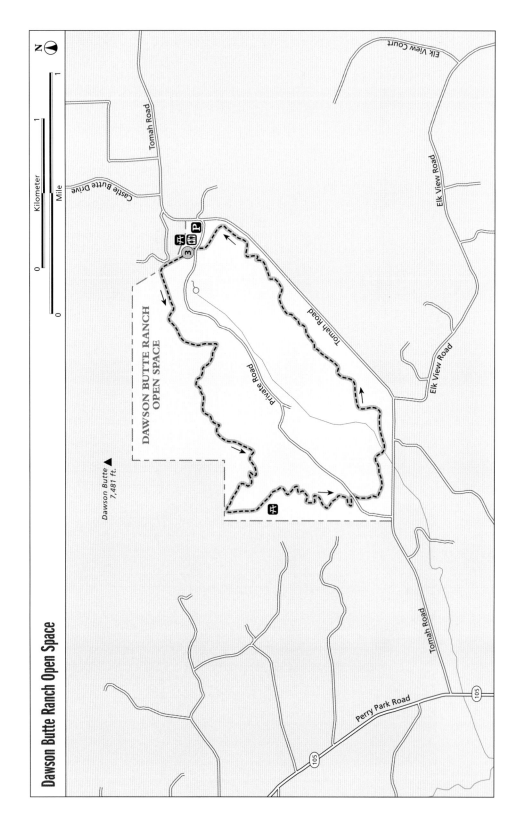

Dawson Butte
7,481 ft.

DAWSON BUTTE RANCH
OPEN SPACE

Castle Butte Drive

Tomah Road

Elk View Court

Elk View Road

Elk View Road

Tomah Road

Tomah Road

Private Road

Perry Park Road

105

105

N

Kilometer

Mile

0   1   1

Dawson Butte Ranch Open Space is a wonderful little area to escape to from the crowded city; enjoy a day in these rolling woodlands with your family (both two- and four-legged members). Come often to see what changes the different seasons bring to this special place.

MILES AND DIRECTIONS

0.0   Start at the trailhead on the north side of the parking lot. Elevation: 6,815 feet. The loop is described here in a counterclockwise direction. You can also start at the trailhead on the south side.

0.9   Reach the junction with Manger Meadow Trail, one of the many bridle paths with horse jumps. Continue straight ahead.

1.4   Over the next 0.5 mile, you'll come to junctions with several bridle paths. All are well marked. Stay on the main trail for hikers and mountain bikers.

2.0   Look to the right; you'll see a picnic table down Picnic Tree Trail. This is a good place for lunch if you'd like to take this spur trail. GPS: N39 17.41' / W104 56.40'

2.8   Reach the junction with the private road. Continue straight ahead on the trail.

3.3   Cross a little creek, which is the low point of the hike.

3.5   At the junction with Tomah Meadow Path, continue straight ahead.

4.4   Reach the four-way junction of the Dawson Butte Trail, Tomah Meadow Path, and Play Pen Path. Continue straight ahead.

5.0   Pass three picnic tables to the right. Play Pen Path comes in from the left. Arrive back at the parking lot.

4 PAWNEE BUTTES

WHY GO?

The Pawnee Buttes protrude 200 to 250 feet above this trail like upside-down vases. The surrounding shortgrass prairie is home to many bird species, including great horned owls, American kestrels, eagles, hawks, swallows, and mountain plover—and these are just a few of the nearly 300 species that make their homes in Pawnee National Grassland. Coyotes, foxes, deer, mountain lions, pronghorns, rattlesnakes, and an assortment of mice, voles, jackrabbits, and prairie dogs call this special place home. Spring fills the prairie with colorful wildflowers and is a great time for bird watching.

THE RUNDOWN

Start: From the Pawnee Buttes (Trail 840) Trailhead
Distance: 3.6 miles out and back
Approximate hiking time: 1.5 to 2.5 hours
Difficulty: Easy
Elevation gain/loss: 30-foot gain / 290-foot loss
Seasons: Year-round except after big snowstorms; summer can be very hot. Spring and fall are best for hiking.
Trail surface: Dirt trail
Other trail users: Equestrians
Canine compatibility: Dogs should be leashed, due to the abundant wildlife.

Fees and permits: None for hiking, except for groups larger than 75 people
Maps: USGS Grover SE and Pawnee Buttes
Trail contacts: Pawnee National Grassland, Greeley; (970) 346-5000; www.fs.usda.gov/arp
Other: Please obey any seasonal closures and avoid disturbing nesting birds. Hawks and falcons nest in the cliffs while others nest in the grasses. Rattlesnakes live in this area too, so keep an eye and ear open for them, and a watchful eye on your dog.

FINDING THE TRAILHEAD

 From I-25 east of Fort Collins, take exit 269A (Ault). Drive 50.4 miles east on CO 14, through Briggsdale, to the sign for Keota at Weld CR 103, just east of mile marker 189. Turn left and drive 4 miles to where the road curves right onto WCR 98. In another 0.8 mile, you're at Keota. Head northeast on WCR 98½. In another 0.3 mile, turn left onto WCR 105. The road turns a few times, but follow the signs for Pawnee Buttes. In 2.9 miles, turn right onto WCR 104 and drive another 3 miles to WCR 111. Turn left. When you reach WCR 110 in 3 miles, continue straight ahead. Drive another 1.2 miles to FR 685, which heads north from a left curve. Turn right and you'll reach the trailhead in 1.2 miles. Turn left into the parking lot. There are no facilities or water at the trailhead or the overlook, another 0.5 mile past the parking lot. Bring water with you. **GPS:** N40 48.83' / W104 00.00'

THE HIKE

Driving from Ault to the Keota turnoff on CO 14, the world around you is a far cry from the nonstop traffic of I-25 and the congestion of the Denver / Boulder / Fort Collins metro areas. Rolling hills of grass stretch to the horizon on each side of the road,

Pawnee Buttes and surrounding area

punctuated with a lone tree here and there. A ranch house may appear in the distance. A few rows of little trees have been planted on the north side of the highway, probably for a windbreak, if the trees can survive the dry, windy climate of Colorado's high plains.

Before you turn into the trailhead parking lot, you'll pass a windmill used to pump water for cattle. Listen to it creak and groan; watch the tail and vane keep the wheel into the wind. To the north you'll see the Cedar Creek wind farm, its 274 turbines generating 300 megawatts of electricity. Located on private land, the wind farm began operation in October 2007. The old and the new are quite a contrast, but each serves its purpose. Unfortunately, large birds, raptors in particular, can't see the rotating turbine blades, and a collision always results in the bird's death.

Colorado was covered by the Cretaceous Seaway from 114 million to 65 million years ago. After the dinosaurs disappeared 65 million years ago, the Rockies were uplifted and volcanoes ejected ash high into the sky. The inland sea receded, but sediments eroded from the mountains to the west covered the old seabed. For more than 10 million years, sandstone, siltstone, and ashy claystone were deposited on the plains, eventually becoming the White River Formation.

The opening acts of the Age of Mammals starred camels, rhinoceros, three-toed horses, and hippopotamus–like animals grazing on the grasslands and woodlands that had developed. Erosion continued to wear down the Rockies, and the deposits on the plains became the Arikaree Formation and the Ogallala Formation, the latter comprising sandstone and conglomerate (rocks and stones cemented together).

Around 5 million years ago, the whole area was uplifted about 5,000 feet. Rivers increased in speed and volume, sometimes fed by melting mountain glaciers. Water eroded through the sediment layers on the plains, especially the softer White River Formation. Some of the harder Ogallala Formation remained, protecting the underlying

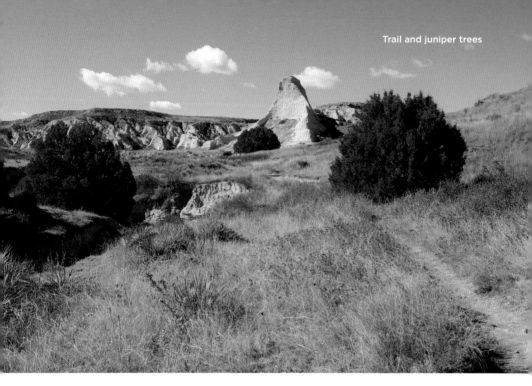

materials. The Pawnee Buttes are remnants of those early plains, as are the Chalk Bluffs to the north. The White River Formation in the Pawnee Buttes area contains one of the prime deposits of vertebrate fossils in the world. Please remember fossils are protected by law and must not be removed from the area.

Erosion continues today, creating the badlands features found along the trail as it drops down a little gully between the trailhead area and Lips Bluff. Just enough moisture allows junipers to grow, with an occasional piñon pine or limber pine for good measure. Prickly pear cactus blooms brightly in mid-June, along with purple locoweed, white yucca, and white prairie phlox. While hiking, you might notice tufted sandwort, a pincushion-like plant that grows on the siltstone barrens in the area. One general aspect of shortgrass prairie is that vegetation covers less than 50 percent of it.

Bison once roamed this area in herds as large as 60 million. Blue grama and buffalo grass satiated these large animals, which moved constantly in search of new food. The grasslands and bison adapted to each other. As settlers moved west to homestead, they turned the sod, exposing the prairie soil to wind erosion. Unlike the bison, cattle continually grazed the same area, giving the grasses no time to recover. With low annual precipitation rates, farming was marginal at best. High winds accompanied the drought of the 1930s, blowing loose soil everywhere. Many people left their farms during this Dust Bowl.

In 1934 the US government created a program to purchase marginal lands. By 1946 the government had purchased 11.3 million acres, of which 5.5 million acres came under the jurisdiction of the Department of Agriculture, and, eventually, the Forest Service. In 1960 about 3.8 million acres were designated as national grasslands. The Pawnee National Grassland consists of 193,060 acres. One of the Forest Service's duties is to manage national grasslands for forage and recreation resources, while another is to manage the

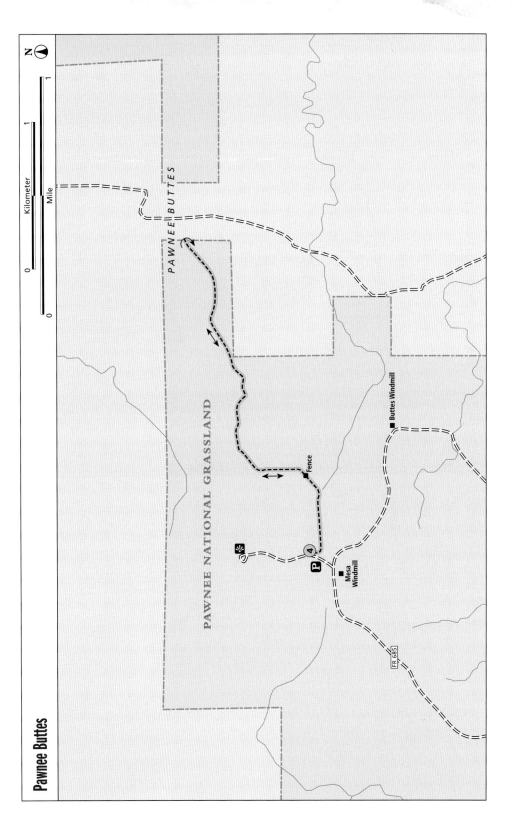

Pawnee Buttes

PAWNEE BUTTES

PAWNEE NATIONAL GRASSLAND

Fence

Buttes Windmill

Mesa Windmill

FR 685

Kilometer

Mile

N

resources to "maintain and improve soil and vegetative cover and to demonstrate sound and practical principles of land use for the areas in which they are located."

Because the buttes are crumbling sandstone, please refrain from climbing them. While you hike, keep an eye out for prairie residents: antelope, deer, rabbits, and, of course, the myriad birds. (And be sure to maintain control over your dog at all times during these wildlife observations.) Enjoy some peaceful time in this unique section of Colorado's Eastern Plains.

MILES AND DIRECTIONS

0.0 Start at the interpretive signs in the parking lot. The trail is to the right. Elevation: 5,420 feet. Hike down the little gully.

0.4 Reach a fence and bulletin board. Just beyond, the trail branches. Go left on the main Pawnee Buttes Trail. The right branch goes to Lips Bluff, which is closed Mar 1 to June 30 to protect nesting birds.

0.6 The trail winds through a little juniper forest.

1.0 An overgrown doubletrack comes in from the right (also closed Mar 1 to June 30). Continue on the main trail to the left.

1.1 A trail comes in from the right. Continue on the main trail to the left.

1.4 A faint trail crosses the main trail. Continue straight ahead on the main trail.

1.5 Arrive at the west butte.

1.8 Arrive at the grassland / private property boundary. Elevation: 5,160 feet. GPS: 40 49.32' / W103 58.48'. You're in between the west and east buttes. Turn around and return the way you came.

3.6 Arrive back at the trailhead.

5 SOUTH SHORELINE TRAIL

WHY GO?

One of the best things about visiting northeastern Colorado is that, even on a sunny weekend day, you'll likely have any trail all to yourself. The South Shoreline Trail evokes the stark beauty of the Great Plains, and it's not uncommon to see a herd of grazing cattle just a few hundred yards from the park's resident American white pelicans, and, even in late summer, plenty of delicate little wildflowers.

THE RUNDOWN

Start: From the Inlet Grove Campground Trailhead
Distance: 6.3 miles out and back
Approximate hiking time: 2 hours
Difficulty: Easy
Elevation gain: 50 feet
Seasons: Spring, fall, winter
Trail surface: Gravel
Other trail users: Equestrians and mountain bikers
Canine compatibility: Dogs must be on leash

Fees and permits: Colorado State Parks entry fee (or annual State Parks Pass)
Maps: USGS North Sterling Reservoir; Colorado Parks and Wildlife North Sterling State Park map at https://cpw.state.co.us/placestogo/parks/NorthSterling/Documents/SouthTrail.pdf
Trail contacts: Colorado Parks and Wildlife—North Sterling State Park, 24005 CR 330, Sterling; (970) 522-3657, https://cpw.state.co.us/placestogo/parks/NorthSterling

FINDING THE TRAILHEAD

From Denver proper, take I-25 north to I-76. Follow I-76 for 112 miles to exit 125 for Sterling. Turn left from the exit ramp onto Highway 6. Head west for 2 miles (over a bridge), then take a right onto North 3rd Street. A slight left gets you onto Sidney Avenue; head north for another 1.5 miles. Take a left onto CR 34 for 1 mile, then right on CR 39. Follow this paved road for 10 miles. (GPS units show several name changes for this road; if you don't turn onto any unpaved roads, you'll be on the right track.) Turn left onto CR 46 (right after the S-shaped curve) and continue west for 2 miles to CR 33. Enter the park at the south entrance. Stop and pay the entrance fee at the station, then stop and grab a map at the kiosk on your right if you'd like. Follow signs for the Inlet Grove Campground; take a left off the main park road, then follow the one-way road around to a small parking area with a bathroom. Park here for the South Shoreline Trail. GPS: N40 45.82' / W103 16.42'

THE HIKE

Let's address the bovine in the room right away: North Sterling State Park is quite a hoof from Denver. All on its own, the South Shoreline Trail isn't the kind of trail you'd ordinarily be drawn to drive several hours for, just to go on a day hike. Oddly, that's actually part of what makes this park really special. Even on a gorgeous weekend in late summer, you'll have no trouble finding peace and quiet on the trail, and it doesn't take the kind of months-in-advance planning to get a campsite that many other Colorado campgrounds require.

You'll cross this footbridge almost immediately after beginning your hike.

Take in views of the bluffs across the reservoir as you stroll along the South Shoreline Trail.

In the right mind-set, even the drive out to North Sterling State Park—whose name-sake reservoir was once called Point of Rocks Reservoir—is beautiful. As you make your way farther north, away from the smog of the big city, you start to see the kind of scenery people must be thinking of when they lump Colorado in with the Midwest—it's not, of course, but that doesn't stop this part of the state from looking very much like Kansas or Nebraska. Small outposts punctuate the endless ranchland along I-76, and, as you get closer to Sterling during the summer months, the sides of the freeway burst to life with infinite sunflower blooms.

North Sterling State Park itself feels like the kind of place you might bring your family for an inexpensive, wholesome vacation. The Inlet Grove Campground, where you'll start your hike, is mostly populated by RVs, and there's a restroom with running water and flush toilets on the premises. You'll start your hike from a small parking area near the end of the one-way loop; it's marked by a sign for the South Shoreline Trail, and there's a vault toilet just a few steps from the parking area.

Almost immediately, you'll cross a bridge that spans the campground's namesake inlet; you can see from its steep, eroded banks that the water often gets quite high. Once you've crossed the bridge, you'll get your first view of the bluffs to the north and of the bigger lake itself. (At low water, keep an eye out for the park's resident flock of pelicans that tends to gather on the mudflats.)

Wind your way along the even, well-maintained gravel path, stopping if you'd like at the trail's occasional benches (there are fewer of these as you make your way closer to the other trailhead at the west end of the trail). There's some shade provided by a few cottonwood groves, but for the most part, expect to be in the sun the whole time you're hiking. Plan your hike for morning or evening, when it tends to be a bit cooler, and bring plenty of water for both you and your dog—there's none available at the western terminus of the trail.

This is an easy hike with virtually no elevation gain. You could walk the trail briskly, but the scenery lends itself to a slower pace, and your pooch will have plenty of scents to sniff along the way. Dogs are required to be on a leash in North Sterling State Park, and it's smart to obey that rule, since the dry climate also means there are plenty of rattlesnakes just off the trail. Slow down and look closely, and you'll see myriad wildflower blooms during the summer months. They're not the big, showy columbines you might see in other areas of the state, but smaller, understated flowers—much like the understated beauty of this landscape.

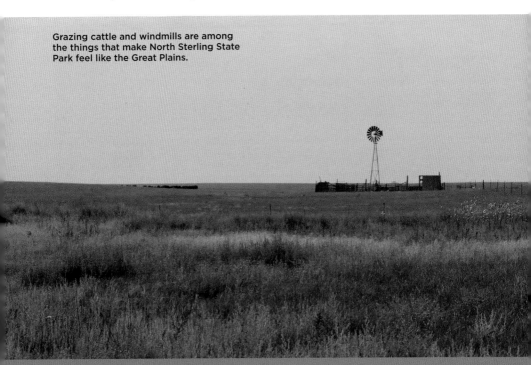

Grazing cattle and windmills are among the things that make North Sterling State Park feel like the Great Plains.

Keep an eye out for delicate wildflower blooms during the summer.

OPTIONS

There's also a parking area at the east trailhead, accessible off CR 33, and at the west end of the trail, off CR 29. Either way, you'll need to pay the park entrance fee at a self-service pay station. If you still haven't gotten your fill of hiking at the end of an out-and-back hike on the South Shoreline Trail, you can head to one of the park's other trails—though they're all quite short, and South Shoreline offers the most sustained hiking. The Balanced Rock Trail, just north of the dam on the east side of the reservoir, visits a park high point for spectacular views—and, if you're a geology buff, it might be of interest to know that a brontothere jawbone fossil was found near this rock formation.

South Shoreline Trail

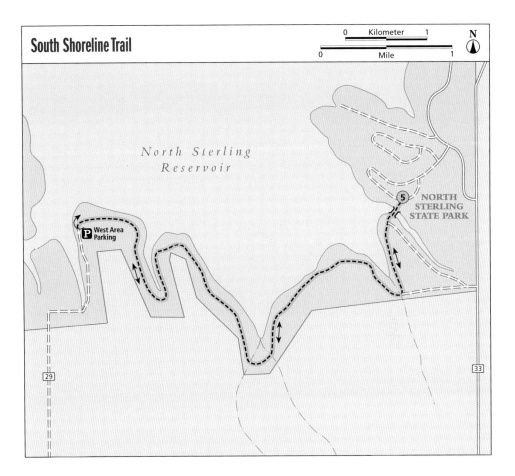

North Sterling Reservoir

West Area Parking

5 NORTH STERLING STATE PARK

29

33

MILES AND DIRECTIONS

0.0 Begin the hike from the Inlet Grove Campground Trailhead.

0.1 Cross a footbridge and gain a handful of feet of elevation.

2.6 The trail nearly doubles back on itself to avoid crossing a swampy inlet.

2.9 South Shoreline Trail moves gradually closer to the banks of the reservoir; there's good fishing access here.

3.1 Arrive at the west area parking. There's a bathroom here, but no water. Retrace your steps.

5.0 There's a bench in a small grove of cottonwoods (along with several picnic tables, which have been overtaken by undergrowth) if you need a shady break before finishing the hike.

6.2 Cross the footbridge again.

6.3 Arrive back at the trailhead.

FRONT RANGE

The easternmost spine of mountains in Colorado, running from the Wyoming border to Colorado Springs, is known as the **FRONT RANGE**. That same moniker refers to the most populated section of the state: Denver, Boulder, Fort Collins, and Colorado Springs are all considered part of the Front Range. (To break things up, we've put Colorado Springs–area hikes into the next section of this book, Southern Front Range.)

The Front Range may be the most crowded swath of Colorado (it's where 80 percent of the population lives), and although it's occasionally disheartening to fight traffic or get up at the crack of dawn to get a reasonable parking space at your favorite trailhead, it's not hard to see why everyone wants to live here: It's gorgeous. The foothills—which are where you'll find my quaint little hometown, Golden—rise steadily into higher, more-rugged peaks. The Front Range is also home to five Fourteeners, so you know it's an exercise in oxygen deprivation.

You'll find all kinds of interesting geology here, too. The unmistakable Flatiron formations, for example, rise prominently from the Boulder foothills and provide the backdrop for some of the area's best hiking. (Boulder County hiking also has the distinction of having the Voice and Sight Tag program, mentioned in the introduction, which allows dog owners to hike with their pups off leash and under voice command.) The Devils Backbone, on page 43, is another geological oddity.

The beauty of the Front Range is that, although you're close to creature comforts, you're also a short drive away from lots of the state's best hiking. When things heat up in the summer, you can escape to the foothills to cool off; when the mercury drops in the winter—which it rarely does for more than a few days at a time; we do, after all, have an annual average of 300 days of sunshine—you'll find plenty of cold-weather hiking if you head south.

For the most part, we've organized hikes in this section from north to south. There's one exception: Cherry Creek State Park's Dog Off-Leash Area is listed first, since it's a great place to practice hiking with your dog off leash before you get to the big leagues.

6 CHERRY CREEK STATE PARK DOG OFF-LEASH AREA

WHY GO?

If you're working on training your dog to be off leash, this is the hike for you: It's the ideal place to work on off-leash commands with your dog in a setting where you can't easily lose control, as the area is mostly fenced, and you'll have a great deal of visibility. It's not a challenging hike, but the 107-acre dog off-leash area (DOLA), complete with a romp in Cherry Creek, will set you and your pooch up for a summer of excellent off-leash hiking wherever pups are allowed to roam free.

THE RUNDOWN

Start: From the Cherry Creek State Park DOLA parking area
Distance: Up to 3 miles
Approximate hiking time: 1 hour
Difficulty: Easy
Elevation gain: 45 feet
Seasons: Year-round
Trail surface: Gravel
Other trail users: Lots of off-leash dogs
Canine compatibility: Dogs allowed off leash if under voice command
Fees and permits: Colorado State Parks entry fee plus day-use fee for Dog Off-Leash Area (pay at entrance station or at self-pay station at the entrance to the DOLA)
Map: USGS Fitzsimmons; Colorado Parks and Wildlife Cherry Creek State Park Dog Off-Leash Area at https://cpw.state.co.us/placestogo/parks/CherryCreek/Documents/DogOffLeashBrochure.pdf
Trail contacts: Colorado Parks and Wildlife—Cherry Creek State Park, 4201 S Parker Road, Aurora; (303) 690-1166; http://cpw.state.co.us/placestogo/parks/CherryCreek/

FINDING THE TRAILHEAD

From Denver, take I-25 south to exit 200 for I-225. Head north on I-225 toward Limon for 3 miles, then take exit 4 onto CO 83 S/S Parker Road. Keep an eye out for signs indicating Cherry Creek State Park; stop and pay the entrance fee plus the day-use DOLA fee. (You can also get into the park with an annual Colorado State Parks Pass, but you'll still need to pay the day-use fee to access the DOLA.) Continue onto East Lehigh Avenue, then take a left onto East Lakeview Road, followed by another immediate left to stay on Lakeview. Take one last left-hand turn onto 12 Mile North, where you'll find the parking area for the DOLA. There's a bathroom at the trailhead. If the trailhead is full, the DOLA is at capacity, and you'll need to wait until someone leaves before more dogs can enter. **GPS:** N39 37.40' / W104 49.84'

THE HIKE

It's impossible to overstate the importance of having a dog under voice command when you're hiking with them off leash. Of course, the DOLA requires that dogs be under control, so this isn't a great training spot if you're just getting to know your dog. Consider working on some basic commands and making sure they'll come when called in a backyard or private, fenced-in area first. Once you have the basics down, though, this is a great spot to test those skills.

The regulations are clear at the Cherry Creek Dog Off-Leash Area.

The DOLA at Cherry Creek—along with a similarly managed plot of land at Chatfield State Park, to the west in Littleton—was originally created as an area to train hunting dogs. The Chatfield Board approved the plan to create these areas in 1983, and in 2006 the Parks and Wildlife Commission placed a moratorium on adding any new dog off-leash areas in the Colorado State Parks. There's no plan to remove these areas or eliminate off-leash privileges, but it's crucial that dog owners stick to the regulations to keep this resource available. (More on that in a moment.)

Keep your pup on leash until you get to the proper start of the DOLA, which has a typical dog park–like entrance station with two gates. Here, you can let your pooch off, but you must carry a leash and at least one waste removal bag per dog (and handlers are allowed to have no more than three dogs with them at any time). These rules are enforced, so be sure you don't set your leash or bag down and forget it at the entrance station.

From the entrance the world is your oyster. A big loop trail will net you nearly 3 miles, but there are several other trails crisscrossing through the DOLA, along with more than one opportunity to take your pup for a dip in Cherry Creek. On a warm day, you'll see tons of other dogs splashing through the water, playing fetch, and swimming in the cool current. If you're walking the loop in a counterclockwise direction, stop in at the first turnoff for the creek for the shallowest spot, where even poor swimmers can get their paws wet and romp around. If your dog is a great fetcher and swimmer, the deeper spots farther along the trail might present a fun challenge.

There's little shade along the way, except down by the creek. You should bring plenty of water for yourself, and it's up to you to decide whether to bring additional water for your dog, or just to let them drink from the creek. (Know, though, that the creek is only accessible for the first mile or so, after which you'll be farther from water.)

As you loop back around toward the entrance station where you started, you'll pass several pastures full of horses for a commercial stable operation. This is a great opportunity to expose your dog to horses that are unlikely to be spooked. Certainly you shouldn't let

Along the way, stop to let your dog cool off in Cherry Creek.

The wide trail in the Cherry Creek State Park DOLA makes for easy hiking, so you can focus on training your dog to be on their best behavior off leash.

your dog charge the fence, barking, but allow them to watch the big creatures, since it's important to desensitize them to other critters they might see out on the trail.

A note on leashes: If you visit the DOLA, don't leave your dog on a leash. It's stressful for dogs to be confined, especially if other dogs around them are approaching or running up to sniff and say hello. It's very possible that you're setting yourself up for a

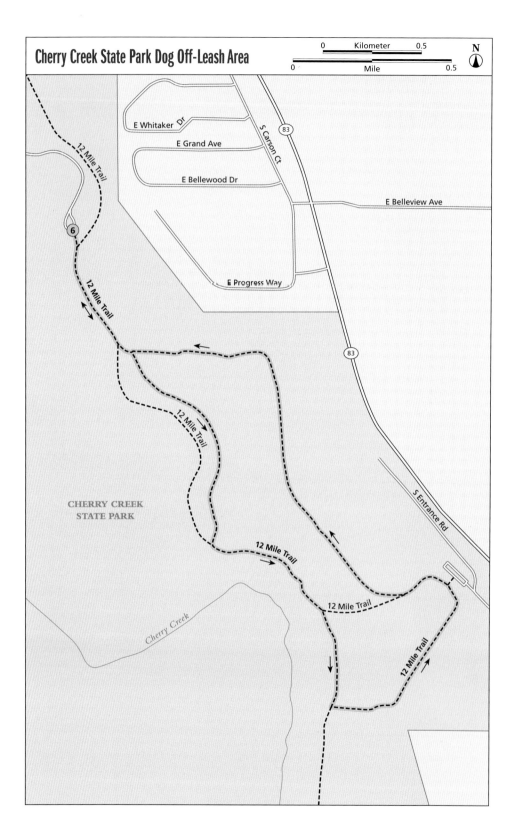

Cherry Creek State Park Dog Off-Leash Area

Kilometer 0 0.5
Mile 0 0.5

N

E Whitaker Dr

E Grand Ave

E Bellewood Dr

S Carson Ct

83

E Belleview Ave

E Progress Way

83

12 Mile Trail

6

12 Mile Trail

12 Mile Trail

S Entrance Rd

CHERRY CREEK
STATE PARK

12 Mile Trail

12 Mile Trail

12 Mile Trail

Cherry Creek

12 Mile Trail

doggie conflict if you keep even an otherwise nonaggressive dog on a leash at an area like the DOLA. If you're still nervous about having your dog off leash in such a big area, consider a few more backyard sessions or visits to your local dog park before you head to the DOLA.

Rangers check regularly to make sure dog handlers are carrying these permits (and that the requisite bag and leash per dog are being carried), so keep it on your person, or expect that you'll be cited. If you plan to visit more than ten times as you train your dog, save a little money by purchasing the annual DOLA pass.

MILES AND DIRECTIONS

0.0 Begin at the DOLA parking lot; pay at the self-service station if you haven't already paid at the entrance station. Keep your dog on a leash as you exit the parking area.

0.2 Enter the DOLA at the double gate. Don't forget to bring your leash and at least one waste bag per dog!

0.9 Take a detour off the main trail and down to the riparian zone around Cherry Creek.

1.1 Let your dog splash around in the creek and walk among the willows until you get to an exit back to the main trail.

1.4 Here's another opportunity to dip down some big stone steps to a deeper part of the creek.

2.2 Pass another entrance station.

2.7 Arrive back at the entrance where you started; leash your dog in the double gate.

2.9 Arrive back at your vehicle. Give your pooch some water!

7 LORY STATE PARK LOOP

WHY GO?

Lory State Park is a well-traveled mountain bike destination—it's earned a name for itself in northern Colorado thanks to its easy access and fairly flowy singletrack—but there are still plenty of "Foot Only"–designated trails, so you can enjoy a bike-free hike. Situated next to Horsetooth Reservoir, trails climb into the nearby montane foothills with ponderosa pine and Douglas fir forests. Wild turkeys hide, mule deer browse, and Abert's squirrels and cottontail rabbits frolic. Lory even has six backcountry campsites available by permit. Thanks to its lower elevation, this is a perfect place to satisfy early-season hiking and camping urges. Arthur's Rock protrudes above the park, providing views of the Fort Collins area. This hike makes a loop using sections of six different trails.

THE RUNDOWN

Start: From the Well Gulch Nature Trailhead by the South Eltuck Picnic Area

Distance: 6.6-mile loop

Approximate hiking time: 2.5 to 4 hours

Difficulty: Difficult due to elevation gain and some steep spots

Elevation gain: 1,670 feet (including three elevation gains/losses)

Seasons: Year-round, except after big snowstorms

Trail surface: Dirt trail, sometimes steep and rocky, sometimes gentle

Other trail users: Some trail sections open to mountain bikers and equestrians, others are hiker-only; hunters in season

Canine compatibility: Dogs must be on leash. There is little to no water along the trail.

Fees and permits: Daily fee or annual parks pass required. Permit required (with fee) for backpacking (overnight camping at designated campsites only). Campfires are not allowed in the backcountry.

Maps: USGS Horsetooth Reservoir; Latitude 40˚ Colorado Front Range

Trail contacts: Lory State Park, 708 Lodgepole Dr., Bellvue; (970) 493-1623; http://parks.state.co.us/parks/lory

Other: Vault toilets but no water. Bring water with you.

FINDING THE TRAILHEAD

From Fort Collins, take US 287 north. Just past mile marker 350, US 287 turns right. Continue straight ahead onto Larimer CR 54G. Drive 2.7 miles through Laporte, then turn left to Rist Canyon (LCR 52E). Turn left after 1 mile onto LCR 23N in Bellvue, drive 1.4 miles south, and then turn right onto LCR 25G. Drive another 1.7 miles to the park entrance and turn left. Pay the entrance fee and stop in the visitor center to check out the interpretive displays. Restrooms and water are available at the visitor center. Drive 0.9 mile south to the South Eltuck Picnic Area, across from the Well Gulch Nature Trail kiosk. **GPS:** N40 34.70' / W105 10.70'

THE HIKE

Fort Collins sits at almost exactly 5,000 feet above sea level, and it's best known as the home of Colorado State University. The school's highly sought-after agricultural

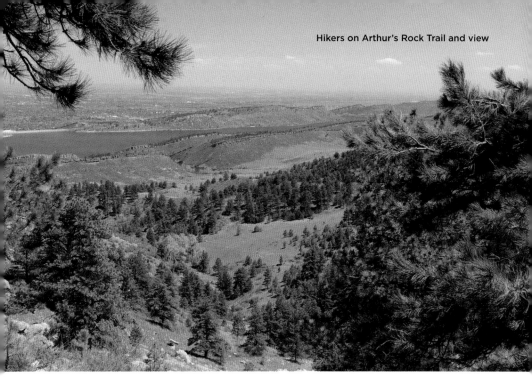

program is telling: Fort Collins is right on the edge of the plains, and there's still plenty of ranchland to the north (it's just a handful of miles from the Wyoming border), east, and south. There's easy access to recreational opportunities like Cameron Pass and Red Feather Lakes, not to mention the short drive to Laramie, where you can get deep into the Medicine Bow National Forest and Wilderness areas just outside of town.

In addition to the nearby recreational opportunities, Fort Collins is an exceptionally dog-friendly town. If there's one thing Coloradans love almost as much as our dogs, it's beer. Combine the two, and you get this northern Colorado town, where dogs are allowed on the patio of nearly every microbrewery, plus in numerous taprooms. There are also a half-dozen very well-maintained off-leash dog parks in town, including several with water features.

Horsetooth Reservoir and adjacent Lory State Park are some of the recreational crown jewels of the Fort Collins area. Lory's history dates back to the early nineteenth century, when fur traders came to the area in search of pelts. In 1836 a party of trappers climbed into the foothills west of the Fort Collins area. Their supplies became too heavy and they decided to hide them. Because the cache included gunpowder, the river near their cache became known as the Cache la Poudre.

One member of this party, Antoine Janise, returned a few years later to settle down; he was just in time for the Gold Rush. He established a settlement called Colona, near present-day Laporte, in 1859, and soon, prospectors arrived to search for gold in tributaries of the South Platte River, including the Cache la Poudre. Settlers continued to arrive, establishing farms to feed themselves and the miners.

One settler was John Kimmons, who homesteaded 160 acres in the area of today's Lory State Park. In 1897 he exchanged his land for John Howard's family ranch in North Park. The Howards appreciated the milder winters near Fort Collins, plus the nearby schools

THE WOOD TICK

Colorado has relatively few poisonous or irritating plants, insects, and reptiles. Be aware, however, of the wood tick, *Dermacentor andersoni*. The small insect is about an eighth of an inch long, with a flat body. Ticks are active from late March into early July and live in grassy, woody, or brushy areas, waiting for a warm-blooded body. Humans and dogs can easily pick up ticks by brushing against vegetation. The tick embeds itself head first into your flesh, with its body sticking out. Unlike mosquitoes, ticks feed on the host's blood for hours. An anchor below their mouths keeps them attached.

The wood tick may carry one of two infections that are threatening to human hosts. If the tick bite goes undetected, a person may develop the virus called Colorado tick fever. Symptoms appear within three to six days after the bite and include head and body aches, lethargy, nausea, vomiting, and abdominal pain. The illness lasts for five to ten days. These wood ticks also carry the bacterium that causes Rocky Mountain spotted fever. Symptoms appear in two to four days, including fever, spotted rash, headache, nausea, vomiting, and abdominal and muscle pain. If Rocky Mountain spotted fever is suspected, seek medical attention immediately, as this illness can be life-threatening.

When hiking during tick season, check yourself (skin, hair, clothes) and your dog often to remove any ticks before they can transmit disease. Applying DEET- and permethrin-based repellents on skin and clothes can help. Wear light-colored clothing so you can see ticks more easily. Tuck loose clothing into your socks and pants. If you find a tick embedded in your skin, grasp the skin as close as possible to the tick with a pair of tweezers and gently pull it straight out. Remove the tick intact. Do *not* leave the head and neck in your skin. Other removal methods, such as covering the insect with alcohol, fingernail polish, or oil, may cause the tick to regurgitate and pass infection on to its host. If you cannot effectively remove the tick, seek medical attention.

for their children. They grew hay, raised cattle, and harvested timber in the foothills. Purchasing adjacent lands over the years, their ranch expanded to 3,600 acres. Stop by Homestead Picnic Area to see the three cedar trees and sandstone slabs where the Howards' house used to stand.

The plains and foothills of Colorado are known to be dry, and early farmers looked to the Cache la Poudre River for relief. G. R. Sanderson built the first irrigation ditch in northern Colorado, diverting water from the Poudre above Bellvue. By 1933 irrigation took a great deal of water from the Poudre and the Big Thompson River to the south. The US Bureau of Reclamation started the Colorado–Big Thompson Project, to divert west-slope water to the thirsty farms and growing population of the east. A 9.75-foot-diameter tunnel, up to 3,600 feet underground, was drilled under the Continental Divide. The Alva B. Adams Tunnel transports water from Grand Lake on the west side of the Continental Divide to Marys Lake near Estes Park on the east. Water from Marys Lake flows through various reservoirs and ultimately to Horsetooth Reservoir, which was completed in 1949.

By 1967, after three generations, ranching became unprofitable for the Howard family. Part of the land was sold and developed into Soldier Canyon Estates, which you'll drive past on your way to the park. The State of Colorado procured the remaining land for the park, which opened in May 1975. A later land purchase added about 100 acres, and presently Lory State Park consists of 2,591 acres. The park is named in honor of Dr. Charles A. Lory, a former president of Colorado Agricultural College (now Colorado State University) and an early settler.

Little waterfall on Well
Gulch Nature Trail

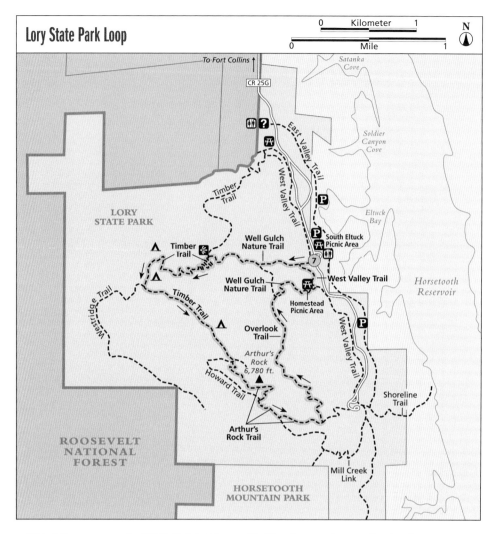

Lory State Park Loop

0 Kilometer 1
0 Mile 1

N

To Fort Collins ↑

Satanka Cove

CR 25G

Soldier Canyon Cove

East Valley Trail

West Valley Trail

Timber Trail

LORY STATE PARK

Eltuck Bay

Timber Trail

Well Gulch Nature Trail

South Eltuck Picnic Area

West Valley Trail

Well Gulch Nature Trail

West Valley Trail

Horsetooth Reservoir

Westridge Trail

Timber Trail

Homestead Picnic Area

Overlook Trail

West Valley Trail

Arthur's Rock 6,780 ft.

Howard Trail

Shoreline Trail

ROOSEVELT NATIONAL FOREST

Arthur's Rock Trail

Mill Creek Link

HORSETOOTH MOUNTAIN PARK

This hike starts at the Well Gulch Nature Trailhead near the South Eltuck Picnic Area. Following Well Gulch through yucca, wooly mullein, and shortgrass prairie, the trail enters ponderosa pine and Douglas fir forests. Watch out for poison ivy along this trail. It then joins the Timber Trail and climbs steadily and sometimes steeply to a ridge. As the trail turns from south- to north-facing slopes, notice how the vegetation changes in response to a slightly cooler and wetter climate on the north faces. At various points check out the excellent views of the Eastern Plains and Fort Collins.

At the ridgeline, numbered poles mark campsites. Near campsites 1 and 2, look straight ahead to see Arthur's Rock. A short trail scrambles to its top for even better views. Return to the main trail and head downhill on the Arthur's Rock Trail, which drops and twists below granite cliffs to the Overlook Trail. This trail travels the edge of forest and plains, climbing and dropping across drainages below Arthur's Rock before finally emerging onto the prairie for the last leg of the loop.

MILES AND DIRECTIONS

0.0 Start at Well Gulch Nature Trailhead by South Eltuck Picnic Area. Elevation: 5,480 feet. Stop at the kiosk for information and a *Well Gulch Self-Guided Nature Trail* brochure.

0.1 Reach the intersection with West Valley Trail. Cross the bridge and turn right onto Well Gulch Nature Trail.

0.5 Come to the intersection of Well Gulch Nature Trail and the access trail to Timber Trail. Continue straight ahead on the access trail to reach Timber Trail.

1.0 Reach a T intersection with Timber Trail. GPS: N40 34.71' / W105 11.51'. Turn left onto the Timber Trail and head uphill. The trail switchbacks up an open, south-facing slope.

1.3 The trail swings left, from a south-facing to a north-facing slope. (**Note:** Check out the change in vegetation with the change in slope aspect.)

2.3 Westridge Trail comes in from the right. Curve left on Timber Trail. (**Note:** The flat ponderosa-filled area is a nice place for a little break. You'll be passing by the designated campsites in this section.)

3.0 Reach the CAMPSITE 1 sign on the left and CAMPSITE 2 sign on the right. As you continue along the trail, Arthur's Rock is ahead.

3.1 Arrive at the three-way junction with Howard, Arthur's Rock, and Timber Trails. Turn left onto Arthur's Rock Trail.

3.2 Come to the intersection with the spur trail to Arthur's Rock summit. GPS: N40 34.09' / W105 11.30' (**Side trip:** Turn left to scramble to the top of Arthur's Rock [6,780 feet] for great views. It's 0.1 mile out and back to the saddle between rock lumps.) Curve right and head downhill on Arthur's Rock Trail. The trail switchbacks and drops down along the side of Arthur's Rock. (**Note:** You'll get a good view of what 1.7-billion-year-old rock looks like.)

3.8 The trail curves right as it drops below the ridge at the end of Arthur's Rock.

4.0 An access trail to a bouldering area is on your right. Continue downhill to the left on Arthur's Rock Trail.

4.3 Reach the intersection with the Mill Creek Link. Turn left at this fork, staying on Arthur's Rock Trail.

4.6 Reach the intersection with Overlook Trail. GPS: N40 33.81' / W105 10.66'. Turn left and follow Overlook toward Well Gulch Nature Trail. Overlook Trail meanders up and down at the edge of the forest but eventually levels out.

5.8 Arrive at the intersection of Overlook Trail and Well Gulch Nature Trail. Turn right and follow the nature trail downhill toward Homestead Picnic Area.

6.3 Reach the intersection of Well Gulch Nature and West Valley Trails. Turn left and walk on West Valley Trail, past Homestead Picnic Area, heading mostly north.

6.5 Reach the intersection of West Valley Trail and Well Gulch Nature Trail. Turn right, cross the bridge, turn right, and return to South Eltuck Picnic Area.

6.6 Arrive back at the Well Gulch Nature Trail kiosk.

8 DOME MOUNTAIN TRAIL

WHY GO?

This trail takes hikers to the summit of 8,450-foot Sheep Mountain, high above the Big Thompson River and its namesake canyon. The trail is well marked with mileage markers and informative signs pointing out information on plant life, erosions, and geology. Be sure your dog is in good health and physical shape for this hike.

THE RUNDOWN

Start: From the Dome Mountain Trailhead near the kiosk
Distance: 9.0 miles out and back
Approximate hiking time: 4 to 5 hours
Difficulty: Moderate to strenuous
Elevation gain: About 3,000 feet
Seasons: Apr to Nov
Trail surface: Varies from smooth in some sections to extremely rocky in others

Other trail users: None
Canine compatibility: Dogs must be under control
Map: Nat Geo Trails Illustrated 101 Cache la Poudre–Big Thompson
Trail contacts: Roosevelt National Forest and the City of Loveland; (970) 295-6600; www.fs.usda .gov/contactus/arp/about-forest/ contactus

FINDING THE TRAILHEAD

From the junction of US 287 and US 34 in Loveland, travel west on US 34 for 14 miles into Big Thompson Canyon, to the Dome Mountain Trailhead on the left. The hike starts at a gate near the restrooms. **GPS:** N40 25.28′ / W105 17.21′

THE HIKE

From the parking area, follow the road up past a gate to a sign pointing to the summit trail. Make a quick left and go up to a second sign near a large pipe on the left. Go left again here; the trail becomes narrow as it clings to the side of a steep hill.

Begin a steep climb to where the trail cuts across a talus slope. Read the first of many informative signs that are located along the trail. This section of the trail travels through a forest of beautiful ponderosa pines and the occasional Douglas fir. Along the trail pointed yuccas and prickly pear cacti grow alongside delicate blooming wildflowers.

The trail switches back steeply in a west-to-east direction, with nice views in both directions. Soon you arrive at the 1-mile marker, with open views to the east. The trail becomes quite steep as you continue to climb high above a narrow gulch to the left.

The terrain stays rocky and continues to switchback up and up. Arrive at the 2-mile marker and begin the steepest section of the hike. The trail becomes quite narrow and very rocky as it travels through a beautiful forest of mature ponderosa pines and weird rock formations. Slide through a natural rock corridor and begin a slight descent to a spring, on the right just before the 3-mile marker. This is a good spot to take a break and offer your dog some water.

At the 3-mile marker the trail stays fairly level and actually drops a bit into a beautiful aspen forest with a small drainage. Enjoy pleasant hiking through the aspen, with views of Sheep Mountain to the north and west.

Dome Mountain Trail

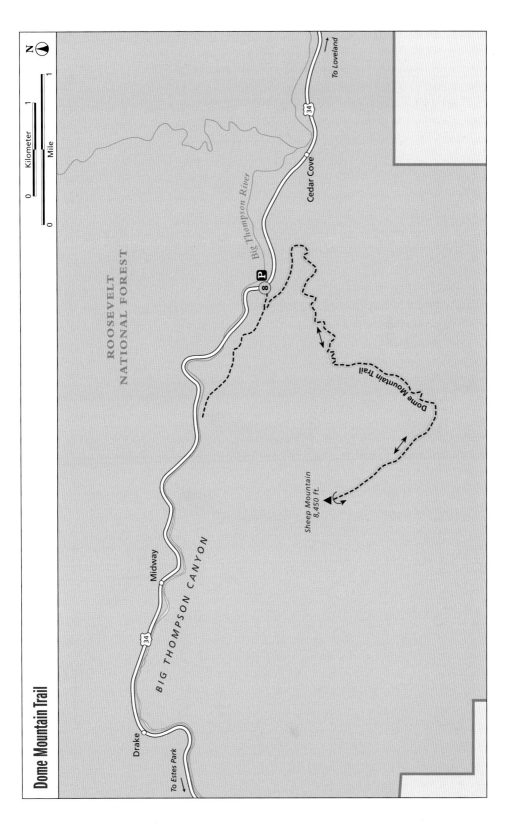

Arrive at the 4-mile marker and cruise up through the rocks to the summit of Sheep Mountain. Enjoy views to the north, and of Loveland and the plains to the east.

After a well-deserved rest, retrace your route back to the trailhead.

MILES AND DIRECTIONS

0.0   Start by passing the gate.

0.2   Go left up a narrow trail.

0.4   Go left, climbing up a steep hill.

0.6   Cross a talus slope.

1.0   Pass a mile marker.

2.0   Pass a mile marker.

2.5   Pass through a natural rock corridor.

2.9   Reach the spring.

3.0   Pass a mile marker.

3.5   Reach the aspen forest.

4.0   Pass a mile marker.

4.5   Arrive at the summit of Sheep Mountain. Retrace your steps.

9.0   Arrive back at the trailhead.

9 DEVIL'S BACKBONE NATURE TRAIL

WHY GO?
Despite its intimidating-sounding name, this pleasant, family-friendly hike is suitable for dogs and kids of all ages. It traces the base of the Devil's Backbone, just west of Loveland. There's little shade on the hike, so although it's open year-round, you'll find the most enjoyable temperatures in the spring and fall shoulder seasons (this is also when you're least likely to arrive and find the trailhead parking lot full).

THE RUNDOWN
Start: From the Devil's Backbone Nature Trailhead
Distance: 2.7-mile lollipop
Approximate hiking time: 1.5 to 2.5 hours
Difficulty: Easy
Elevation gain: 200 feet
Trail surface: Smooth
Seasons: Year-round

Other trail users: Mountain bikers and equestrians
Canine compatibility: Dogs must be on leash
Maps: USGS Larimer County CO; Larimer County Open Space / Devil's Backbone map
Trail contacts: Larimer County Parks and Open Lands; (970) 498-7000; www.larimer.org/naturalresources

FINDING THE TRAILHEAD
From the intersection of US 287 and US 34 in Loveland, go west on US 34 for 4.8 miles to Glade Road. Turn right onto Glade Road and make an immediate right turn onto Wild Lane. Travel 0.3 mile on Wild Lane to the Devil's Backbone Trailhead and parking area. **GPS:** N40 24.42' / W105 09.08'

THE HIKE
Devil's Backbone Open Space is a significant landmark in Larimer County. Not only is it visually striking—you can't miss it protruding distinctly as you drive by on Highway 34—it's also the first open space area in the county, and it's a habitat for all kinds of wildlife, including nesting raptors. It once served as the habitat for prehistoric mammals, including an elephant-like creature with five-foot-long tusks whose remains were found in what's now the Devil's Backbone Open Space. You're less likely to find fossils these days, but if you keep your eyes peeled, you might see a Bell's twinpod, a yellow wildflower that grows here, in a handful of spots in Boulder and Jefferson Counties, and literally nowhere else on the planet.

Of course, you should always keep dogs on a leash where it's required, but you should take extra precautions here. If your dog happens to be a terrible lizard-chaser, like a certain West Texas Dirt Dog I know, be on the lookout for the little guys and keep your pup extra close to avoid an encounter.

From the parking area, walk north on a road up to the trailhead kiosk. Grab a Devil's Backbone Nature Trail map. The map explains local history, geology, flora, and wildlife surrounding the Devil's Backbone area. (There's also water available at the trailhead.)

Devil's Backbone Nature Trail

0   Kilometer   0.5

0   Mile   0.5

N

The Keyhole ■

Devil's Backbone Nature Trail

DEVIL'S
BACKBONE
OPEN SPACE

Hidden Valley Drive

Big Thompson River

To
Estes
Park

34

Glade Road

9
P

Wild Lane

Plaster
Mill Road

To Loveland

34

Past the kiosk the trail follows a road leading to the Wild Lane Bed and Breakfast. Go right just before the bed-and-breakfast, following the sign for the Devil's Backbone Trail, up to a gate. Stay right of the gate and curve around the side of a small hill, with an irrigation ditch on your left and a house down to the right.

Cross two wooden footbridges at the 0.3-mile point and climb a small hill toward a trail junction. There are good views to the north, and in the early summer months, yuccas, lupines, and other wildflowers bloom on the east-facing hill. Continue north.

Arrive at a trail junction; for this hike, go right. The Devil's Backbone Nature Trail travels through a nice area of mahogany oak, cacti, and hills filled with yuccas. At around the 1-mile mark a good view of Devil's Backbone can be seen to the west.

Continue north up to a trail junction at the 1.3-mile mark, where a new trail and loop continue to the north and east. For this hike, go left on the Devil's Backbone Nature Trail and angle back to the south and up toward the Keyhole (a keyhole-shaped rock formation caused by erosion). Arrive at the Keyhole and a metal post marked 6. Time to bring out the map and read about how the Keyhole was formed.

Follow the trail along Devil's Backbone, keeping your map handy for quick reference. Reach a metal post marked 5 at the 1.7-mile mark. Learn who used to roam these lands millions of years ago. The trail crests a small hill at the 1.8-mile mark and offers great views to the north, south, and east. Large yuccas line the trail and tall prairie grass fills the open hillsides as you continue in a southerly direction back to the trailhead.

At the 2-mile mark, reach a metal post marked 3 and read the map. The trail makes a slight decline, and you soon arrive at the first trail junction. Go straight and retrace your route back to the trailhead and the end of the hike.

If you decide to explore this open space area further after your hike, note that dogs are not allowed on the Rimrock Trail or in the Coyote Ridge Natural Area.

MILES AND DIRECTIONS

0.0   Start by following the road toward the bed-and-breakfast.

0.3   Cross two wooden footbridges.

0.5   The trail forks; go right.

1.3   The trail forks; go left.

1.5   Arrive at the Keyhole.

2.2   Continue straight at the trail junction.

2.7   Arrive back at the trailhead.

WHY GO?

This strenuous day hike reaches the alpine summit of Mount Audubon (13,223 feet) via a long, 4-mile march. Wildflowers, panoramic high alpine views, and alpine lakes make it well worth the effort. There are stunning views of Pawnee Peak, Mount Toll, Paiute Peak, Sawtooth Mountain, and Rocky Mountain National Park to the north. This is a very popular trail that sees a fair amount of traffic in the summer months. Your best bet to avoid the crowds is to do the hike midweek.

THE RUNDOWN

Start: From the Beaver Creek Trailhead
Distance: 8.0 miles out and back
Approximate hiking time: 4 to 6 hours
Difficulty: Strenuous
Elevation gain: About 3,200 feet
Seasons: Late June to early Oct
Trail surface: Well-traveled trail on the lower section, with very loose, rocky tread to the summit
Other trail users: None

Canine compatibility: Dogs must be on leash
Map: Nat Geo Trails Illustrated 102 Indian Peaks/Gold Hill
Trail contacts: Boulder Ranger District, USDA Forest Service; (970) 295-6600; www.fs.usda .gov/contactus/arp/about-forest/ contactus
Other: Camping is available at Brainard Lake Recreation Area.

FINDING THE TRAILHEAD

From the junction of CO 93 (Broadway) and CO 119 (Canyon) in downtown Boulder, go west on CO 119 for 18 miles to Nederland and the junction with CO 72. Go west on CO 72 for 10 miles to CR 102. Turn left onto CR 102 to the Brainard Lake Recreation Area and the Mitchell Lake Trailhead parking area. **GPS:** N40 04.60' / W105 34.52'

THE HIKE

The hike starts at the Beaver Creek Trailhead, located at the Mitchell Lake Trailhead parking area above Brainard Lake. Access the well-marked Beaver Creek Trail on the north side of the parking area. The trail is well maintained and makes a gradual climb to a shelf and the Mount Audubon Trail. After about 0.5 mile of easy hiking through a dense spruce forest, the trail makes a sharp right turn up a steep switchback, with views out to the east.

At 1.3 miles the Beaver Creek Trail goes right down to Coney Flats Road. The Mount Audubon Trail continues straight. The trail takes a tight line up through a stand of twisted krummholz and a small boulder field. You are gaining considerable altitude at this point, as the pine trees disappear behind you. The trail cuts over a small, beautiful stream and up through a stunning alpine meadow to a snowfield.

At 2.5 miles the trail makes a sharp right away from a snowfield and climbs steeply through a boulder field to a broad, flat ridge with excellent views of the surrounding alpine peaks. At 3.5 miles the trail goes left, up a steep, rocky trail to the summit. There are a number of side trails that shoot off from the main trail and take a steep scramble to the summit. Follow the cairns and stay on the main trail. It is easier to gain the summit following the main trail, and less intrusive to the surrounding alpine environment. At 4 miles you arrive at the summit of Mount Audubon.

The last section of the hike lies above timberline and is exposed to violent lightning storms. Get an early start and try to be off the summit by noon during the thunderstorm season. The last mile of the trail gains 1,000 feet and can be very strenuous for those not acclimated to altitude. Take a break at one of the many rock shelters on the summit and enjoy the spectacular alpine scenery from this beautiful peak.

C. C. Parry, a botanist, and zoologist J. W. Velie climbed the mountain in 1864 and named the peak after the famous naturalist, who never set foot in Colorado.

After you've summited, retrace your steps to the trailhead.

MILES AND DIRECTIONS

0.0 Start from the parking area and access the signed Beaver Creek Trail.

0.4 The trail cuts right up a steep switchback.

1.3 At the junction with the Beaver Creek Trail, continue straight on the Mount Audubon Trail.

1.9 Enjoy great views of the surrounding peaks and Blue Lake.

2.5 Climb steep switchbacks to a ridge.

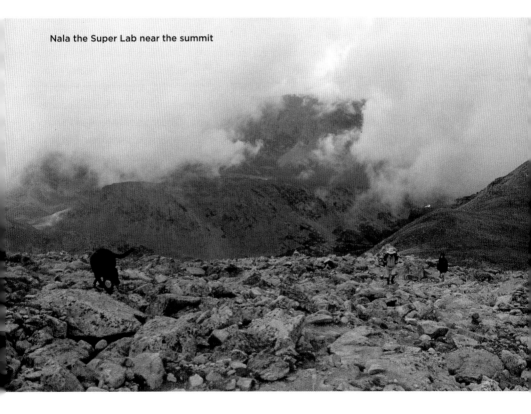

Nala the Super Lab near the summit

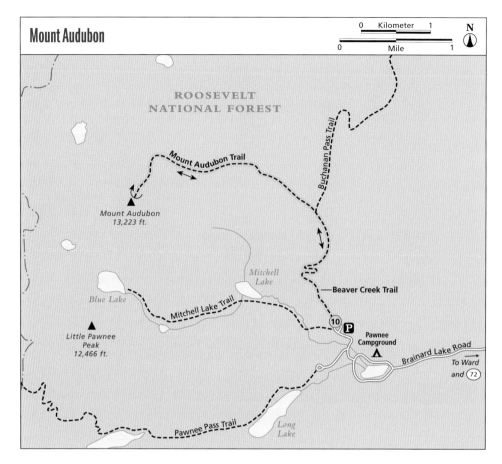

3.5 Climb steep switchbacks to the summit.

4.0 Arrive on the Mount Audubon summit. Retrace your steps.

8.0 Arrive back at the trailhead.

11 BLUE LAKE

WHY GO?

This short hike in the Indian Peaks Wilderness Area leads to a beautiful alpine lake surrounded by Indian Peaks' signature craggy summits. Due to the rocky and sometimes wet and snowy conditions of the trail, you may want to consider outfitting pooches with sensitive paws with weather-appropriate booties.

THE RUNDOWN

Start: From the Mitchell Lake Trailhead
Distance: 5.0 miles out and back
Approximate hiking time: 2.5 to 4 hours
Difficulty: Moderate
Elevation gain: About 1,000 feet
Seasons: June to Oct
Trail surface: Well-traveled and rocky on the lower section, with loose, rocky, and wet conditions up to Blue Lake. Expect to find snow on the upper section of the trail well into June.
Other trail users: Equestrians
Canine compatibility: Dogs must be on leash
Map: Nat Geo Trails Illustrated 102 Indian Peaks/Gold Hill
Trail contacts: Boulder Ranger District, USDA Forest Service; (970) 295-6600; www.fs.usda .gov/contactus/arp/about-forest/ contactus

FINDING THE TRAILHEAD

From the junction of CO 93 (Broadway) and CO 119 (Canyon) in Boulder, go west on CO 119 for 18 miles to Nederland and the junction with CO 72. Go west on CO 72 for 10 miles to CR 102. Turn left onto CR 102 to the Brainard Lake Recreation Area and the Mitchell Lake Trailhead parking area. **GPS:** N40 04.60' / W105 34.52'

THE HIKE

This hike may be short, but you'll get plenty of bang for your buck. Beautiful views, spectacular wildflowers, lovely alpine lakes—this hike has it all. It's certainly worth the trip, but know that if you're headed to the trailhead on a summer weekend, you'll need to leave the house early to find parking; that's just one of the things about living on the Front Range. The parking lot fills up quickly in summer, and finding a space after early morning can be a problem.

The hike begins at the Mitchell Lake Trailhead, located near the restrooms at the Mitchell Lake Trailhead parking area. The Mitchell Lake Trail begins at an elevation of 10,472 feet and climbs to 11,352 feet (at Blue Lake) in just under 2.5 miles. The start of the trail is wide, level, and somewhat rocky. At the 0.2-mile mark you enter the boundary of the wilderness area, and the trail wanders through dense, tall spruce trees.

At around the 0.3-mile mark, cross over Mitchell Creek on a wooden footbridge. After the footbridge the trail climbs gently to Mitchell Lake, with wildflowers and spectacular views of Mount Audubon (13,223 feet), Little Pawnee Peak, Mount Toll, and Paiute Peak. Mitchell Lake is a shallow, 14-acre lake that is stocked with cutthroat trout and is quite popular with anglers. The meadow around the lake is filled with wildflowers

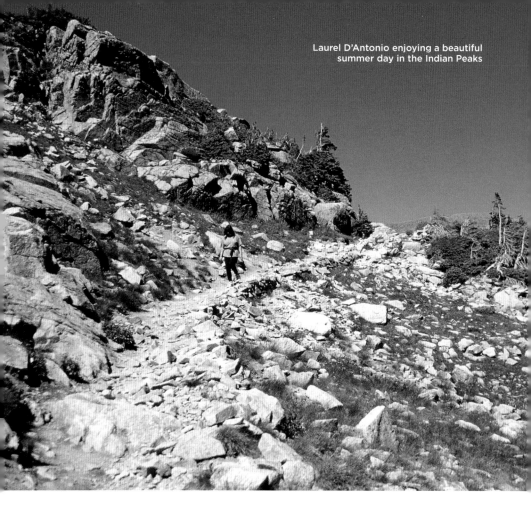

that grow profusely in the moist, fertile soil. Blanketflowers, alpine primrose, mountain lupines, mountain-avers, goldenbanner, and globeflowers are just a few of the flowers that blossom around Mitchell Creek and Mitchell Lake.

At the 1-mile mark the trail crosses over Mitchell Creek again, on a makeshift bridge of logs and fallen trees. After Mitchell Creek the trail climbs on log steps to a meadow with good views of the surrounding peaks. This is another place to stop and enjoy the views and the wildflowers. Wooden walkways guide you through the marshy area of the meadow and up to the drier, rocky section of the trail.

At around the 2-mile mark the trail cuts across a snowfield, following rock cairns, with Mitchell Creek and Little Pawnee Peak on the left. At the 2.5-mile mark Blue Lake appears in a cirque below the towering summits of Mount Toll and Paiute Peak. Blue Lake covers almost 23 acres, is almost 100 feet deep, and is stocked with cutthroat trout.

Take a lunch break and enjoy the panoramic views and alpine splendor; then retrace your steps to the trailhead.

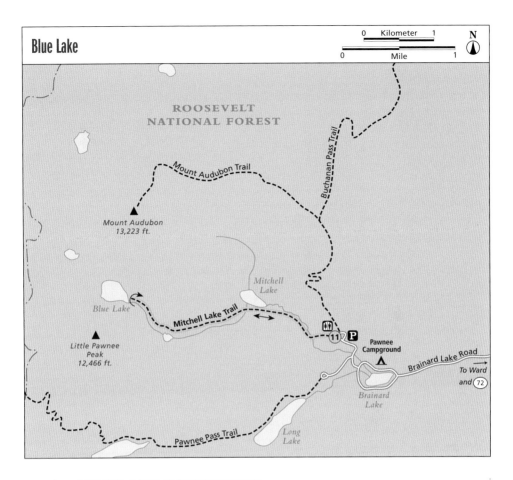

Blue Lake

ROOSEVELT
NATIONAL FOREST

Mount Audubon Trail

Buchanan Pass Trail

Mount Audubon
13,223 ft.

Mitchell
Lake

Blue Lake

Mitchell Lake Trail

Little Pawnee
Peak
12,466 ft.

11

P

Pawnee
Campground

Brainard Lake Road

To Ward
and 72

Brainard
Lake

Pawnee Pass Trail

Long
Lake

0   Kilometer   1

0   Mile   1

N

MILES AND DIRECTIONS

0.0   Start on the Mitchell Lake Trail.

0.2   Arrive at the Indian Peaks Wilderness boundary.

0.8   Arrive at beautiful Mitchell Lake.

1.0   Cross over Mitchell Creek.

1.5   Enjoy alpine meadow and ponds.

2.5   Arrive at Blue Lake. Retrace your steps.

5.0   Arrive back at the trailhead.

12 BEAR PEAK

WHY GO?

It's a strenuous hike to the summit of one of Boulder's most visible landmarks. The Bear Peak Trail follows Bear Creek up beautiful Bear Canyon, then makes a steep ascent up the Bear Peak West Ridge Trail to the summit. Expect beautiful vistas and blooming wildflowers during the summer months. This isn't one of the trails in the Voice and Sight Tag program; dogs must be kept on a leash here regardless of how well they respond to your voice commands (and there's a hefty fine if you're cited). It's worth the trade-off, though; trails accessed from the National Center for Atmospheric Research (NCAR) parking lot are significantly less crowded than the Chautauqua trails.

THE RUNDOWN

Start: From the Walter Orr-Roberts Trailhead
Distance: 7.4-mile lollipop
Approximate hiking time: 4 to 5 hours
Difficulty: Strenuous
Elevation gain: About 2,000 feet
Seasons: Year-round
Trail surface: Well-traveled and smooth up to the Bear Canyon Trail.

From there on, the trail is rocky and steep.
Other trail users: Equestrians
Canine compatibility: Dogs must be on leash
Map: USGS Eldorado Springs
Trail contacts: City of Boulder Mountain Parks and Open Space; (303) 441-3440; www.boulder colorado.gov

FINDING THE TRAILHEAD

From the junction of Broadway and Table Mesa Drive in Boulder, go west on Table Mesa for 2.4 miles to NCAR, where you'll find parking and the trailhead.
GPS: N39 58.45' / W105 16.28'

THE HIKE

From the parking area, access the Walter Orr-Roberts Weather Trail on the west side of NCAR. Follow this informative trail for a short 0.2 mile to a kiosk and a sign pointing to the Mesa Trail. Drop a short distance, then climb steeply to a water tower.

From the water tower, follow signs for the Mesa Trail, staying left at all trail junctions. At the 1.2-mile mark you arrive at the junction of the Mesa Trail and Bear Creek. Go left up the steep, wide road to a junction with the Mesa Trail and the Bear Canyon Trail on the right.

Turn right onto the Bear Canyon Trail, passing a utility tower and power lines. The trail becomes rockier and begins to climb steeply. It crosses Bear Creek several times and winds through several patches of aspens, willows, and cottonwoods. Wildflowers grow profusely along the creek, as do ferns and other flowering shrubs.

At the 3.1-mile mark you arrive at a beautiful, small meadow and a trail junction. The Green-Bear Trail goes to the right. You go left and up on the Bear Peak West Ridge Trail into the pines. The trail climbs steeply through the pines to an open area at an old fence line. The trail cuts to the left and away from private property. Here views open to the west to Walker Ranch Open Space, the Indian Peaks, and Mount Meeker (13,911 feet) to the north.

The trail begins to climb a steep hillside with numerous granite boulders. At around the 4.2-mile mark the trail forks to the left, climbing a series of steep, granite steps. Before you know it you are standing below the pointed summit of Bear Peak. Follow the trail through the rocks to the north ridge, past the Fern Canyon Trail, and scramble up the north ridge to the summit proper. Take a long rest and enjoy the spectacular views in all directions.

After your rest and photo session, go back down the ridge to the Fern Canyon Trail. Go right and down the very steep Fern Canyon Trail to a saddle. The trail is loose and rocky and drops over 2,000 feet in 1.4 miles, a real knee-tweaker. Fern Canyon is a narrow, densely vegetated canyon filled with spectacular rock formations, aspens, and pine trees. The trail in several sections is made of steep steps and wooden stairs.

The trail breaks out of the narrow canyon and you arrive at a junction with Shanahan North Trail. Continue straight on the Fern Canyon Trail, dropping to the Mesa Trail. Wildflowers bloom along the trail and in the open areas. Go left on the Mesa Trail, down to Bear Creek. From here, retrace your route back to NCAR and the parking area.

Awesome views from the summit of Bear Peak

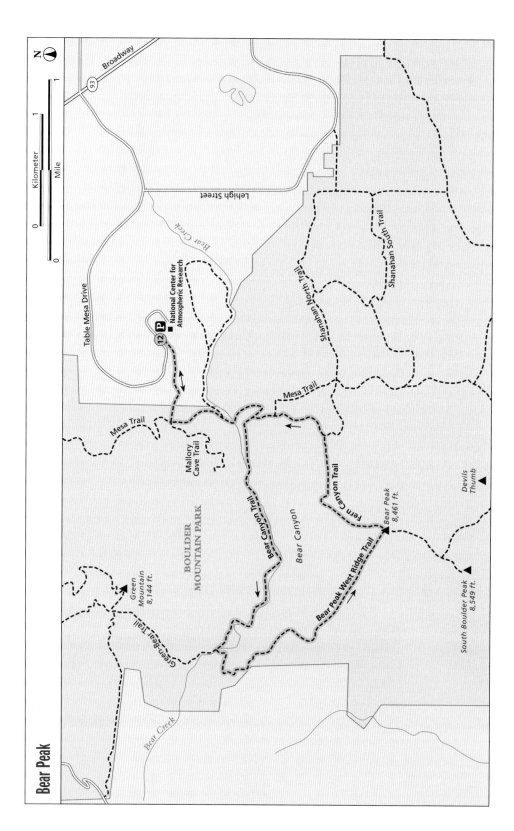

Bear Peak

MILES AND DIRECTIONS

0.0 Start behind NCAR on the Walter Orr-Roberts Trail.

0.2 Arrive at a kiosk and sign for the Mesa Trail.

0.7 Pass a very large water tank.

1.2 Arrive at a junction with the Mesa Trail and Bear Creek.

1.4 Arrive at a junction with Bear Canyon Trail.

3.1 Arrive at a junction with Green-Bear Trail.

4.7 Arrive at the spectacular summit of Bear Peak.

4.8 Arrive at a junction with Fern Canyon Trail.

5.6 Arrive at a junction with Shanahan North Trail.

6.0 Arrive back at a junction with Mesa Trail.

7.4 Arrive back at NCAR, the trailhead, and the parking area.

13 WALKER RANCH LOOP

WHY GO?

This popular hike leads around the old homestead of James Walker. Beautiful views, excellent wildflowers, and good fishing along South Boulder Creek are the main attractions on this hike.

THE RUNDOWN

Start: From the South Boulder Creek Trailhead and parking area
Distance: 7.4-mile loop
Approximate hiking time: 3 to 4.5 hours
Difficulty: Moderate
Elevation gain: Minimal
Seasons: Year-round
Trail surface: Extremely rocky in places

Other trail users: Mountain bikers and equestrians
Canine compatibility: Dogs must be on leash
Maps: USGS Boulder County; Boulder County Open Space/Walker Ranch map
Trail contacts: Boulder County Open Space; (303) 678-6200; www.bouldercounty.org/government/dept/pages/pos.aspx

FINDING THE TRAILHEAD

From the intersection of Broadway and Baseline Road in Boulder, travel 7.5 miles west on Baseline, which becomes Flagstaff Road and climbs up past Flagstaff Mountain. Turn left into the South Boulder Creek Trailhead and parking area at Walker Ranch. **GPS:** N39 57.05' / W105 20.15'

THE HIKE

From the trailhead, go through the gate and begin a nice descent to South Boulder Creek. The Walker Ranch Loop Trail follows an old road and passes several rock formations on the right. At the bottom of the hill, cross a small stream and then go right along beautiful South Boulder Creek.

The trail goes upstream to a bridge. Cross the bridge and go left up the steep hill. Crest the steep part of the hill, where the trail bends to the right, and enjoy excellent views to the west. This trail is extremely popular with mountain bikers, so be aware of their presence, especially on weekends.

The trail becomes level just past a small rock garden and travels past a gate and down through a beautiful forested area. Climb up a hill and through another gate, where the trail drops you onto Reservoir Road. Go left up the road for 0.1 mile to a trail on the left. Go left up the trail and arrive at Crescent Meadows. Turn left onto the Walker Ranch Loop Trail, heading to the east and through the open meadow. There are great views to the west, and wildflowers light up the meadow in late spring and early summer.

At around the 3.5-mile mark, the trail leads you into a dense forest and starts to drop in elevation. Travel past several rocky sections and through a small, open meadow. Arrive at a sign warning mountain bikers to dismount. Follow rock-and-log steps steeply down to South Boulder Creek and a bridge. This is a good spot to take a break with your dog and admire the scenery. South Boulder Creek runs wild through this section, and the deep pools of water are crystal clear and excellent for fly fishing.

Walker Ranch

ROOSEVELT
NATIONAL FOREST

To Boulder and
Baseline Road

Flagstaff Road

Meyers Homestead Trail

Meyers
Homestead

Gross
Reservoir

South Boulder Creek

Columbine Gulch Trail

Eldorado Canyon Trail

To Eldorado
State Park

WALKER
RANCH PARK

Reservoir Road

Crescent Meadow Trail

ELDORADO
CANYON
STATE PARK

WALKER
RANCH
PARK

72

72

N

0 Kilometer 1

0 Mile 1

A young deer getting its new antlers

Cross the bridge and turn left, passing the Eldorado Canyon Trail on the right. Begin a good climb through the ponderosa and spruce trees to a junction with the Columbine Gulch Trail at the 5.8-mile mark. Go left on this narrow trail into a narrow, forested gulch. Pass a small stream, then begin a steep ascent past several switchbacks. A beautiful stretch brings you up and out of the gulch to a ridge and excellent views. Go right and up a gentle grade, following the Columbine Gulch Trail past a recent burn area and back to the trailhead.

Once the site of the largest cattle ranch on the Front Range, Walker Ranch is now a beautiful piece of open space land that provides a glimpse into Boulder County history. James Walker first came to the area for health reasons, and thrived in the fresh mountain air and peaceful setting of open meadows and mountain terrain. Hope you do the same on this hike.

MILES AND DIRECTIONS

0.0   Start from the parking area and pass through a gate at the kiosk.

1.0   Cross over a small stream.

1.5   Cross a bridge over South Boulder Creek.

2.4   Pass Reservoir Road.

4.5   Begin a serious steep, rocky descent.

4.7   Cross a bridge over South Boulder Creek.

5.8   Go left on the Columbine Gulch Trail.

7.4   Arrive back at the trailhead.

14 MARSHALL MESA

WHY GO?
Kids, dogs—the entire family—will enjoy this beautiful Front Range hike on a great trail system with wonderful vistas in a park-like setting.

THE RUNDOWN

Start: From the Marshall Valley Trailhead parking area
Distance: 3.3-mile loop
Approximately hiking time: 1.5 to 3 hours
Difficulty: Moderate
Elevation gain: About 150 feet
Seasons: Year-round; can be snow-packed in winter months
Trail surface: Smooth and hard-packed, with short rocky sections

Other trail users: Mountain bikers and equestrians
Canine compatibility: Dogs must be on leash or voice control
Map: Boulder County Open Space/ Marshall Mesa
Trail contacts: Boulder County Open Space; (303) 678-6200; www .bouldercounty.org/government/ dept/pages/pos.aspx

FINDING THE TRAILHEAD

From Boulder, access Broadway (CO 93) south to the intersection with Marshall Road (CO 170). Turn left onto Marshall Road and make a quick right into the trailhead parking area. **GPS:** N39 57.18' / W105 13.89'

THE HIKE

Dogs must be leashed in the Marshall Mesa parking area; beyond that, the Voice and Sight Tag program means that dogs and their humans who have passed their test and paid their fees can enjoy some off-leash time. Fees to enroll a dog who responds to voice commands in the program vary, depending on where you live. City of Boulder residents pay the lowest amount, followed by Boulder County residents who don't live in the city of Boulder. While non–Boulder County residents pay the highest amount, consider that it's about the same cost as the fine you would have to pay if you're caught with your dog off-leash and no tag. Fees cover one person and one dog; you can add another household human or dog to your permit for an additional amount.

Start from the trailhead parking area and walk south into an open field on the Marshall Valley Trail. Hike through cactus, prairie grass, and yucca to a trail junction at a wooden bridge. Follow the Community Ditch Trail up a short hill with great views to the east, west, and north. Arrive at the top of the hill and panoramic views. Go right, following the Community Ditch Trail and enjoying more great views. The trail follows the ditch on your left. This is a great place to let your dog swim on hot summer days. Pass several trail junctions, staying on the Community Ditch Trail to a junction with the Coal Seam Trail. Turn right onto this beautiful trail; wildflowers are profuse here during the spring and summer months. Arrive back at the trailhead and parking area.

This is a very popular hiking and biking trail in the Boulder area. It can be extremely busy during the weekends. Get to the parking area early, and be respectful of other trail users. Share the trail and be courteous; a smile to fellow users goes a long way.

Marshall Mesa

0   Kilometer   0.5

0   Mile   0.5

N

To Boulder

93

Marshall

170

Cowdrey Draw

P

14

Marshall Valley Trail

Coal Seam Trail

170

Community Ditch Trail

Marshall Lake

Greenbelt Trail

CITY OF BOULDER
OPEN SPACE

Coal Creek

P

93

128

To Golden

MILES AND DIRECTIONS

0.0 From the parking area, head south and access the Marshall Valley Trail. Follow the Marshall Valley Trail left into an open field.

0.9 Reach a junction with the Community Ditch Trail just past a bridge. Veer right on the Community Ditch Trail and climb a hill to a trail junction.

1.2 Arrive at a trail junction; turn right, following the Community Ditch Trail.

1.4 Continue straight on the Community Ditch Trail.

2.2 Continue straight on the Community Ditch Trail.

2.3 Arrive at a junction with the Greenbelt Trail. Continue straight on the Community Ditch Trail.

2.7 Arrive at a junction with the Coal Seam Trail. Turn right onto the Coal Seam Trail.

3.3 Arrive back at the trailhead parking area.

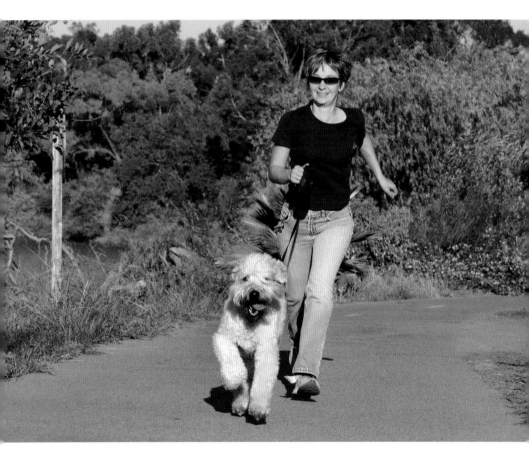

A dog's natural gait is usually faster than ours, so it can be difficult for them to adjust to our slower pace, particularly on narrow or steeper trails.

15 ELDORADO CANYON TRAIL

WHY GO?

This beautiful hike leads along towering rock walls. The trail travels up a south- and west-facing hillside through North Draw, with spectacular views of the Indian Peaks, the Continental Divide, Denver, and towering, sheer rock walls. It's an iconic rock-climbing area, so you'll likely see folks scaling Eldo's sheer cliffs as you enter the park.

THE RUNDOWN

Start: From the Eldorado Canyon Trailhead, just north of the parking area

Distance: 5.8 miles out and back

Approximate hiking time: 2.5 to 3.5 hours

Difficulty: Moderate

Elevation gain: 1,000 feet

Seasons: Year-round

Trail surface: Smooth in parts, extremely rocky in others

Other trail users: Equestrians

Canine compatibility: Dogs must be on leash

Maps: USGS Boulder County; Colorado State Parks/Eldorado Canyon State Park map

Trail contacts: Colorado State Parks; (303) 866-3437; www.parks.state .co.us

FINDING THE TRAILHEAD

From the intersection of Broadway and Baseline in Boulder, travel south on Broadway (CO 93) to CO 170. Go right on CO 170 for 4.4 miles to the entrance/fee station and parking area for Eldorado Canyon State Park. Pay the day-use fee and follow the dirt road up to the ranger station, parking area, and trailhead. **GPS:** N39 55.49' / W105 17.37'

THE HIKE

From the parking area at the ranger station, walk north up some steps and cross the road to access the Eldorado Canyon Trailhead. Begin a steep climb into North Draw on the Eldorado Canyon Trail. Much work has been done on the lower section of the trail to eliminate cutting switchbacks, so stay on the main trail.

You gain altitude quickly as the trail climbs up into North Draw. Great views open to the north, of Shirttail Peak and towering rock walls that are popular with rock climbers from around the world. Eldorado Canyon has been a popular spot for rock climbers since the 1950s, and has been at the forefront of Colorado rock climbing.

At around the 0.4-mile mark, the trail climbs through a series of steep switchbacks across a steep hillside. At the top of the switchbacks, a climbers' trail on the right leads to the Rincon Wall. Continue straight on the Eldorado Canyon Trail.

The trail becomes level and views open to the west, onto the Indian Peaks and the Continental Divide. Cacti, yuccas, and other sun-loving plants grow on the west-facing hillside, which becomes quite colorful with blooming flowers and cacti during the late spring and early summer months.

At around the 1.3-mile mark, the trail climbs five steep switchbacks and enters a dense pine forest. Large, colorful boulders line the trail; look for a small spring that seeps out

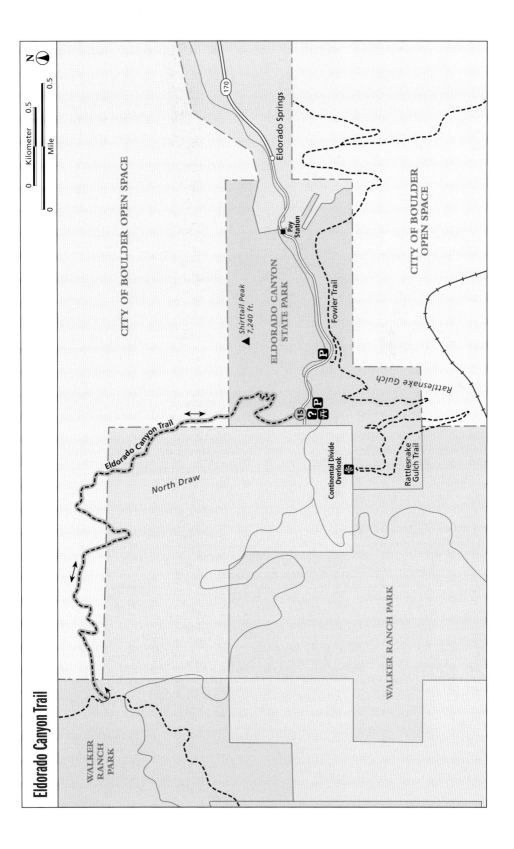

Eldorado Canyon Trail

CITY OF BOULDER OPEN SPACE

CITY OF BOULDER OPEN SPACE

ELDORADO CANYON STATE PARK

▲ *Shirttail Peak* 7,240 ft.

Eldorado Canyon Trail

North Draw

Fowler Trail

Rattlesnake Gulch

Rattlesnake Gulch Trail

Continental Divide Overlook

WALKER RANCH PARK

WALKER RANCH PARK

Eldorado Springs

Pay Station

15

170

0   Kilometer   0.5

0   Mile   0.5

N

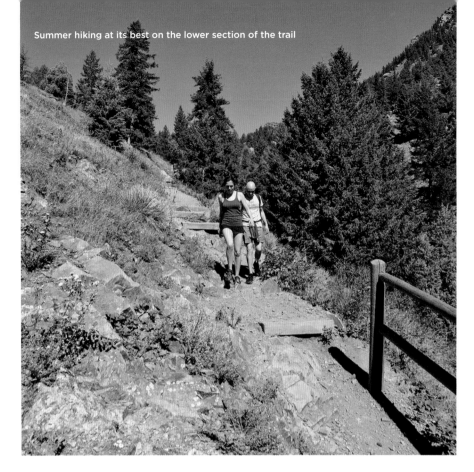
Summer hiking at its best on the lower section of the trail

from one of the boulders, just to the right of the trail. The trail curves to the west and crosses over a small seasonal drainage via a wooden footbridge.

Beyond the footbridge the trail begins a modest climb up through the pines to an open meadow filled with yuccas and small ponderosas, with great views to the east, south, and west. South Boulder Peak (8,549 feet) looms high above to the northeast. The trail cuts a straight line across the meadow and climbs a short, rocky section, gaining a small ridge and high point with great views south to Eldorado Mountain.

At around the 2.9-mile mark, the trail begins to drop and goes right, down into Walker Ranch Open Space. This is the turnaround point of this hike. Feel free to drop down to Walker Ranch and South Boulder Creek for more mileage and views. Otherwise, retrace your steps to the trailhead.

MILES AND DIRECTIONS

0.0   Start by heading up into North Draw on the Eldorado Canyon Trail.

0.5   A climbers' trail to Rincon Wall goes right.

1.3   Arrive at a series of steep switchbacks.

2.9   Arrive at the turnaround point and great views to the west.

5.8   Arrive back at the trailhead.

16 BEAVER BROOK TRAIL

WHY GO?

While most of the Golden valley bakes in the sun, much of the Beaver Brook Trail remains shady all day long. You can do the trail as an out-and-back option all the way from the Beaver Brook Trailhead at the Chief Hosa exit off I-70 (that makes it a long 18 miles), set up a shuttle or have a friend pick you up either there or at the Windy Saddle Trailhead, or (my personal favorite) do an out-and-back of just about any length you'd like from the Windy Saddle end on Lookout Mountain. Whatever you choose, it's a lovely hike with stellar views and plenty of shade.

THE RUNDOWN

Start: From the Windy Saddle Trailhead
Distance: Up to 20 miles, if you do the whole trail, out and back
Approximate hiking time: Up to 8 hours, if you hike the whole trail
Difficulty: Moderate
Elevation gain: 2,073 feet, if you hike the whole trail
Seasons: Year-round
Trail surface: Singletrack dirt path, occasionally rocky
Other trail users: Hikers only

Canine compatibility: Dogs must be on leash
Maps: USGS Morrison and Evergreen; Jefferson County Open Space map at https://www.jeffco.us/DocumentCenter/View/14152/Beaver-Brook-map-brochure
Trail contacts: Jefferson County Open Space, 700 Jefferson County Parkway, Ste. 100, Open Space Building, Golden; (303) 271-5925; https://www.jeffco.us/1440/Windy-Saddle-Park

FINDING THE TRAILHEAD

From downtown Golden, head south on Washington Avenue and take a right on 19th Street. The road crosses Highway 93 just west of the Colorado School of Mines campus and begins climbing up Lookout Mountain. Follow Lookout Mountain Road for 3 miles until you see the entrance to Windy Saddle Park on the right. **GPS:** N39 44.19' / W105 14.72'

THE HIKE

Golden, Colorado, butts up against the foothills, and is in many ways the gateway to the Rockies. Out-of-towners often picture Denver as a mountain town, but in reality, it's way out on the plains—Golden, the state's former capital, is more like what they're envisioning. It was founded during the gold rush of the late nineteenth century, and in the intervening years, it's grown considerably. Visitors to the high country pass just south of Golden on I-70; the mountains are also accessible via Highway 6, which runs up Clear Creek Canyon; the creek runs right through downtown Golden.

Golden itself remains an attractive tourist destination; there's ample hiking, mountain biking, rock climbing, and even tubing and whitewater kayaking available without ever getting in a car. It's also a hub for outdoor enthusiasts, and is home to several specialty bike and climbing shops, along with several excellent restaurants and breweries. (Its most famous tenant is the gargantuan Coors Brewery.)

One of the town's most prominent features is Mount Zion, which has a prominent "M" made up of white rocks on its east-facing slope. M stands for Mines; the Colorado School of Mines is an engineering college whose campus is on a picturesque hillside in town. Visitors often mistake Mount Zion for Lookout Mountain, the peak just behind it, which is home to Buffalo Bill's grave site, along with a museum and visitor center, and the Lookout Mountain Nature Center.

A drive up windy Lookout Mountain road is a great way to see the town from an up-high vantage point, and it's also the best way to access Windy Saddle Park, the eastern terminus of the Beaver Brook Trail. In the summer months, the hiking in and around Golden is virtually shade-free: North and South Table Mountains are high mesas with few tall trees, which also means that rattlesnakes abound. (In fact, North Table Mountain was recently discovered to contain a hibernaculum, the scientific word for a gigantic rattlesnake den filled with countless snakes. Parts of the trail are often closed during the peak season, when dozens of snakes are out sunning themselves on the rocks.)

Beaver Brook, on the other hand, is quite shady even when it's hot: The trail is largely along north faces, and its less-desert-like climate means the snakes aren't out in force the way they are on some of Golden's other popular hikes. That's not to say you won't see a rattler on the Beaver Brook Trail—that's a possibility anywhere in Golden.

The first several miles of the Beaver Brook Trail from Windy Saddle are fairly flat, with only small ups and downs. There are a few rocky sections, though the trail remains fairly well-defined throughout them. The trailhead is shared with mountain bikers, but they're required to take a left-hand turn less than a quarter-mile from the trailhead, and from there hikers have the trail to themselves to take in views of Clear Creek and its namesake canyon.

There are a few spots on this trail that will likely require hands to scramble over rocks, and a few fairly exposed cliffy sections. None are overly technical, though with a dog on a leash, you should be aware of them and keep your dog under control as you approach.

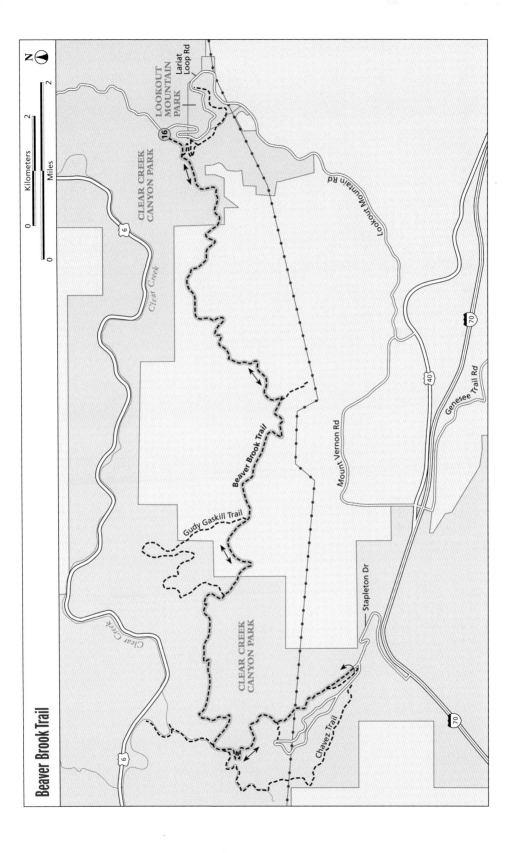

Beaver Brook Trail

N

Kilometers
0   2

Miles
0   2

Clear Creek

6

CLEAR CREEK
CANYON PARK

16

LOOKOUT
MOUNTAIN
PARK

Lariat Loop Rd

Lookout Mountain Rd

Beaver Brook Trail

Gudy Gaskill Trail

Mount Vernon Rd

40

70

Genesee Trail Rd

Clear Creek

6

CLEAR CREEK
CANYON PARK

Stapleton Dr

Chavez Trail

70

The Beaver Brook Trail winds along mostly in the shade. North Table Mountain is on the left in the distance.

When in doubt, scramble down first, then call your dog to you; it's much safer than allowing an eager canine to pull you down over the rocks.

Mountain lions and black bears have occasionally been spotted in this vicinity, so this is not a good hike to do alone at dawn or dusk. For the most part, though, you'll see only other happy hikers and their pups strolling along as you hike, which you can do for a quick midday jaunt, or for a beast of an 18-mile workout.

OPTIONS

You can also begin your hike at the Beaver Brook Trailhead at Genesee Mountain Park, which you'll access via I-70. Take exit 254 (one exit past the iconic bison herd) and turn right, essentially into a U-turn. Follow Stapleton Drive down a steep hill and park in the parking area. Follow signs for the Beaver Brook Trail.

MILES AND DIRECTIONS

0.0   Begin at the Windy Saddle Trailhead.

0.2   The trail splits and mountain bikers must exit. Keep right to stay on Beaver Brook.

0.6   Cross the brook, which may or may not be running.

0.8   This brief rocky, exposed section may require hands for scrambling.

1.1   Reach an overlook where there's a great stopping point to peer into Clear Creek Canyon.

2.0   Cross another, slightly larger stream. This is a good spot to let your pooch grab a drink and cool off.

2.3   A steady uphill climb from 6,800 feet to 7,750 feet begins.

5.2   Reach the high point of the Beaver Brook Trail and begin descending. Grades reach 25 percent on this descent.

6.7   Arrive at the lowest-elevation point on this hike (6,566 feet) and begin the ascent to the Beaver Brook Trailhead.

9.0   Arrive at the Beaver Brook Trailhead (7,417 feet). Arrange for pickup, or retrace your steps back to Windy Saddle Park.

SOUTHERN FRONT RANGE

The Front Range designation generally refers to the Denver Metropolitan Area, including Fort Collins, Boulder, and Golden, typically on down to Littleton. South of that area, though, "Front Range" doesn't quite apply, although "Southeast Mountains" doesn't feel quite right, either. With that in mind, the hikes in the Colorado Springs area have been grouped in a **SOUTHERN FRONT RANGE** section for this book.

There's a significant military presence in the Springs, including the US Air Force Academy, Fort Carson (an army base), and Forts Peterson and Schriever, both Air Force bases. The city—the second-most populous in Colorado—is also home to the Team USA Olympic Training Center. You'll find plenty of reasons to be patriotic when you take in the views around town.

Colorado Springs sits at the base of 14,115-foot Pikes Peak. The peak was the namesake for Katherine Lee Bates's original version of what would later become "America the Beautiful," and it's not hard to see why. Although sprawling Colorado Springs has taken over many miles east of town, climb Pikes or any of its satellites, and you'll still see plenty of purple mountains' majesty and amber waves of grain.

17 SUSAN G. BRETAG / PALMER LOOP

WHY GO?

This loop hike follows four different trails and offers spectacular views of the Garden of the Gods and Pikes Peak. Dogs will have lots of smells to sniff at the various trail forks, as horses and mountain bikers are known to travel the various trails.

THE RUNDOWN

Start: From the trailhead on the north side of the main Garden of the Gods parking lot
Distance: 2.6-mile loop
Approximate hiking time: 1 hour
Difficulty: Moderate
Elevation gain: 200 feet
Seasons: Year-round
Trail surface: Singletrack dirt path and doubletrack paved trail
Other trail users: Mountain bikers and equestrians on parts of the trail

Canine compatibility: Dogs must be on leash
Fees and permits: None
Map: USGS Cascade
Trail contacts: Colorado Springs Parks, Recreation, and Cultural Services, 1401 Recreation Way, Colorado Springs, CO 80905-1975; (719) 385-5940; www.springsgov.com
Other: Colorado Springs city park rules apply.

FINDING THE TRAILHEAD

From I-25, take exit 146 and drive west on Garden of the Gods Road until it dead-ends at 30th Street against the mountain front. Turn left (south) onto 30th Street and drive south to Gateway Road, opposite the Garden of the Gods Visitor and Nature Center. Turn right (west) onto Gateway Road and follow it until it merges with Juniper Way Loop, a one-way loop road that encircles the main Garden of the Gods zone. Turn right (north) onto the one-way road and follow it to a large parking lot on the left. The trailhead is at the north side of the parking lot at a crosswalk. **GPS:** N38 53.00' / W104 52.63'

Alternatively, approach from I-25 and downtown Colorado Springs by driving west on Cimarron Street / US 24 from I-25 to Ridge Road, 0.5 mile past 31st Street. Exit right and follow Ridge Road north to a stop sign at Colorado Avenue. Cross Colorado Avenue (the road may be busy) and drive up a steep hill on Ridge Road to the Garden of the Gods. At Juniper Way Loop, go right and drive to the main parking lot on the north side of the park.

THE HIKE

This pleasant hike follows parts of four different trails around the main red-rock zone of the Garden of the Gods. The first section, following Palmer Trail, climbs onto ridges west of North and South Gateway Rocks before dipping down to the Scotsman Picnic Area. The next segment follows Scotsman Trail back to the central Garden zone, where it picks up the paved Perkins Central Garden Trail. The last part follows the Susan G. Bretag Trail north up a broad valley east of the rock formations.

The trails are singletrack except for a wide concrete sidewalk section. Expect great views and a close-up, intimate experience with the unique rock formations and the transitional ecosystems found here. Most of the trail is quiet, with few other hikers, although the section through the main Garden zone is busy. The trail also crosses the park roads four times. Be sure to use the crosswalks.

Start the hike at the trailhead on the north side of the main parking lot off Juniper Way Loop. Walk north across the road to a trail junction. Go left on the Palmer Trail. The trail coming in from the right, the Susan G. Bretag Trail, is the return trail. The first trail segment on the Palmer Trail, named for General William Jackson Palmer, the founder of Colorado Springs, runs 1.2 miles from the junction to the Scotsman Picnic Area, southwest of the central Garden zone.

Paralleling the road, the Palmer Trail goes northwest through copses of scrub oak before arcing south. It slowly gains elevation and after 0.3 mile reaches a scenic overlook. Walk 75 feet southeast off the trail for the best view and photo opportunity. All the main rock formations—North Gateway Rock, South Gateway Rock, Gray Rock, Keyhole Rock, Montezuma Ruins, and the Three Graces—tower to the south, their ragged outlines etched against the sky.

Past the overlook the trail turns west and contours through a shallow canyon before climbing onto east-facing slopes opposite North Gateway Rock, the park's highest formation. The trail continues climbing through a piñon pine and juniper woodland until it reaches a high point and then descends to a shoulder. This is another great viewpoint. Note the Kissing Camels, a small arch perched atop North Gateway Rock on the left, and the Weeping Indian, the white rock profile of an Indian face on South Gateway Rock. Continue south down the trail and reach a junction 0.8 mile from the trailhead. From here a short trail heads left to the central Garden zone. Stay straight on the Palmer Trail, ignoring another side trail that jogs over to the road 100 feet farther down.

The Palmer Trail passes beneath the west face of the Giant Footprints, a couple of tilted slabs composed of 220-million-year-old Fountain Formation sandstone, then descends southwest parallel to the park road through scrub oak for 0.4 mile. When the trail reaches the edge of the road at 1.2 miles, you're opposite the Scotsman Picnic Area. Cross the road to a parking lot and cross a bridge. A restroom, open in summer only, is to your left. Go right on the Scotsman Trail.

Follow the Scotsman Trail northeast for 0.36 mile. The sandy trail, often used by horses, slowly climbs. At an obvious junction, keep left and hike to the Juniper Way Loop road. Cross the road just north of a parking area and follow a trail into the central Garden zone.

The next 0.5 mile of trail follows the paved Perkins Central Garden Trail, the Garden's most popular trail. Hike north and then east on the paved path, passing north of the Three Graces and Montezuma Tower, both slender spires popular with rock climbers. At an obvious T junction, go left (north) and hike to the Gateway, the huge gap between North and South Gateway Rocks. At the trail junction here below the dedication plaque, turn right onto a paved trail and walk 0.15 mile east to Juniper Way Loop.

The last trail segment follows the Susan G. Bretag Trail for 0.5 mile back to the trailhead and parking lot. Cross the road at a crosswalk and turn left onto the marked trail. Follow the wide trail north in a valley between rock formations on the west and a hogback to the east. The trail crosses a meadow covered with grass and yucca. After 0.3 mile it reaches a Y junction with the Dakota Trail. Keep left and follow the Susan G. Bretag Trail, which bends northwest. End your hike at the start of the Palmer Trail. Cross the road back to the trailhead. If you're thirsty or need the facilities, a water fountain and restrooms are located on the southeast side of the parking lot.

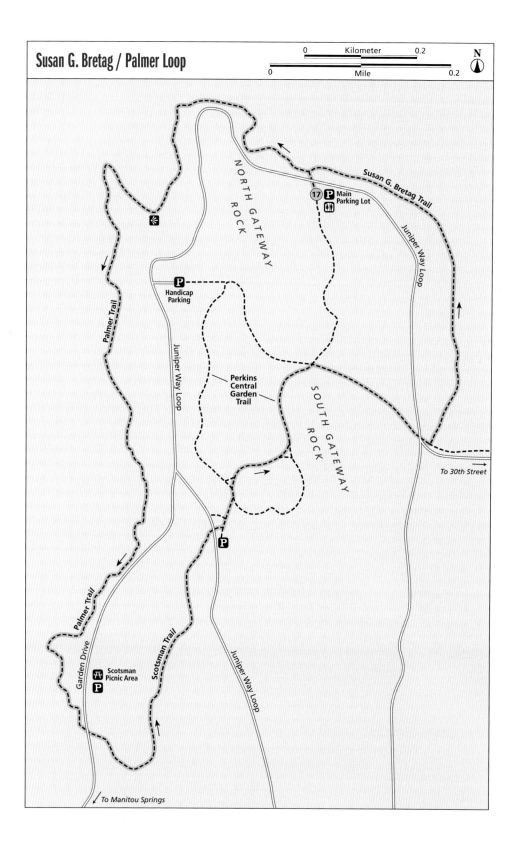

Susan G. Bretag / Palmer Loop

0 Kilometer 0.2
0 Mile 0.2

N

NORTH GATEWAY ROCK

Susan G. Bretag Trail

17 P Main Parking Lot

Juniper Way Loop

Palmer Trail

P Handicap Parking

Perkins Central Garden Trail

SOUTH GATEWAY ROCK

To 30th Street

P

Palmer Trail

Garden Drive

Scotsman Trail

Scotsman Picnic Area

P

Juniper Way Loop

To Manitou Springs

MILES AND DIRECTIONS

0.0 Start at the trailhead on the north side of the main Garden parking lot. Cross the road to a T junction and turn left (west) onto the Palmer Trail.

0.3 Come to a scenic overlook on the left.

0.8 Reach a junction with a short trail to the Garden zone on the left. Go straight.

1.2 Reach a road opposite the Scotsman Picnic Area. Cross the road to the left and then cross a bridge to reach Scotsman Trail. Go right.

1.6 End the Scotsman Trail at Juniper Way Loop. Cross the road to the central Garden zone. Follow the trail straight to the paved Perkins Central Garden Trail.

2.1 End the Perkins Central Garden Trail at the Juniper Way Loop on the east side of the park. Cross the street and turn left (north) onto the Susan G. Bretag Trail.

2.6 End the Susan G. Bretag Trail at the junction with the Palmer Trail. Go left across the road to return to the trailhead and parking lot.

18 LOWER BARR TRAIL

WHY GO?

The Barr Trail is the standard route up Fourteener Pikes Peak, which is among Colorado's most famous summits. The trail is a whopping 13 miles one-way, but even if you're not up for a literal marathon-length hike, this great day hike follows the trail's first 3 miles up Mount Manitou. You'll get excellent views of the surrounding mountains.

THE RUNDOWN

Start: From the Barr Trailhead on Hydro Street
Distance: 6.4 miles out and back
Approximate hiking time: 3 to 5 hours
Difficulty: Moderate
Elevation gain: 1,600 feet
Seasons: Year-round; cold and icy in winter
Trail surface: Wide singletrack dirt path

Other trail users: Runners
Canine compatibility: Dogs must be on leash
Fees and permits: None
Map: USGS Manitou Springs
Trail contacts: Pike National Forest, Pikes Peak Ranger District, 601 S. Weber St., Colorado Springs, CO 80903; (719) 636-1602; www.fs.usda.go

FINDING THE TRAILHEAD

To reach the Barr Trailhead from I-25, take the Cimarron Street / US 24 exit and drive west on US 24 for 5.4 miles to the first Manitou Springs exit. The exit ramp circles onto Manitou Avenue. Turn right and drive west on Manitou Avenue for 1.4 miles (following signs for the cog railroad) to a roundabout at its intersection with Ruxton Avenue. Turn left (southwest) at the roundabout onto Ruxton and travel 0.8 mile, past the cog railroad depot to Hydro Street. Turn right (northwest) onto Hydro Street and drive uphill 0.1 mile to the parking area and trailhead. (**Note:** The parking lot is usually full, especially in the morning. If it is, park on Ruxton Avenue below the cog railroad depot. Do not park in the cog railroad parking lots.) **GPS:** N38 51.34' / W104 56.04'

THE HIKE

Pikes Peak, looming 8,000 feet above Colorado Springs, is one of America's most famous mountains. The summit of the 14,115-foot peak is accessible by road—in fact, it's among the highest paved roads in North America, second only to the road up Mount Evans, a little farther north—and the Barr Trail, which climbs 12.6 miles from Manitou Springs to the summit.

For many years, visitors could also ride a cog railway to the top of Pikes Peak, which made for a novel experience. In 2018, however, the railway did not reopen for the summer, and after careful evaluation, it was determined that the infrastructure of the railway had run its course. No more costly repairs are being considered for the railway in the foreseeable future, so unless you're driving to the summit, the only way up is via your own two feet (or four feet, as the case may be).

Barr Trail is a difficult hike up Colorado's thirty-first-highest peak, not an easy day hike. If you're not up for a marathon-length hike (and even if you are, many dogs would

Lower Barr Trail

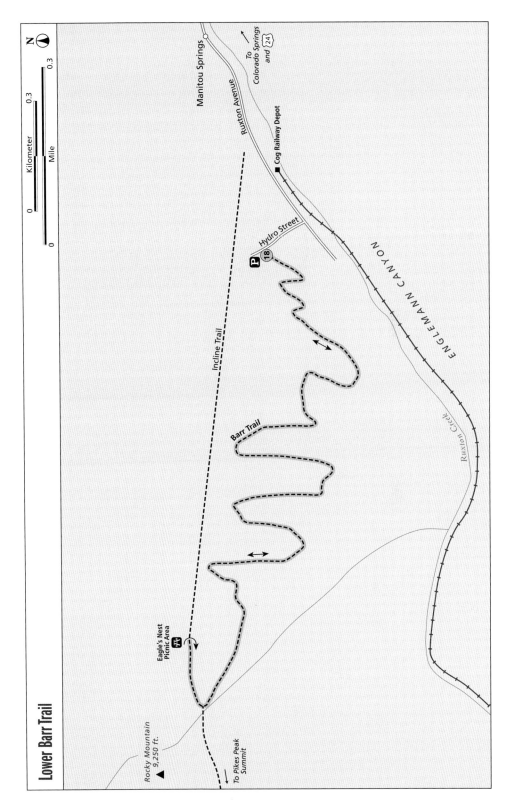

Rocky Mountain
9,250 ft.

To Pikes Peak
Summit

Eagle's Nest
Picnic Area

Incline Trail

Barr Trail

ENGLEMANN CANYON

Ruxton Creek

Hydro Street

P 18

Cog Railway Depot

Ruxton Avenue

Manitou Springs

To
Colorado Springs
and 24

N

Kilometer
0   0.3

Mile
0   0.3

not be up to the challenge), take on this shorter, 6.4-mile round-trip hike up the trail's lower section and sample some of its best terrain and views.

The hike switchbacks up the eastern face of 9,250-foot Rocky Mountain, a spur of Mount Manitou, and features easy grades on the wide trail, fabulous views, and moderate hiking. Wear sturdy shoes, maintain a steady pace, and carry water and energy drinks in summer. At the top you'll be rewarded for your efforts.

Begin the hike at the trailhead at a parking area on Hydro Street. Hike up switchbacks on the trail, which traverses back and forth across the mountain's east face above Englemann Canyon to the south. After 0.3 mile you reach a trail junction. Bend sharply right on Barr Trail. As you slowly climb through scrub oak, ponderosa pine, and Douglas fir, great views unfold of Manitou Springs below, the red rocks of Garden of the Gods to the northeast, and sprawling Colorado Springs beyond. Hiking up Barr Trail from Manitou Springs to the summit is like taking a telescoped journey from Mexico to the Arctic, passing through almost all the major ecological life zones.

A trail marker at 1 mile announces the elevation as 7,200 feet. Past here, large granite boulders line the trail. You pass a lofty rock outcrop at 1.8 miles that offers spectacular views of Englemann Canyon to the south. This is a good picnic spot and, if you're tired, a turnaround point.

Barr Trail continues west, alternately traversing steep slopes and climbing switchbacks up the south-facing side of Rocky Mountain. Rocky slopes spill into the canyon, and if you look closely, you'll spot the tracks of the cog railroad below. Farther along, the trail ducks through a tunnel of boulders that have fallen against one another like giant dominoes and passes a small concrete tunnel on the right. At 2.6 miles you reach a trail junction at No Name Creek. To finish the hike, turn right onto Incline Trail. (Barr Trail continues straight west from the junction, toward Barr Camp and the Pikes Peak summit.)

Follow the flat, wide Incline Trail east past a granite cliff to a trail fork. Go left (east) on the upper trail, which heads slightly downhill to the EAGLE'S NEST TRAIL sign at 3 miles. Keep right (east) on the descending trail to a stunning overlook and the hike's turnaround point at Eagle's Nest Picnic Area. From this lofty perch you'll enjoy an eagle's view of the city below, spreading east to the tawny prairie and the distant horizon.

Catch your breath, take a drink of water, and rest your feet for a few minutes. Now tighten your boot laces and head back the way you came. The return trip, all of it downhill, goes fast. Remember the trail junctions on the way down. Stick to the well-beaten trail and you'll be fine.

MILES AND DIRECTIONS

0.0   Start at the Barr Trailhead at the parking area on Hydro Street.

0.3   At the junction, go right on the main trail.

1.0   Pass the 7,200-foot elevation marker.

1.8   Rest at the overlook rocks. (**Option:** Turn around here for a 3.6-mile round-trip hike.)

2.6   Reach the Incline Trail intersection. Turn right onto the Incline Trail.

3.2   Come to the Eagle's Nest Picnic Area, the hike's turnaround point. Retrace your steps.

6.4   Arrive back at the trailhead.

19 HORSETHIEF FALLS

WHY GO?

A steady climb leads to Horsethief Park, a high mountain meadow, and ends at a cascading waterfall on the western slope of Pikes Peak.

THE RUNDOWN

Start: From the parking area near the old Little Ike Tunnel
Distance: 2.2 miles out and back
Approximate hiking time: 1 to 2 hours
Difficulty: Moderate due to technical terrain
Elevation gain: 460 feet
Seasons: Best from May through Oct; snowy in winter
Trail surface: Dirt path
Other trail users: Mountain bikers and equestrians

Canine compatibility: Dogs must be on leash
Fees and permits: None
Maps: USGS Pikes Peak and Cripple Creek North
Trail contacts: Pike National Forest, Pikes Peak Ranger District, 601 S. Weber St., Colorado Springs, CO 80903; (719) 636-1602; www.fs.usda.gov
Other: Snowshoes required in winter

FINDING THE TRAILHEAD

From I-25, take the Cimarron Street / US 24 exit (exit 141) and head west. Drive up US 24 through Ute Pass and Woodland Park to the town of Divide. Go left in Divide onto CO 67. Drive 9.2 miles south on CO 67, pass a closed-off tunnel on the left, and go around a curve. The gravel parking area and trailhead is on the left at the other end of the old Little Ike Tunnel. **GPS:** N38 50.06' / W105 08.24'

THE HIKE

Located off CO 67, an oft-traveled route between Divide and the historic mining town of Cripple Creek, the Horsethief Falls Trail (Trail 704B) offers the solitude and beauty of the Rocky Mountains without straying far from the beaten path. The singletrack dirt trail ends at the crystalline falls, which spills over a jumble of granite boulders. The waterfall is most dramatic in early summer, when it's swollen with snowmelt from Sentinel Point, a spur of Pikes Peak. Although steep at the beginning, the trail is perfect for families, kids, and dogs. It's also a great winter hike on snowshoes.

You'll get most of the elevation gain out of the way on the first half-mile of this hike. Departing from the right corner of the parking lot at 9,740 feet, the trail climbs briskly above the road and rounds a wide switchback. The path traverses above a blocked-off area above the old tunnel, then zigzags back right and enters forested north-facing slopes in a deep valley.

The sound of the highway traffic fades as the wide track steadily ascends, traversing a shelf across a steep slope. Small moss-covered granite boulders are strewn about the hillside beneath a dark evergreen forest, offering plenty of shade, and the distant sound of rushing water drifts up from the valley below.

After scrambling over a short rocky section, the trail finally levels out at 0.6 mile and edges alongside a gently rushing creek in lovely Horsethief Park to a trail junction with

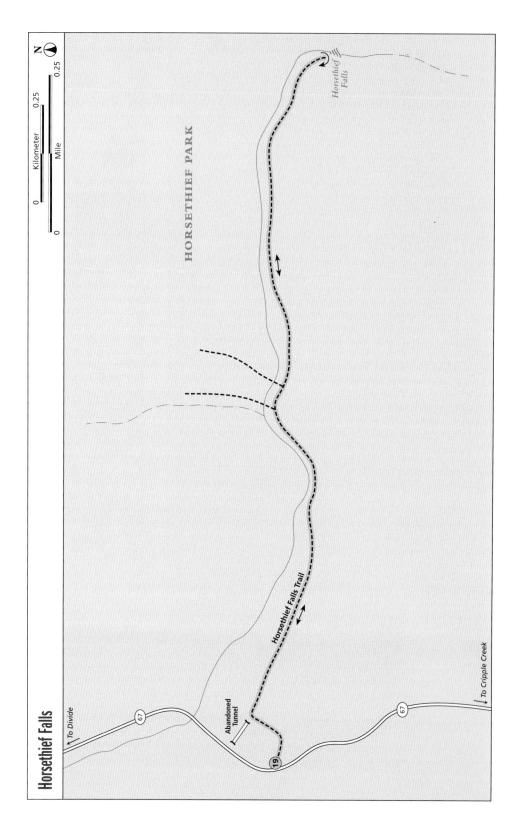

Horsethief Falls

HORSETHIEF PARK

Horsethief Falls

Horsethief Falls Trail

Abandoned Tunnel

19

67

67

To Divide

To Cripple Creek

N

Kilometer
0   0.25

Mile
0   0.25

the Ring the Peak Trail system. Go straight on the main trail; pass beside placid ponds created by beaver dams and head east along the edge of a broad meadow. Across the valley, stands of young aspen, gleaming gold in September, cling to hills that rise from the grassy basin. The trail, slowly climbing up Horsethief Park, is a scenic delight. Also look for cabin ruins, perhaps used by the horse thieves for which the park is named.

Sentinel Point, a prominent pointed summit on the west side of Pikes Peak, looms directly ahead. At 0.7 mile the trail jogs back into the woods at a marked junction with the Pancake Rocks Trail. Go straight and rejoin the willow-lined stream.

After meandering through a forest of tall spruce and fir trees, the trail terminates at the base of Horsethief Falls at 1 mile. The cold mountain stream rushes over the center of an eroded boulder and cascades down a section of granite bedrock. Cross logs over the stream to rest on rocks on the north side, or climb the hillside for 0.1 mile to a perch above the falls at 10,200 feet. Either choice is perfect for a quiet picnic or nap in the sun. In dry years, little water tumbles down the falls.

After exploring Horsethief Falls, return as you came; it's a quick 1.1-mile hike downhill from the falls to your car.

MILES AND DIRECTIONS

0.0 Start at the trailhead on CO 67.

0.6 The steep climb ends and the trail reaches Horsethief Park. Go straight at the junction with Ring the Peak Trail.

0.7 Go straight at the junction with Pancake Rocks Trail.

1.0 Arrive at the base of Horsethief Falls.

1.1 Reach the top of Horsethief Falls. Retrace your path downhill to the trailhead.

2.2 Arrive back at the trailhead.

WHY GO?

A classic hike flanked by towering sandstone walls follows an old road in the heart of Red Rock Canyon Open Space.

THE RUNDOWN

Start: From the trailhead at the east side of the park's main parking lot

Distance: 2.2 miles out and back

Approximate hiking time: 1 to 2 hours

Difficulty: Easy

Elevation gain: 150 feet

Seasons: Year-round

Trail surface: Doubletrack dirt path

Other trail users: Runners, mountain bikers, equestrians

Canine compatibility: Dogs must be on leash

Fees and permits: None

Maps: USGS Manitou Springs; trail map available at park website (below)

Trail contacts: Colorado Springs Parks, Recreation, and Cultural Services, 1401 Recreation Way, Colorado Springs, CO 80905-1975; (719) 385-5940; www.springsgov .com

FINDING THE TRAILHEAD

Red Rock Canyon Open Space is directly south of Garden of the Gods and US 24. To access the area from downtown Colorado Springs and I-25, take the Cimarron Street / US 24 exit (exit 141) and drive west about 3.5 miles toward the mountains. Access the parking areas and trailheads by turning left (south) onto Ridge Road from US 24, which is the only left turn between 31st Street and the first Manitou Springs exit. Use extreme caution turning on and off the busy highway. Drive south on Ridge Road for 0.1 mile and turn left into the park. Drive through a roundabout and go left. Park at the first parking area. (**Note:** Portable toilets and a map are located at the trailhead at the east end of the lot. Additional parking is available at a lot at the end of the park road to the southeast.) **GPS:** N38 51.08' / W104 52.71'

THE HIKE

The Red Rock Canyon Trail explores its namesake canyon, which is the centerpiece of the open space park of the same name. The City of Colorado Springs purchased the park's 787 acres in 2003. Red Rock Canyon itself is a mile-long canyon lined with ruddy sandstone cliffs and floored by scrub oak, cottonwood trees, and grassy meadows. The canyon also harbors archaeological and historical sites, including a quarry that operated from 1886 until 1915.

Begin the hike from the trailhead at the east side of the main parking lot, located on the north side of the park opposite US 24. Portable toilets and a trail map are at the trailhead. An alternative parking area is located past the first parking area at the end of the park road below Red Rock Canyon. If you park here, knock 0.4 mile off your hike.

The first trail segment runs east and then south for 0.35 mile before joining an old road. Just east of the trailhead is a junction with the Mesa and Greenlee Trails, which head south up a closed road. Continue straight and pass the left side of a biking area. Past here the wide trail bends south. Follow the trail between the south parking area and a sandstone cliff that was quarried in the nineteenth century. The trail slowly climbs and

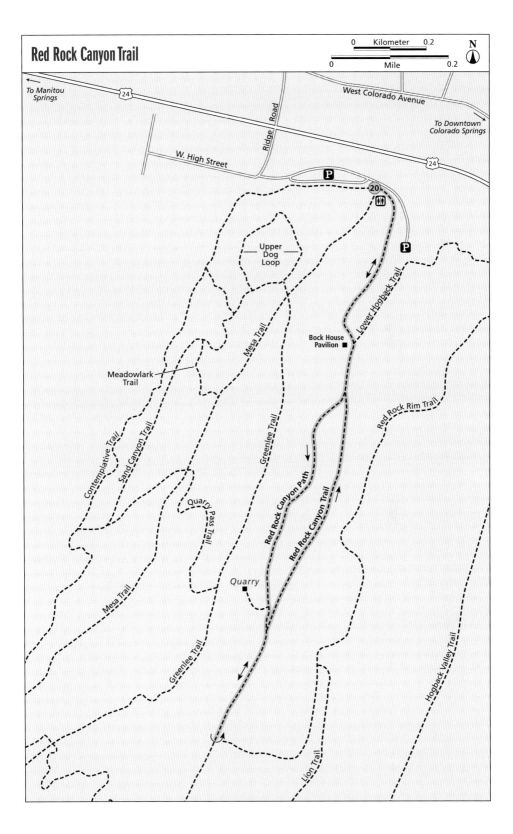

Red Rock Canyon Trail

0   Kilometer   0.2

0   Mile   0.2

N

To Manitou Springs

24

West Colorado Avenue

Ridge Road

To Downtown Colorado Springs

W. High Street

24

P

20

P

Upper Dog Loop

Lower Hogback Trail

Mesa Trail

Bock House Pavilion

Meadowlark Trail

Red Rock Rim Trail

Contemplative Trail

Sand Canyon Trail

Greenlee Trail

Red Rock Canyon Path

Red Rock Canyon Trail

Quarry Pass Trail

Mesa Trail

Quarry

Greenlee Trail

Hogback Valley Trail

Lion Trail

then bends east to join the old Red Rock Canyon road. (If you started from the south parking area, it's 0.15 mile to this point.)

Hike up the road 0.1 mile, passing a locked gate, to the site of the old Bock house, now a picnic and rest pavilion. Red Rock Canyon once belonged to John George Bock, who assembled the house during the 1920s and 1930s.

After Bock's death his two sons, John and Richard, wanted to build a World Trade Center here with golf courses, luxury homes and condos, a shopping center, office buildings, a sports arena, and thirteen lakes. They were unable to get the area rezoned, so in the 1970s it was turned into a landfill and gravel pit. In the 1990s another developer attempted to resurrect the Bock plan but was denied annexation by both Manitou Springs and Colorado Springs, leaving the door open for its purchase as parkland.

The next trail section follows the old road on the east side of the canyon for 0.4 mile to its junction with Quarry Pass Trail. (*Side trip:* For an alternative hike, go right at the pavilion and descend stone steps to a small lake. Bear right and follow the singletrack 0.5-mile Red Rock Canyon Path, a hiker-only trail, along the west side of the canyon to the Quarry Pass Trail junction. For a diversion, go right and follow the Quarry Pass Trail 0.1 mile up to the nineteenth-century stone quarry, a historic site. The sandstone blocks quarried here were loaded on train cars on a railroad spur that ran into the canyon and then shipped to Denver, Kansas, and Texas. The stone, however, didn't weather well, and the canyon's quarries closed by 1915. This side trail climbs to the quarry. Make sure you climb the stone staircase into the quarry. After visiting the quarry, retrace your steps back to the main trail.)

The last trail segment continues south for 0.25 mile on the old road, steadily climbing a hill to a major junction and the hike's turnaround point at 6,400 feet. Take a minute and enjoy the view. Directly west across the wooded canyon is the Wiggins Wall and a deep defile called Black Bear Canyon. This and the other cliffs in Red Rock Canyon are popular with rock climbers, who enjoy more than one hundred established climbing routes. From this high point, retrace the trail north to the parking lot.

OPTIONS

Several excellent loop hikes fan out from the end of the Red Rock Canyon Trail. The best hike continues south up the canyon for 0.15 mile before turning west up a deep canyon. Follow the 1.3-mile Roundup Trail up and out of the canyon, then dip across the heads of a couple shallow canyons before descending north to the southern end of the Contemplative Trail. This 3.5-mile loop hike is an excellent easy day hike.

MILES AND DIRECTIONS

0.0 Begin at the trailhead at the east end of the park's main parking lot.

0.35 Reach a junction with a closed dirt road.

0.45 Reach the pavilion and lake.

0.85 Arrive at the junction with Quarry Pass Trail. Go straight.

1.1 End the first half of your hike at the top of a hill at a three-way trail junction. Turn around and hike back toward the trailhead.

2.2 Arrive back at the trailhead.

21 MOUNT CUTLER TRAIL

WHY GO?

Climb through a pine and fir forest in North Cheyenne Cañon Park to the summit of 7,164-foot Mount Cutler, which offers panoramic views of Colorado Springs. With easy terrain and little elevation gain, this is a nice starter hike as you get to know a dog or begin introducing them to hiking.

THE RUNDOWN

Start: From the Mount Cutler Trailhead
Distance: 1.9 miles out and back
Approximate hiking time: 1 to 2 hours
Difficulty: Easy
Elevation gain: 367 feet
Seasons: Year-round; icy in winter
Trail surface: Singletrack dirt trail
Other trail users: Runners

Canine compatibility: Dogs must be on leash
Fees and permits: None
Map: USGS Manitou Springs
Trail contacts: Colorado Springs Parks, Recreation, and Cultural Services, 1401 Recreation Way, Colorado Springs, CO 80905-1975; (719) 385-5940; www.springsgov .com

FINDING THE TRAILHEAD

From I-25, take the Nevada Avenue / CO 115 exit (exit 140 B). Drive south on South Nevada Avenue / CO 115 for about a mile and turn right (west) onto Cheyenne Road. Follow Cheyenne Road for 2.6 miles to its end at Cheyenne Boulevard. (If you approach via Cheyenne Boulevard, stay right on Cheyenne Boulevard at this intersection.) Go left (west) on Cheyenne Boulevard for 0.1 mile to a Y intersection. Turn right, through an open gate, into North Cheyenne Cañon Park. Drive 1.4 miles up the park road to the Mount Cutler Trailhead on the left. **GPS:** N38 47.50' / W104 53.23'

THE HIKE

Peaceful North Cheyenne Cañon is a gem tucked away on the southwest side of Colorado Springs; it feels remote, but doesn't require a long commute. Just beyond charming residential districts, a winding road climbs west into this spectacular canyon, which is also one of the city's oldest parks.

The hike up Mount Cutler is the easiest and most accessible summit climb in the Pikes Peak region. Expect great views across North and South Cheyenne Cañons, an easy grade, peaceful pine and fir woods, and airy exposure on the last section. Be careful, and watch your children and dog as you hike along the exposed trail above South Cheyenne Cañon, especially if you make the short hike out to the east summit, which perches above dangerous and vertical cliffs. Some of the footing is on loose, slippery gravel scattered atop the granite bedrock.

Mount Cutler offers stunning panoramic views from its rounded summit of dark forests spilling down steep mountainsides, the North and South Cheyenne Creek drainages, towering granite formations, and tumbling Seven Falls, as well as vistas of Colorado Springs and the high plains to the east. The wide trail climbs steadily but is an easy climb,

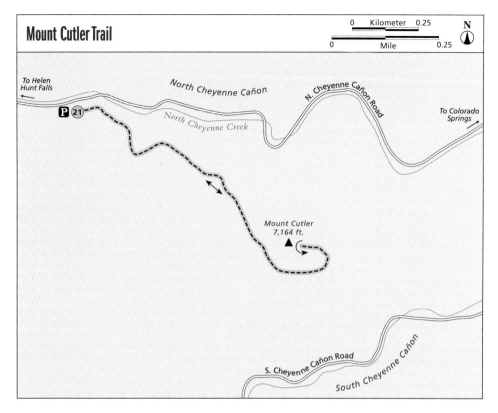

0   Kilometer   0.25

N

0   Mile   0.25

To Helen
Hunt Falls

North Cheyenne Cañon

N. Cheyenne Cañon Road

To Colorado
Springs

North Cheyenne Creek

Mount Cutler
7,164 ft.

S. Cheyenne Cañon Road

South Cheyenne Cañon

with a thrilling touch of exposure as you traverse across the west- and south-facing shoulders of the mountain.

From the parking lot and trailhead at 6,797 feet in North Cheyenne Cañon, hike up the broad, well-used path through a dense evergreen forest that provides welcome shade in summer. The trail gently climbs and at 0.26 mile reaches an overlook with views of distant downtown Colorado Springs. The trail continues climbing, crossing steep slopes littered with fallen trees. The trail flattens out briefly beneath a squat rock tower, then bends through a gully and climbs again, reaching an outlook at 0.4 mile. An excellent view opens across the cliff-lined canyon to the sprawl of Colorado Springs.

At 0.5 mile is a saddle that separates North and South Cheyenne Cañons. The Mount Muscoco Trail heads right here. Keep straight ahead on the well-trod path for Mount Cutler. The trail traverses onto the dry southwest side of the mountain. Below, sparse pines cling to rocky soil. The narrow trail edges across an exposed slope, with steep cliffs and drop-offs to your right. Keep your children and your dog in check here. As you hike, look down to the right from the trail and you'll glimpse Seven Falls cascading far below.

The trail continues spiraling upward onto the south slope, passing a trail marker at a switchback at 0.75 mile. Keep left and scramble up the final steep trail section to 7,164-foot Mount Cutler's broad rounded summit at 0.95 mile. The summit offers 360-degree views, with the city and vast plains spreading east to the distant horizon and the monumental peaks of the Front Range looming to the west.

To return to the trailhead from Mount Cutler's summit, follow the trail in reverse. It's all downhill, and the views are just as good as on the way up.

OPTION

Go left (east) from the main trail on one of two trails. A short distance east of the main path, these two join together. Follow the trail another 0.25 mile east to Cutler's lower summit. This lofty perch, surrounded by airy cliffs, yields superb views of Colorado Springs and the Broadmoor Hotel area below.

MILES AND DIRECTIONS

0.0   Begin at the Mount Cutler Trailhead.

0.4   Arrive at an overlook.

0.5   Reach the saddle separating North and South Cheyenne Cañons.

0.95 Arrive at the summit of Mount Cutler. Retrace your steps toward the trailhead.

1.9   Arrive back at the trailhead.

22 THOMPSON MOUNTAIN

WHY GO?

This interesting hike makes a rolling loop through part of the Deer Haven Ranch. The trail winds through ponderosa pines, Douglas firs, and meadows. Open areas, including a side trip to Thompson Point, provide nice views of Pikes Peak, the Wet Mountains, and the Sangre de Cristo Range.

THE RUNDOWN

Start: From the Wilson Creek (Trail 5827A) Trailhead
Distance: 7.6-mile lollipop
Approximate hiking time: 3.5 to 5.5 hours
Difficulty: Difficult due to elevation gain
Elevation gain/loss: 1,420-foot gain / 420-foot loss
Seasons: Year-round except after big snowstorms
Trail surface: Single- and doubletrack dirt trail
Other trail users: Equestrians, mountain bikers, hunters (in season)

Canine compatibility: Dogs must be under control
Fees and permits: None
Maps: USGS Gribble Mountain and Rice Mountain; Nat Geo Trails Illustrated 137, Pikes Peak/Cañon City
Trail contacts: Bureau of Land Management, Royal Gorge Field Office, Cañon City; (719) 269-8500; www.blm.gov/co/st/en/fo/rgfo.html
Other: No facilities at the trailhead. Minimal water is found along the trail; bring your own.

FINDING THE TRAILHEAD

From the intersection of CO 115 and US 50 in Cañon City, drive west on US 50 about 9.5 miles, past the Royal Gorge turnoff (restaurants and motels here), to CO 9. Turn right onto CO 9 and head north approximately 8.7 miles to Fremont CR 11. Turn right onto FCR 11, watching for deer along this twisty paved road. (You're on the Gold Belt Scenic Byway.) Drive 5.3 miles to the DEER HAVEN RANCH sign, just past mile marker 5, and turn right onto FCR 69, a well-graded narrow dirt road. Drive slowly to avoid collisions with oncoming traffic or cattle because this area is open range. Drive 3.3 miles to the WILSON CREEK TRAIL (Trail 5827A) sign and turn right. Park immediately in the meadow. **GPS:** N38 36.62' / W105 20.98'. (**Note:** Drive the extra 0.2 mile to the trailhead bulletin board *only* if the road is dry and you have high clearance. The road can be extremely wet and muddy, and driving through the mud only makes the muddy area larger. Even Bureau of Land Management (BLM) vehicles have occasionally gotten stuck on this road.)

THE HIKE

One of the beauties of BLM land is that there tend to be fewer regulations; you won't see the kinds of leash laws on many BLM tracts that you do in, say, a state park or county-run open space. It's a double-edged sword, however; cattle are also allowed to run free, so if your dog has a tendency to chase cows, keep them on a leash (or at least bring a leash so you can control your dog if you see some grazing critters).

There's a long, colorful history here. Charlie and Lee Switzer first started cattle ranching in the Thompson Mountain area back in the 1870s. Their 640 acres covered open

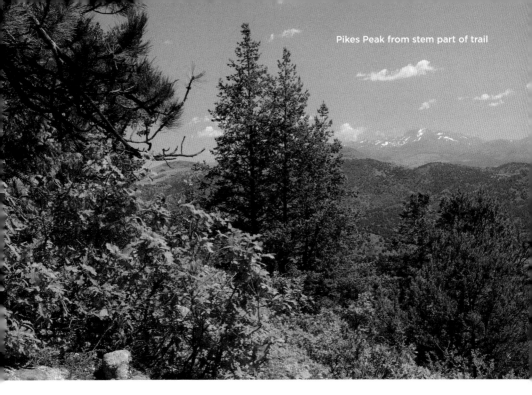

range, rolling hills, and fields of bunchgrass. During the Cripple Creek–Victor gold rush, they supplied beef to the miners. Around 1900 Toll Witcher bought the ranch from the Switzers, then sold it to Lon Gribble in 1914 or 1915. During World War I the price of cattle rose. With his profits Gribble built a new house in 1917. While digging the base-ment, he struck solid rock in one corner. After digging four feet into the rock, he struck water. Gribble constructed a water tank of sorts and built the kitchen right above it. The two-story house had two bedrooms downstairs and four upstairs, a big fireplace, and a full basement. Lumber for the house was hauled from Cañon City with a four-horse team. The house cost $12,000 to build, a substantial sum in those days. You passed the historic house (still a private residence) on the way to the trailhead.

Gribble also established a sawmill, with a Case tractor to run it. He hired a worker to run the mill and others to cut the timber. He sold the lumber to the coal mines south of Cañon City for mine props. By 1932 cattle prices had fallen and a hard winter took its toll on Gribble's ability to pay his loans, resulting in foreclosure on Gribble's ranch.

According to a story titled "Last Wilson Creek Roundup," in the June–July 1976 *Frontier Times*, Dud Van Buskirk, who was Lon Gribble's brother-in-law, bet Gribble that Fred Short could hold a cow by the tail for five minutes. Short walked into the herd of cattle and grabbed the tail of a two-year-old heifer. The heifer ran as fast as she could, out of the herd and up along the fence. Fred was hanging on. After about 100 feet, the heifer decided to head back to the herd, "stopped right quick and turned back down the fence. Fred, however, just kept going—about 10 feet to a step—till he fell and lit on his face."

In 1940 Floyd Murphy bought the old Switzer Ranch and actually made it profitable. He grazed a string of relay horses and was one of the best relay riders in America. He also grazed cattle. He sold the ranch about ten years later at $10 per acre.

Water trough along trail

After several other owners, the Richard King Mellon Foundation and the Conservation Fund of Arlington, Virginia, bought the land, then donated it to the Bureau of Land Management in 1992 to "provide significant wildlife habitat, riparian, and wetland habitat, recreation opportunities, protect scenic quality and to improve stewardship and access to adjoining public land." The donation amounted to 4,900 acres. On National Trails Day in 1993, a groundbreaking ceremony was held to initiate the current trail. The Rocky Mountain Back Country Horsemen and the Medicine Wheel Bicycle Club have steadily worked on the trail.

The hike starts up a drainage, then turns up another drainage at a check dam. The first part climbs steadily through the forest, then up a ridge. As you gain elevation, keep an eye open to the right for views of Pikes Peak. In a beautiful ponderosa pine forest, the trail is marked with brown carsonite signs. Mica flecks sparkle in the trail.

Pass through a gate at 2.2 miles, then descend through a flower-filled meadow to a pond where the loop part of the trail begins. Take the left fork first. The trail follows occasional trail markers. It heads down another drainage to a metal cattle trough. From the descending trail you can see the rocky knob of Thompson Point. After the cattle trough the trail heads up a broad drainage to a saddle. A spur trail, Trail 5827B, heads to the left, to Thompson Point. Wilson Creek Trail (Trail 5827A) turns right here and eventually climbs, descends, and climbs again to an open area with views of Cap Rock. Turn right here and follow the two-track trail that winds through forest and meadow and back to a gully. Turn right at the gully and walk back to the first pond and dam to end the loop. Head back to your vehicle the way you came.

Thompson Mountain covers a large area, its gentle ridges surrounding drainages and meadows. It's definitely not the typical Colorado pointy-topped mountain.

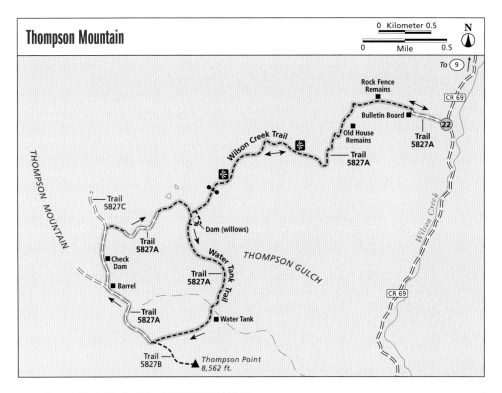

Thompson Mountain

0 Kilometer 0.5
0 Mile 0.5
N

MILES AND DIRECTIONS

0.0 Start in the meadow near the WILSON CREEK TRAIL (Trail 5827A) sign. Elevation: 7,620 feet. Hike up the dirt road.

0.2 Reach the bulletin board for the trail. Please stop and read the area information and regulations.

0.4 Look for an old rock fence to your right.

0.6 Curve left at the directional sign.

0.7 Reach the remains of an old one-room house with corrugated siding.

1.2 The trail reaches a saddle and turns right up the ridge. (**Note:** During the next 0.4 mile, look to the right for views of Pikes Peak through the trees.)

2.2 Reach a fence and gate. Elevation: 8,250 feet. GPS: N38 36.28′ / W105 22.51′. Use the metal gate to the left—remember to close the gate behind you. The trail descends the meadow to a trail junction sign. (**Note:** Nice views to the southwest of the Wet Mountains and the Sangre de Cristo Range.)

2.4 Reach the junction of Water Tank Trail and Thompson Mountain Trail. The loop trail is really across the gully to the west. You can turn left onto Water Tank Trail and follow the trail through the trees, turning right to cross the little dam. However, willows are overtaking the top of the dam. Instead, head toward the gully to the west on the north side of the pond and make your way to the other side. The trail comes to a T intersection. The loop in the trail starts here. Turn left and follow the trail through the forest, then descend toward a creek.

3.0 Enter a meadow. Look downhill as you hike and you'll see a circular water tank, a narrow water trough, and a creek. Head to the water tank.

3.1 Drop down past the metal water tank and cross the creek. GPS: N38 35.67' / W105 22.56'. You'll find the trail on the other side, which takes you up and around into a grassy open meadow and drainage. Head uphill toward a saddle.

3.6 Reach the saddle and a trail junction. Turn right and follow the two-track Trail 5827A uphill. (***Note:*** Look to your left for some interesting rock formations.) (***Side trip:*** If you'd like to hike up to Thompson Point, turn left onto Trail 5827B. Out-and-back distance to Thompson Point is about 1 mile, to a point beyond the rocky outcropping.)

3.8 Follow the trail downhill to the right. As you approach a gully, the road turns left and starts heading uphill again.

4.1 Enter an open area with a rusted barrel stuck in the ground to your right. Continue uphill on the trail to a check dam at mile 4. Continue along the trail to the left of the dam.

4.4 Enter an open, flat area with three trail posts. Elevation: 8,580 feet. GPS: N38 36.08' / W105 23.27'. Trail 5827A turns right while Trail 5827C goes straight ahead and starts heading slightly downhill. Turn right here and follow Trail 5827A as it curves toward some ponderosas. (***Note:*** There are great views of various hills ahead, with Thompson Point and the Sangre de Cristo and Wet Mountains behind you.)

4.9 Arrive in an open meadow. A big rock outcropping is on your left. Continue across the meadow toward ponderosas. The trail curves a little to the left, then the right. You'll come to a gully, then turn right and follow the trail back to the start of the loop.

5.2 Reach the trail junction sign for Water Tank Trail and Thompson Mountain Trail. Head uphill and return the way you came.

7.4 Arrive back at the trailhead bulletin board.

7.6 Arrive back at the parking area in the meadow.

23 NEWLIN CREEK TRAIL

WHY GO?

The Newlin Creek Trail meanders up a narrow canyon. It follows what's left of an old logging road. Floods and time have deteriorated the trail to the point that it's often hard to tell that it was once a road. Rocky cliffs hang over the trail in spots, and little cascades punctuate the creek. The most interesting features of this hike lie in the destination meadow. An old steam boiler, flywheel, and chimney are all that remain of a sawmill operation.

THE RUNDOWN

Start: From the Newlin Creek (Trail 1335) Trailhead near Florence Mountain Park
Distance: 5.0 miles out and back
Approximate hiking time: 2.25 to 4 hours
Difficulty: Difficult due to elevation gain
Elevation gain: 1,400 feet, plus lots of little undulations at creek crossings
Seasons: Best from mid-May to late Oct
Trail surface: Dirt trail with numerous creek crossings, rocky in places

Other trail users: Equestrians and hunters (in season)
Canine compatibility: Dogs must be on leash
Fees and permits: None
Map: USGS Rockvale
Trail contacts: San Isabel National Forest, San Carlos Ranger District, Cañon City; (719) 269-8500; www.fs.usda.gov/psicc
Other: No facilities at the trailhead. Bring water in case the creek is low. Treat water obtained from Newlin Creek.

FINDING THE TRAILHEAD

From the intersection of CO 115 and CO 67 in the middle of Florence, drive south on CO 67 for 4.3 miles to Fremont CR 15. The intersection is marked as NATIONAL FOREST ACCESS and for the Newlin Creek Trailhead. Turn right onto FCR 15. The road forks in 2.7 miles; stay on FCR 15 by driving on the right fork. The road turns to dirt in another 0.9 mile. The road forks in another 0.8 mile; stay right, following the sign to Florence Mountain Park. The entrance to the mountain park is designated by two big log posts on either side of the road in another 1.2 miles. At the junction in another 0.1 mile, marked AMPHITHEATER, go straight. In another 0.2 mile, there's an intersection where you continue straight, then pass the caretaker's house on the left. Follow the signs to Newlin Creek Trailhead. In 0.5 mile, pass the national forest boundary sign; the road narrows. It's another 0.1 mile to the trailhead. The trailhead is about 10.8 miles from the middle of Florence. **GPS:** N38 16.00' / W105 11.30'

THE HIKE

Newlin Creek is nestled in the northeastern end of the Wet Mountains. Early explorers, such as the Gunnison Expedition of 1853–1854, perceived that rain constantly fell on this mountain range and named it accordingly. Streams ran high in late winter and early spring, and summer thunderstorms flooded creek beds. Newlin Creek was probably named after a local by the same name who lived in Locke Park to the west.

Boiler and flywheel

Oil was discovered near the town of Florence in 1881, and some wells are still producing oil today. Coal mining also became a big industry in the late 1800s. Coal Creek lies just north of Newlin Creek. The discovery of silver on the west side of the Wet Mountains created booming mining towns such as Silver Cliff and Westcliffe. Coal and silver mines needed much timber for shoring up mine shafts and for residential and commercial buildings. The forests of the Wet Mountains provided an opportunity for an entrepreneur to supply lumber to industries on both sides of the range.

Today an old steam boiler, a relic of this boom era, lies rusting amid aspen trees next to Newlin Creek. Some bricks lie near its base. Pipes point in different directions, and the flywheel sits forlorn and disconnected. Exactly how much time it took to haul this equipment from Cañon City or Florence is unknown, but it must have been quite an effort. Look carefully at the boiler for an interesting gargoyle-type face and other inscriptions.

This hike is great in high summer, when it's hot enough that your pooch will be glad to splash around in the numerous creek crossings. Still, a word of caution about stream crossings: If you're heading this way in the spring or early season, when the runoff is high, you may find yourself unable to cross; if the water is running high or especially swiftly, save the remainder of this hike for another day. The same goes if there's a lot of rain in the forecast. Newlin Creek has been known to flash-flood, so avoid heading out after heavy rain.

The hike follows Newlin Creek up to the steam boiler meadow. Between rock slides and floods, it's hard to tell today that any type of wagon road existed along the creek. The trail twists through forests of Douglas fir, ponderosa pine, and Gambel oak. A picnic table sits just before the trail slips between steep canyon walls. Enjoy the fancy wooden bridge that crosses Newlin Creek, since you'll be using rocks and logs to cross creeks numerous times over the duration of the hike. Watch the creek for mini waterfalls and cascades. Look up occasionally for interesting pointy cliffs and rocks. Farther up the canyon you'll hike along an open slope with Gambel oak above, then head back into the trees, where the undergrowth is dotted with red columbine, heart-leafed arnica, Wood's rose, strawberries, pussytoes, and some nice aspen.

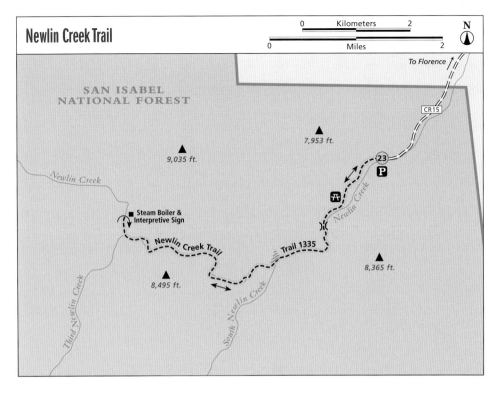

A few creek crossings later, you enter a little meadow on the left (west) side of the creek. An interpretive sign outlines the history of the equipment beyond, along with a location diagram. The old boiler and other equipment lie among the trees. Remember the equipment is protected as historical items under the Antiquities Act. Please do not climb on or disrupt the remains. The meadow is a wonderful picnic spot. Enjoy and return the way you came.

MILES AND DIRECTIONS

0.0 Start at the trailhead parking area for Newlin Creek Trail (Trail 1335). Elevation: 7,000 feet. Please sign the trail register.

0.5 Come to a picnic table.

0.6 The trail crosses Newlin Creek on a wooden bridge with handrails.

0.9 The trail goes through an area of big boulders with rocks in the trail.

1.0 Come to the first of many creek crossings without a bridge.

1.5 Reach a nice 4-foot-high waterfall off to the right of a creek crossing.

1.7 There's a tricky creek crossing on slopey rock (like slickrock).

2.5 Arrive in a little meadow. A nice interpretive poster explaining the history of the boiler and location of artifacts is to your right. Elevation: 8,400 feet. GPS: N38 15.71' / W105 13.00'. Return the way you came.

5.0 Arrive back at the trailhead.

24 CRAGS TRAIL

WHY GO?

After a short climb, this hike leads through serene meadows below granite cliffs and boulder-strewn hillsides, with excellent views of Pikes Peak's northern shoulders.

THE RUNDOWN

Start: From the Crags Trailhead by the restrooms at Crags Campground
Distance: 4.0 miles out and back
Approximate hiking time: 2 to 3 hours
Difficulty: Easy
Elevation gain: 700 feet
Seasons: Best from Apr through Oct; snowy in winter
Trail surface: Singletrack dirt trail
Other trail users: Mountain bikers

Canine compatibility: Dogs must be on leash
Fees and permits: None
Maps: USGS Pikes Peak and Woodland Park
Trail contacts: Pike National Forest, Pikes Peak Ranger District, 601 S. Weber St., Colorado Springs, CO 80903; (719) 636-1602; www.fs.usda.gov
Other: Skis or snowshoes required in winter

FINDING THE TRAILHEAD

Take the Cimarron Street / US 24 exit (exit 141) from I-25. Follow US 24 west for about 24 miles up Ute Pass and through Woodland Park to the town of Divide. Turn left (south) onto CO 67 and drive 4.3 miles south to a left (east) turn onto Teller CR 62, marked with a CRAGS CAMPGROUND sign. Follow the rough dirt road through the Rocky Mountain Mennonite Camp for 3.2 miles to Crags Campground on the left. Park on the right in a parking lot surrounded by a split-rail fence. The trailhead is across the road, next to the restrooms. Alternatively, hike up the road through the campground to the Crags Trailhead at its east end. **GPS:** N38 87.13' / W105 11.96'

THE HIKE

With its gentle grades and unsurpassed mountain beauty, the Crags Trail (Trail 664) may be the perfect day hike in the Pikes Peak region. The trail slowly climbs up a subalpine valley below high summits, offering all the exposure and views of a full-fledged mountain ascent, but your thighs and lungs won't feel the burn like they would if you climbed neighboring 14,115-foot Pikes Peak. The valley the trail winds up is beautiful in summer, with wildflower-strewn meadows, warm temperatures, and plentiful wildlife.

Take your time on this hike. Although the trail is relatively easy, its starting elevation is 10,040 feet and it ends at 10,800 feet. If you're coming from sea level, watch for altitude sickness, including headache and nausea. On summer afternoons, watch for severe thunderstorms with lightning moving across The Crags. Carry a raincoat and retreat to your car if you see incoming bad weather. Drinking water is available at the campground.

From the trailhead by the restrooms, the trail crosses Fourmile Creek, and the most difficult part of the hike begins. The trail switchbacks up a steep hillside, quickly gaining elevation before leveling off above Crags Campground. Curve around a hillside and drop back down to a trail junction. Stay to the left, minding the trail marker for The Crags and paralleling the tumbling creek.

0   Kilometer   0.6

0   Mile   0.6

N

10,817 ft.

THE CRAGS

10,855 ft.

To 67

CR 62

Crags
Campground

Fourmile Creek

P

24

The trail passes through a jumbled boulder field before opening into a broad, grassy expanse. The trail heads east up the narrowing valley before reaching a broader meadow. Here the creek makes wide meanders across the valley floor, its banks densely lined with willows. Outcroppings of granite line the hillside to the left. Aspen trees and tall Engelmann spruce and subalpine fir trees stand sentinel-like along the edge of the meadow. Ahead rises Pangborn's Pinnacle, a mighty stone dome that towers above the valley.

The Crags Trail briefly jogs to the left, climbing higher before dropping back into the meadow. Approaching a large granite dome on the north, the trail splits. Keep to the right track, with the cliff to the left. The trail then tracks through a swampy marshland before climbing back onto solid ground.

The bare northwest shoulder of Pikes Peak looms to the right, and other cliffs and crags fill steep slopes above the narrowing valley. When the valley crimps down, the trail passes a cliff to the right at 1.2 miles. This is an excellent place to rest on its bedrock slabs, enjoying the trickle of the creek and taking in the valley you just hiked up. This is also a good turnaround point, since the next 0.5-mile trail segment gains lots of elevation and is heavily wooded.

Continue hiking up a narrow canyon on the rustic trail and then climb an abrupt, steep gully. Watch the trail—it can be easy to lose as it switches back and forth over tree roots and lumpy boulders. Eventually you'll reach a high saddle at 1.7 miles. The trail goes left here and climbs to a small summit with a big view and the trail's end point at 2 miles. This is a great place to sit down and enjoy breathtaking, expansive views. To the east is a huge granite buttress called Old Ironsides; farther east are the Pikes Peak Highway, a couple of reservoirs, and the flat top of the Rampart Range. On a clear day you can even see the distant prairie horizon. Also check out the ancient weathered limber pines that inhabit this windswept ridge.

To return, retrace the trail. Take care to remain on the trail as you descend the wooded gully below the saddle.

MILES AND DIRECTIONS

0.0   Start at the Crags Trailhead next to the campground restrooms.

1.2   The trail passes a cliff to the right. (***Option:*** Turn around here to avoid the trail's steepest section.)

1.7   Reach the saddle and follow the trail to the left.

2.0   The trail ends with summit views. Retrace your steps.

4.0   Arrive back at the trailhead.

WHY GO?

This hike will take you down the Levsa Canyon Nature Trail, followed by about 2.6 miles of the Reilly Canyon Trail. Winding through piñon pine and juniper forest gives you an idea of the land through which early settlers traveled, especially on the Mountain Branch of the Santa Fe Trail (where I-25 now exists). The suggested turnaround point is a bench where the trail approaches Trinidad Lake and has a good view of the dam. Look for deer in some of the meadows. While hiking, you can catch views of Fishers Peak, as well as the old coal mines and town sites on or below the south shore.

THE RUNDOWN

Start: From the Trinidad Lake State Park campground
Distance: 6.4 miles out and back with a loop
Approximate hiking time: 2.5 to 4.5 hours
Difficulty: Moderate due to length and a few steep sections
Elevation gain/loss: 390-foot gain / 360-foot loss
Seasons: Year-round except after big snowstorms

Trail surface: Dirt trail with a few steep sections
Other trail users: Mountain bikers
Canine compatibility: Dogs must be on leash
Fees and permits: Daily entrance fee or annual parks pass required
Map: USGS Trinidad West
Trail contacts: Trinidad Lake State Park, Trinidad; (719) 846-6951; http://parks.state.co.us/parks/trinidadlake

FINDING THE TRAILHEAD

From Trinidad, drive 3.9 miles southwest on CO 12 from its intersection with I-25 to the Trinidad Lake State Park entrance. CO 12 is the Scenic Highway of Legends, so follow the scenic byway signs. Turn left onto the park road. The entrance station is about 0.5 mile on the left. Stop and pay the entrance fee. Drive less than 0.1 mile and turn right at the campground entrance. At the fork in the road, turn left and drive to the restrooms, where parking and water are available (take water with you). The trailhead is across from the restrooms. **GPS:** N37 08.65' / W104 34.18'

THE HIKE

The Mountain Branch of the Santa Fe Trail passed near what is today Trinidad Lake State Park. I-25 basically follows the old trail over Raton Pass, just south of the city of Trinidad. These lands were home to many Native American tribes: Comanche, Kiowa, Cheyenne, Arapaho, Jicarilla Apache, and Ute. They traveled over the plains, hunting bison, elk, antelope, and deer and creating trails that laid the foundation for the Santa Fe Trail.

What we now know as New Mexico belonged to Mexico and the Spanish in the early 1800s. Spain prohibited trade between the United States and Santa Fe. In 1821 the Mexican people revolted against Spanish rule and gained their independence.

One American entrepreneur, William Becknell, left Franklin, Missouri, in August 1821 and headed to Santa Fe with trade goods on pack animals. He traveled over Raton Pass,

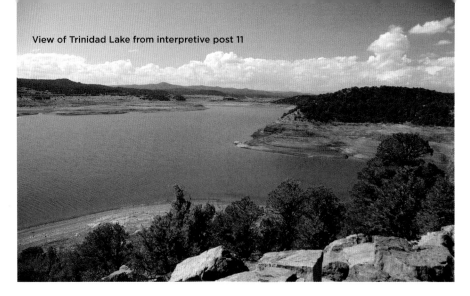

View of Trinidad Lake from interpretive post 11

taking two days to roll boulders out of the way so his pack animals could pass. This route later became the Mountain Branch of the Santa Fe Trail. Becknell reached Santa Fe in mid-December and quickly exchanged his goods for gold, silver, fur, and mules.

Becknell then returned to Missouri by an overland route that avoided Raton Pass, arriving home in January 1822. Later that year, he traveled back to Santa Fe with more trade goods, using wagons on the 780-mile overland route, which became known as the Cimarron Cutoff. The round-trip between Missouri and Santa Fe took two to three months.

Raton Pass provided many challenges to early trail users. Before crossing the pass, people camped along the Purgatoire River on the east side, a welcome relief after the endless dry prairies. The town of Trinidad was founded here around 1862. From a travel account written in 1846, progress could be as little as 600 to 800 yards a day as men hauled wagons by hand over the great rocks. It took five days to cross the pass, a distance of about 30 miles. In one spot, it was so narrow that one false step would send mules, wagons, and people to a certain death.

As you hike the Reilly Canyon Trail, imagine driving a horse-drawn wagon through the area. Some of the trail appears fairly negotiable, while other sections, dropping into the canyons and ravines, would be a bit dicey.

The route starts at the trailhead near the campground. Hike up the first part of Levsa Canyon Nature Trail, then take the right fork and follow the Reilly Canyon Trail for about 2.2 more miles (the mileage noted on the bulletin board starts at this intersection). The trail drops into Levsa Canyon, then climbs out and wanders across a high stretch. Dropping down another little canyon to a flat stretch, the trail then climbs to a big slab of slickrock and descends to Trinidad Lake. A bench to rest on awaits you. From here you can see the dam at the east end of the lake.

If you want to add some mileage, hike another 1.4 miles west to Reilly Canyon itself, for a 9-mile round-trip. Either way, on the way back, take the right fork at the Levsa Canyon Nature Trail / Reilly Canyon Trail intersection and continue back along the nature trail. It drops, climbs, and drops, providing good views of the area across the lake where coal mines and towns resided before the dam was built, plus of Fishers Peak (9,655 feet) to the south. Watch for blue piñon jays and deer as you hike.

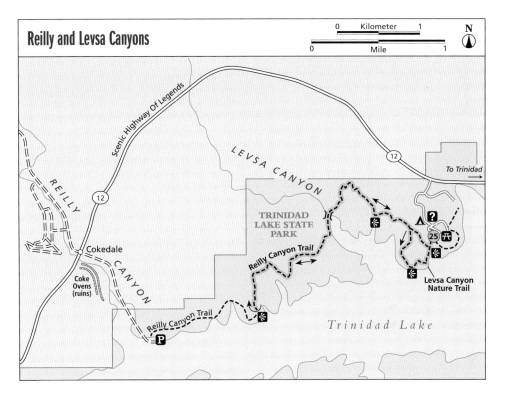

Reilly and Levsa Canyons

Scenic Highway Of Legends

LEVSA CANYON

REILLY CANYON

Cokedale

Coke Ovens (ruins)

TRINIDAD LAKE STATE PARK

Reilly Canyon Trail

Reilly Canyon Trail

To Trinidad

Levsa Canyon Nature Trail

Trinidad Lake

MILES AND DIRECTIONS

0.0 Start at the trailhead near the campground restrooms. Elevation: 6,340 feet.

0.05 At the fork, go right to follow the Levsa Canyon Nature Trail.

0.1 At the fork, take the right branch of the Levsa Canyon Nature Trail and head uphill.

0.3 Arrive at the intersection of the Reilly Canyon Trail and Levsa Canyon Nature Trail. Turn right onto Reilly Canyon Trail.

1.5 Cross the bridge in Levsa Canyon.

2.6 There's a mound of slickrock on the right.

2.9 Reach a bench and a view of the dam. This is the turnaround point. Elevation: 6,370 feet. GPS: N37 08.18' / W104 35.59'

5.6 Come to the trail intersection of Reilly Canyon Trail and Levsa Canyon Nature Trail. Turn right (more like straight) onto Levsa Canyon Nature Trail.

5.9 Reach a bench at sign #11 for the nature trail with a nice view of Trinidad Lake.

6.3 Reach the other end of the Levsa Canyon Nature Trail loop. Take the trail on the right. At the next intersection, turn left.

6.4 Arrive back at the trailhead.

NORTH OF I-70

The terrain in the northern half of the state is often less busy than its Colorado neighbors to the immediate south. It's home to fewer Four-teeners and not accessible via I-70, both of which reduce the number of visitors it sees. Don't let that fool you; there's no shortage of prime, dog-friendly hiking in northern Colorado. Much of it is accessible via I-25, which heads north from Denver to Fort Collins and eventually into Wyoming.

26 KELLY LAKE

WHY GO?

Beautiful Kelly Lake sits snuggled in a glacial basin between a high ridge to the west and the craggy Medicine Bow Mountains to the east. Overnight backpacking is the best way to explore this pleasant area, but don't rule out a long day hike to visit this little jewel. The trail starts out on logging roads through meadows, crosses two forks of the Canadian River, and passes through old timber cuts. The middle section of the hike travels on logging roads and singletrack trail. The final section is singletrack, gaining elevation to a scenic high alpine valley full of wildflowers.

THE RUNDOWN

Start: From the trailhead at the end of Jackson CR 41
Distance: 13.6 miles out and back
Approximate hiking time: 7 to 9 hours
Difficulty: Most difficult due to length
Elevation gain/loss: 2,545-foot gain / 400-foot loss
Seasons: Best from July through Sept
Trail surface: Dirt trail, rocky in a few areas
Other trail users: Equestrians and mountain bikers, snowmobiles in winter
Canine compatibility: Dogs must be on leash

Fees and permits: Daily entrance fee or annual parks pass required
Maps: USGS Gould, Johnny Moore Mountain, and Rawah Lakes; Nat Geo Trails Illustrated 114 Walden/Gould and 112 Poudre River/Cameron Pass
Trail contacts: State Forest State Park, 56750 Highway 14, Walden; (970) 723-8366; http://parks.state.co.us/Parks/StateForest
Other: Campfires are prohibited in the backcountry, so bring a stove. If you're backpacking, please sign the trailhead register. Remember to treat any water from streams and lakes before drinking.

FINDING THE TRAILHEAD

From Walden, drive 19.2 miles east on CO 14 to the KOA Campground and entrance to State Forest State Park. Turn left onto Jackson CR 41, drive 0.2 mile to the entrance station, and pay the fee. Continue driving on JCR 41 for 8.4 miles, past several turnoffs (4WD roads, campgrounds, and picnic areas). Watch for cattle and moose along the road. Arrive at the loop at the end of JCR 41. Parking is on the west side, along with a vault toilet. The trail starts at the northeast end of the loop. Bring your own water as none is available at the trailhead. **GPS:** N40 36.87' / W106 01.30'

THE HIKE

State Forest State Park has an unusual history. When Colorado became a state on August 1, 1876, the federal government granted about 3 million acres of land and 4 million acres of mineral rights to the state to help fund public education. Sections 16 and 36 in every township became state school lands. The Colorado State Board of Land Commissioners (SLB) manages these areas. In 1938 a land exchange between the SLB and the USDA Forest Service occurred. Sections 16 and 36 in various national forests in Colorado were

exchanged for national forest land near Gould, creating 70,980 contiguous acres. In 1953 the Colorado legislature passed legislation establishing the Colorado State Forest (CSF). Grazing, forestry, and recreation continued as it had before the designation.

CSF became a state park in 1970, and two years later the SLB leased the land to what has become Colorado State Parks for recreation management. The forest resource management contract was awarded to the Colorado State Forest Service. The state forest service was created by the Colorado legislature in 1955 as a division of what is now Colorado State University in Fort Collins. The state forest service provides protection and management of the state's forests (versus the national forests) and educates private landowners in forested areas about fire prevention and protection.

Today, the state forest service uses adaptive management strategies to maintain a healthy forest. Some techniques include timber harvesting, researching and monitoring harvest results, wildlife monitoring (signs of healthy habitat) in conjunction with the Colorado Division of Wildlife, water-quality monitoring (in particular for sediment loads), and livestock grazing from July through September to stimulate healthy range and forest.

State Forest State Park offers a wealth of recreation opportunities year-round. Four campgrounds with more than 200 developed campsites, some first-come, first-served dispersed camping, and six cabins are available for your getaway. (Unlike in many state park–run lodging facilities, dogs are allowed in the State Forest State Park huts; you'll just need to pay an additional fee per night to bring your pooch along.) Never Summer Nordic, Inc., operates eight yurts (round Mongolian tents on wooden platforms) and two huts, available year-round. If you plan to stay at a yurt, note that pets are allowed in all the Never Summer Yurts, but only during the snow-free months.

Moose were reintroduced to North Park in 1978 and 1979. These huge ungulates can grow to six feet tall at the shoulder, weigh up to 1,000 pounds, and reach 9.5 feet long. Their long spindly legs give them a top-heavy appearance. They typically live in forested areas near lakes and marshes. They graze on grasses, bushes, and underwater vegetation in summer, and on willows in winter. Being huge creatures, they have few predators and seldom show fear of humans. Extremely protective of their young and their private space, they will chase humans and dogs—and they are fast. Keep an eye out for these magnificent creatures while you're hiking, and give them plenty of space.

The hike starts by descending a ridge to the South Fork of the Canadian River through a lodgepole pine forest. The red dead trees have been killed by the mountain pine beetle. After crossing several meadows the trail meanders through an aspen forest with colorful flowers. At about mile 4.3 the trail winds along the base of a boulder field, then climbs steeply uphill. Purple monkshood and larkspur line the path. By mile 6, you're in a beautiful alpine valley with Engelmann spruce, subalpine fir, marshy areas, and gorgeous wildflowers. Kelly Creek sparkles in the sun. The trail climbs steeply up a ridge, passing a little waterfall. Suddenly Kelly Lake appears down in its bowl, craggy peaks bordering its east side. If you're camping, please remember to camp at least 200 feet away from streams, lakes, and trails. Enjoy this special nook in State Forest State Park!

Facing page: Kelly Lake

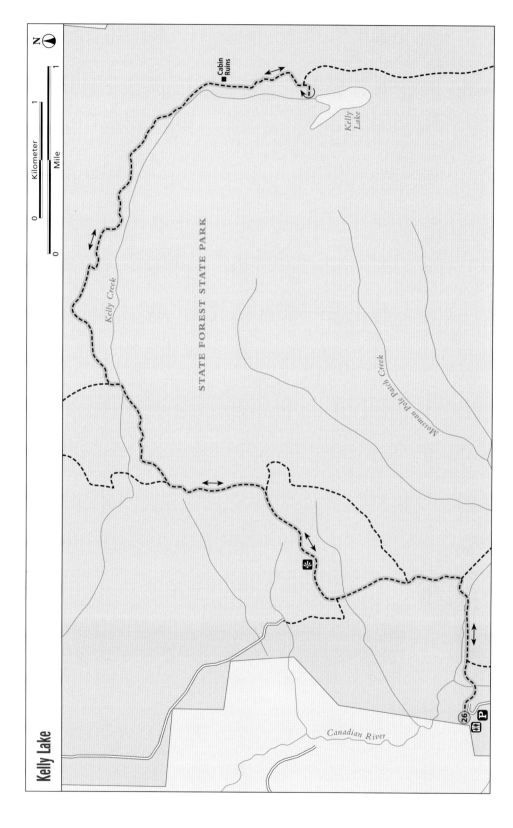

Kelly Lake

N

Kilometer
0   1

Mile
0   1

STATE FOREST STATE PARK

Cabin
Ruins

Kelly
Lake

Kelly Creek

Mossman Pole Patch Creek

Canadian River

26

P

MILES AND DIRECTIONS

0.0 Start at the trailhead at the end of JCR 41. Elevation: 8,660 feet. The low point of this hike, near the South Fork of the Canadian River, is at 8,540 feet.

0.75 An unmarked trail goes left. Continue hiking up the road.

0.8 Reach the junction with a trail to the North Fork Canadian yurt. Continue to the left up the road.

1.2 Reach the junction with the doubletrack trail to Kelly Lake and Clear Lake. Turn left. GPS: N40 37.15' / W106 00.49' (*Option:* You can continue walking up the road. Skip ahead to mile 3.0.)

1.6 Reach the junction with the trail to Clear Lake. Continue straight ahead and uphill.

1.8 Reach a point with a nice view to the northwest of the Mount Zirkel Wilderness and North Park.

2.4 Arrive at the junction with a closed road. Walk a few more feet uphill to another road and turn left onto that road, heading north.

3.0 Reach the junction with the Kelly Lake Trail. Turn right onto the singletrack trail. GPS: N40 38.29' / W105 59.90'

4.7 Reach the top of a steep section. You're entering a narrow valley. The trail crosses Kelly Creek several times in the next 1.3 miles. The trail can be wet and muddy in this section.

6.1 Look for cabin ruins to your left. After a few more creek crossings, the trail climbs steeply for the last 0.6 mile. You'll drop about 70 feet from a ridge (10,875 feet) to the lake.

6.8 Arrive at Kelly Lake. Elevation: 10,805 feet. GPS: N40 37.64' / W105 57.54'. Enjoy lunch and the beautiful scenery or set up your campsite. Return the way you came.

13.6 Arrive back at the trailhead.

WHY GO?

The Seven Lakes Trail (Trail 1125) to Seven Lakes starts on the gentle Red Elephant Nature Trail, passing through lodgepole, spruce, and fir forest. Turning west, it climbs gently to the Mount Zirkel Wilderness boundary near Big Creek Falls. The trail wanders along Big Creek, then climbs a very steep section with many switchbacks. Excellent views of Big Creek Lakes can be seen from several viewpoints. The next section goes through old-growth forest and into flower-filled meadows just below Seven Lakes. The lakes are in a high, open area with views of Red Elephant Mountain and the Continental Divide. The lakes are a peaceful backpacking destination.

THE RUNDOWN

Start: From the Seven Lakes Trailhead near Big Creek Lakes Campground
Distance: 12.2 miles out and back
Approximate hiking time: 5 to 9 hours (recommended 2- to 3-day backpack)
Difficulty: Difficult due to length and one steep section
Elevation gain/loss: 1,773-foot gain / 60-foot loss
Seasons: Best from mid-June to mid-Oct
Trail surface: Dirt trail with some flat sections, occasional rocks and mud, and one section of many steep switchbacks
Other trail users: Equestrians, anglers, mountain bikers (not within the wilderness), hunters (in season)
Canine compatibility: Dogs must be on leash on the Red Elephant Nature Trail (about the first mile), then under control on the rest of the trail
Fees and permits: Day-use fee payable at the trailhead parking lot; America the Beautiful pass accepted (display in vehicle window). Group size limit: No more than 15 people per group with a maximum combination of 25 people and pack or saddle animals in any group.
Maps: USGS Pearl and Davis Peak; Nat Geo Trails Illustrated 116 Hahns Peak/Steamboat Lake
Trail contacts: Medicine Bow–Routt National Forest, Parks Ranger District, Walden; (970) 723-2700; www.fs.usda.gov/mbr
Other: The access road is closed about 13 miles from the trailhead in winter. Snowmobile or cross-country ski on the road; the trail is neither maintained nor marked for winter use.

FINDING THE TRAILHEAD

From Walden, drive north a little more than 9 miles on CO 125 to Cowdrey. Turn left onto Jackson CR 6W. The road becomes gravel in about 5 miles. Drive a total of 18.8 miles from Cowdrey to FR 600 / JCR 6A. Turn left. The road narrows as it enters the national forest. Be careful of oncoming vehicles as the road is not wide enough for two cars. Drive 5 miles to the junction with FR 689. Turn left, staying on FR 600. In 0.7 mile, enter the Big Creek Lakes Campground; go straight ahead at the campground entrance. Follow the hiker signs. There's a bulletin board with the campground fee station and rules 0.5 mile from the entrance. Continue another 0.2 mile and turn left into the Seven Lakes Trailhead. Water is available at the campground. A vault toilet is located in the center of the parking circle. A day-use self-service pay station is located by the trailhead bulletin boards. Please sign the trail register. **GPS:** N40 55.88' / W106 37.15'

THE HIKE

The Mount Zirkel Wilderness was one of the original five Colorado wilderness areas designated by Congress in the Wilderness Act of 1964. This area around Big Creek Falls and Seven Lakes was added in 1993.

In 1867 Congress authorized a geological and natural resource survey along the fortieth parallel. Clarence King, just five years out of the Sheffield Scientific School at Yale, was appointed Geologist in Charge of the Geological Exploration of the Fortieth Parallel. King hired two assistant geologists, three topographic aides, two collectors, a photographer, and support men. He chose well-educated scientists who had studied at Yale or Harvard, and the geologists had even completed advanced studies in German universities. One geologist was Ferdinand Zirkel, who developed a common classification system for American and European rocks. For his contribution to science, a peak in the Park Range was named after him in 1874.

The Park Range forms the backbone of the Mount Zirkel Wilderness area. As the range stretches north toward Wyoming, it becomes known as the Sierra Madre. Part of the Sierra Madre near Seven Lakes produces the Encampment River, which flows north into the North Platte River. On the other side of the Continental Divide, the Elk River drains many of the high valleys, feeding its water into the Yampa River and eventually into the Colorado. The Park Range is composed mainly of Precambrian metamorphic rocks like gneiss and schist, with some granite interspersed. These rocks are around 1.7 billion years old. Glaciers covered the area at various times, and Seven Lakes are probably one result.

This area escaped the miners' shovels and road building. The land has not been altered or changed by humans as much as in other parts of Colorado. The Continental Divide by Seven Lakes appears to be a gentle ridge. The area hosts a spectacular display of July wildflowers, including paintbrushes, red elephants, pussytoes, penstemons, blue gentians, and varieties of yellow composites. Red Elephant Mountain (11,569 feet) raises its head and watches over the entire trail to Seven Lakes. This peak apparently reminded someone a long time ago of an elephant head and trunk. Can you see it?

The first part of the trail follows the Red Elephant Nature Trail. Pick up a nature guide at the trailhead. A forest fire swept through this area in the 1920s, and the resulting lodgepole forest had little deadfall compared to the older, moister spruce-fir forest. Fire is important to the natural health of the forest, creating different vegetation pockets that support various plants and animals. However, by 2005 the mountain pine beetle had invaded the lodgepole forest, killing many of the trees. The USDA Forest Service has removed many dead lodgepole, which pose a danger to hikers and could generate a hot fire. In several places, nice plank bridges cross wet areas. A lily pad–covered pond lies nestled in a cradle of trees.

After the trail turns west to follow Big Creek, an open area provides good views of Upper Big Creek Lake. A prominent cliff face towers above the wilderness boundary. Just beyond, down a little trail to the left, is Big Creek Falls. Not overly huge, the falls is still impressive. Take a break and enjoy the cool creek and falls before heading on. Beetle-kill trees are not removed in the wilderness area, so be aware of possible falling trees, especially on high-wind days.

The trail stays close to Big Creek for a while, then gradually climbs up a flower-filled section of trail with numerous seeps. Cow parsnip, pearly everlasting, and alder line the

trail. After crossing an unnamed creek, take a quick break, since the trail climbs steeply from here. More than fifteen switchbacks take you up 750 feet in 0.5 mile. The trail then levels out and rolls gently through a nice old-growth forest past some beautiful meadows. A final climb threads through flower-filled meadows and on to Seven Lakes.

Follow the faint trail to the left of the first lake to reach the biggest lake, which is stocked yearly with native trout. There is a nice campsite above the largest lake, at an appropriate distance from the water. The Forest Service requests that all camps be located at least 200 feet away from lakes, other water sources, and trails, and that no new campfire rings be built. Use existing fire rings, make a mound fire, or preferably use a stove. Be aware of lightning danger in open areas.

While visiting Seven Lakes, take time to explore the open spaces up to the Continental Divide to the south, or maybe take a side trip up Davis Peak to the north.

Facing page: Big Creek Falls

MILES AND DIRECTIONS

0.0 Start at Seven Lakes Trailhead near Big Creek Lakes Campground. Elevation: 9,020 feet. Head up Seven Lakes Trail (Trail 1125). The Red Elephant Nature Trail shares the trail. (Pick up a nature guide at the trailhead.)

1.25 The Red Elephant Nature Trail breaks left. Stay right, continuing on Seven Lakes Trail.

2.3 Reach the wilderness boundary sign. Big Creek Falls is off to the left. Elevation: 9,200 feet. GPS: N40 54.55' / W106 38.17' (**Option:** For a shorter hike, turn around and return the way you came for a moderate 4.6-mile out-and-back.)

3.4 Come to a creek crossing.

4.3 Reach the top of a steep climb with switchbacks.

5.1 Come to a nice meadow on the left, followed by an old-growth spruce forest.

5.7 Reach a trail junction with the Buffalo Ridge Trail (Trail 1151). Stay to the left and head uphill

6.0 Come to a trail junction with Seven Lakes Trail and the trail to Seven Lakes. Stay to the left (more straight ahead) and hike to the lakes.

6.1 Reach the first of the Seven Lakes. (**Side trip:** Hike an additional 0.25 mile to view the biggest of the Seven Lakes. Elevation: 10,733 feet. GPS: N40 53.78' / W106 40.98') Otherwise, return the way you came.

12.2 Arrive back at the trailhead.

28 SILVER CREEK TRAIL

WHY GO?

Silver Creek Trail starts out on closed logging roads, rising slightly to the Sarvis Creek Wilderness boundary. From here the trail mostly heads downhill, with a few uphills for variety. Silver Creek is a sparkling, crystal-clear stream, very worthy of its name. Interesting granitic formations appear occasionally on the north side of the trail. Lodgepole pine, Engelmann spruce, subalpine fir, aspen, and eventually ponderosa pine trees line the trail. This area is great for a quiet getaway, except during hunting season, which starts at the end of August.

THE RUNDOWN

Start: From the east Silver Creek (Trail 1106) Trailhead on Red Dirt Road

Distance: 12.4 miles point to point (with opportunities for camping and an out-and-back return)

Approximate hiking time: 5 to 8 hours

Difficulty: Difficult due to length

Elevation gain/loss: About 300-foot gain / 2,060-foot loss (plus little undulations)

Seasons: Best from mid-June through Oct

Trail surface: Dirt trail

Other trail users: Equestrians and hunters (in season)

Canine compatibility: Dogs must be under control

Fees and permits: None. Group size limit: No more than 15 people per group with a maximum combination of 25 people and pack or saddle animals in any one group. Camping and campfires are prohibited within 200 feet of all streams and trails.

Maps: USGS Gore Mountain, Tyler Mountain, and Green Ridge; Nat Geo Trails Illustrated 119 Yampa/Gore Pass

Trail contacts: Medicine Bow–Routt National Forest, Yampa Ranger District, Yampa; (970) 638-4516; www.fs.usda.gov/mbr/

Other: FR 100 is closed by winter snow about 14 miles from the trailhead. The trail is neither maintained nor marked for winter use.

FINDING THE TRAILHEAD

With shuttle: From Yampa, drive 8 miles north on CO 131 to Routt CR 14. Turn right onto RCR 14 and drive about 3.5 miles to RCR 16. Turn right onto RCR 16, following the LYNX PASS signs. Drive 1.6 miles, then turn left by some condo buildings to stay on RCR 16. In 1.3 miles, turn right, and continue on RCR 16 for another 5.4 miles. The trailhead is past mile marker 8, on the left side. There is parking on the left by the trailhead. Leave one car here. Continue south about 13.5 miles on RCR 16, which becomes FR 270, to Gore Pass Road (CO 134). Turn left onto CO 134 and drive 3.1 miles east to FR 250. Turn left onto FR 250. At the first fork, stay left. At all junctions, stay on FR 250, driving for 11.1 miles to Red Dirt Road (FR 100). The last mile of FR 250 is a little rough, and low-clearance vehicles should go very slowly. Turn left onto Red Dirt Road (FR 100). Drive 5 miles north. The trailhead is on the left side of the road, past mile marker 11. You can camp near the east trailhead—remember to stay at least 200 feet from streams, trails, and the road. There are no facilities at either trailhead. **GPS:** N40 11.87' / W106 36.36'

Without shuttle: From Kremmling, drive west and north on US 40 about 6 miles to CO 134 / Gore Pass Road. Turn left onto Gore Pass Road and drive about 4.2 miles west to Red Dirt Road (FR 100). At the first two forks, stay right. At the third fork at FR 101 (also Grand CR 191), around mile 4.8, stay left. In another 1.7 miles, reach FR 250 and stay right. Follow the signs for Buffalo Park. The trailhead is on the left side of the road, about 11.6 miles from Gore Pass Road.

THE HIKE

Silver Creek Trail traverses the southern part of the Sarvis Creek Wilderness, designated by Congress in 1993. This wilderness is unique because it is not composed of "rocks and ice" like so many other national forest wilderness areas in Colorado. Although heavily forested, its pristine and primitive nature qualified it for wilderness status.

The Sarvis Timber Company harvested trees in the Service Creek area in the mid-1910s using portable mills. Old-timers insist the area's original name was Sarvis. Some mapmaker, however, decided that "sarvis" was a common mispronunciation of the word "service," and placed the name "Service Creek" on the map. The wilderness area designation tried to right the incorrect spelling by using Sarvis.

The Civilian Conservation Corps (CCC) built much of the Silver Creek Trail. After the 1929 stock market crash and the subsequent Great Depression, 13.6 million Americans were unemployed by 1933. That year Congress passed the Emergency Conservation Work Act, creating what became known as the CCC. Young, unemployed, unmarried men between the ages of eighteen and twenty-five were eligible to join. Conservation of natural resources—reforestation, forest fire fighting, erosion control, trail building and maintenance, development of state parks, and other public works—became the CCC's mission. The US Army built camps, the government furnished food and clothing, and

Bend in Silver Creek

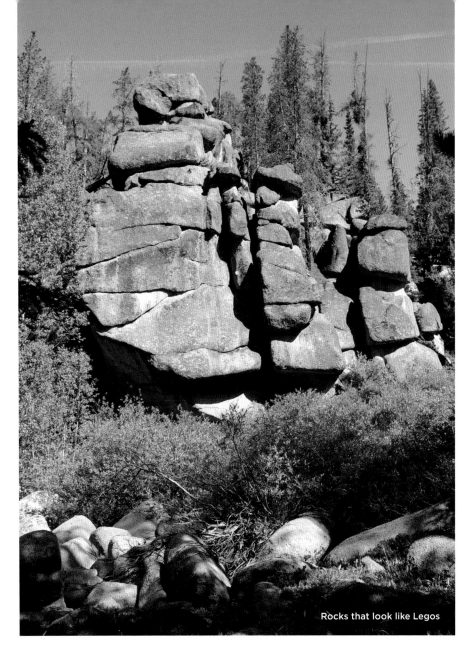
Rocks that look like Legos

the Departments of the Interior and Agriculture provided work projects and leadership. Each man earned $30 per month, of which $25 was sent home to his family.

The CCC is credited with building 46,854 bridges, 3,116 fire lookout towers, and 318,076 dams to help with erosion control, plus numerous buildings and trails. By 1937 the CCC employed more than 500,000 young men, working on projects all over the United States. The army operated more than 2,500 camps to house all the workers.

The men of the CCC performed excellent work. According to Forest Service personnel, the CCC workers who built the Silver Creek Trail created one that is easy to maintain. It has great drainage, rolling dips, and cribbed walls. Moss now covers the rock walls, making them difficult to see.

From the east trailhead, the hike follows several old logging roads, now closed to motorized travel. The trail gradually gains elevation to the wilderness boundary, which is nearly the highest point of the trail. From here you drop into the Silver Creek drainage, with marshy meadows hidden behind trees to the south. The granite rocks along the trail take on some interesting shapes. After crossing a marshy section, the remains of a log cabin rest on the left. The former occupants are unknown, but the notched logs still show careful work by the cabin's builder. "Shiprock" sticks up its prow to the right a little farther down the trail. Colorful aspens frame the boulders in the fall.

As you round a ridge, check out the view down the drainage. The various lumps and cliffs of rock are composed of Precambrian granite (quartz monzonite). Precambrian rocks formed over 600 million years ago when molten magma oozed up into other rocks, cooled slowly, and became the granite you see today. Granite tends to erode like an onion peels, hence some of the rounded shapes. The red trees, or ghost trees, were killed by mountain pine beetles in the 1990s and early 2000s. Although these tiny insects are part of the natural forest cycle, they reproduced in epidemic proportions due to drought, which weakened trees, making them more susceptible to the beetles. Very cold winters kill many beetles, but winters have been relatively mild. Treating the acres of trees involved became impossible. Be aware that these dead trees can fall at any time, particularly in high winds. Park your car and place your tent away from them. Be careful while hiking, too, and keep your dog with you on the trail here.

Sometimes Silver Creek runs swiftly down a tiny canyon, leaping over little cascades. Other times it broadens and sparkles in the sun. Deep pools attract fish; sit and watch for a while. Some good campsites can be found up on low ridges to the north of the trail—an appropriate 200-plus feet from the trail and creek, but close enough to fetch water easily. While you hike and camp, remember to use your Leave No Trace skills!

About two-thirds of the way into the hike, the trail crosses Silver Creek at a wide spot. The trail then swings away from the creek and eventually traverses a steep slope, leaving the creek far below. After topping the ridge, you drop down on south- and west-facing slopes. The vegetation changes here, adapting to the dryness and heat. Ponderosa pines, Gambel oaks, sagebrush, and grasses replace the lodgepole and spruce-fir forest.

This area is very popular during hunting season. Bow and black-powder hunters are plentiful during September. Be considerate and wear some blaze-orange clothing and tie a bright orange bandanna around your dog's neck.

MILES AND DIRECTIONS

0.0 Start at the east Silver Creek (Trail 1106) Trailhead, by the bulletin board. Elevation: 9,730 feet. Walk back to the road, turn left, and walk up the road, over the creek to the trail.

0.1 Silver Creek Trail starts to the left of the road at the big mounds of dirt used to close the old logging road to motorized vehicles. Hike up the dirt mound onto the doubletrack Silver Creek Trail.

1.5 The trail forks; turn left and walk up the old logging road.

1.6 Reach the wilderness boundary sign. Elevation: 9,840 feet. GPS: N40 12.37' / W106 37.47'

2.5 The cabin remains are on the left. GPS: N40 12.19' / W106 38.37'

3.6 Round a ridge with a good view down the Silver Creek drainage.

8.0 Cross Silver Creek. Elevation: 8,900 feet. GPS: N40 12.86' / W106 43.48' (***Note:*** Be careful in early summer when the creek runs high. The current may be swift.)

10.2 Reach the wilderness boundary sign. GPS: N40 13.02' / W106 45.08'

11.5 Top a ridge and begin the final descent to the west trailhead.

11.6 The trail forks; stay to the left (actually go straight downhill as there's a viewpoint off to the right).

12.3 Reach the Silver Creek west trailhead bulletin board. If you're coming up from this direction, please stop to read up-to-date area information. (***Note:*** From here to the trailhead parking, you'll be on private property. The Forest Service has permission for the trail to cross here. Please respect the private property!)

12.4 Arrive at the west Silver Creek Trailhead. Elevation: 7,960 feet. GPS: N40 13.33' / W106 46.73'

WHY GO?

Coyote Trail winds past limestone caves, through a lush riparian and forested area, then climbs above for a bird's-eye view of Rifle Falls. Kids of all ages will love exploring the caves. Bring a flashlight for the largest one. Squirrel Trail crosses East Rifle Creek and winds through Gambel oak forest to the base of a red sandstone cliff. The trail continues along the Grass Valley Canal, which takes water to Harvey Gap Reservoir. Hiked together, the trails make a lopsided figure eight through a naturally and historically interesting area along East Rifle Creek.

THE RUNDOWN

Start: From the Rifle Falls State Park picnic ground
Distance: 1.8-mile double loop
Approximate hiking time: 1 to 2 hours
Difficulty: Mostly easy with some steep sections
Elevation gain: 140 feet (two at 70 feet each)
Seasons: Year-round except after snowstorms
Trail surface: Paved road, dirt road, dirt trail

Other trail users: Wheelchair users (on first part of Coyote Trail), anglers, mountain bikers
Canine compatibility: Dogs must be on leash
Fees and permits: Daily entrance fee or annual parks pass required
Maps: USGS Rifle Falls; Nat Geo Trails Illustrated 125 Flat Tops SW/Rifle Gap
Trail contacts: Rifle Falls State Park, Rifle; (970) 625-1607; parks.state.co.us/parks/riflefalls

FINDING THE TRAILHEAD

From I-70's exit 90 for Rifle, head north on CO 13 through town. In about 4 miles, turn right onto CO 325 and drive another 4 miles to Rifle Gap Reservoir. Stay on CO 325, which turns right and goes over the dam. Drive another 5.6 miles to the Rifle Falls State Park entrance. Pay the fee here or at the self-serve kiosk. Turn left and drive 0.2 mile through the campground to the picnic area. Park here. A vault toilet and water are available. **GPS:** N39 40.58' / W107 41.92'

THE HIKE

Lined with red sandstone and limestone cliffs, Rifle Falls State Park is a showplace with a 60-foot triple waterfall, lush riparian and forested areas, wildlife habitat, and a nice picnic area and campground. Two trails, named after local inhabitants, wander through the park for a complete tour. Interpretive signs along Coyote Trail explain the natural and social history of the area.

The original configuration of Rifle Falls consisted of one wide sheet of water, with some early pictures showing multiple ribbons of water. In 1908 the Rifle Light, Heat, and Power Company was incorporated to provide electricity to the town of Rifle. This group built the first hydroelectric plant in Colorado by diverting part of East Rifle Creek through a pipe descending the cliff at Rifle Falls. As a result, Rifle Falls became two ribbons of water plus the pipeline. Thirteen miles of transmission cable linked Rifle with the power plant. In town, 8 miles of wires, twenty-five streetlights, and wiring for most buildings were installed. Rifle received its first electricity from the power plant

Rifle Falls from overlook

Various stories exist about how Rifle Creek was named. Most stories develop the theme of someone leaving or finding a rifle leaning against a tree along the creek. Another legend refers to a custom of cowboys firing their rifles at a roundup ground near the confluence of the three creeks.

Trail along Grass Valley Canal

on December 31, 1909. The company merged with Public Service Company in 1926. Public Service sold the property to the Colorado Game and Fish Department in 1959, at which time the plant was closed. The stone power plant was torn down in 1971. With the removal of the pipe, the falls have reverted to three streams of water.

The cliffs that create the falls are made of calcium carbonate from creeks flowing underground in limestone deposits upstream. Thousands of years ago the creek ran over some obstacle, which geologists believe was a giant beaver dam. The water left deposits that developed into today's cliffs. You can approach the falls from various sides, getting sprayed no matter which way you choose. To the right of the falls, Coyote Trail winds past limestone caves, created by water eroding the cliff from the inside out. Some are shallow, while one is large enough (90 feet) to need a flashlight to explore. Bats live in these caves, so be respectful if they are hanging out. The caves contain interesting formations, such as flowstone, popcorn stone, and stalactites hanging from the ceiling. Watch your head as you hike from cave to cave. One place in particular has very low clearance.

Outside the caves, cottonwoods, box elders, chokecherry trees, hawthorns (emphasis on thorns), coyote willows, and a little stream line the trail. Blue Steller's jays squawk overhead. The trail curves around and up until you are on top of the cliff. The Bobcat Trail to the Rifle Fish Hatchery branches to the north just before the falls. (The hatchery was completed in 1954 as the largest trout hatchery in the state.) Old metal pipes and wooden water diversions still remain from the hydroelectric plant days. The quickly flowing water disappears over the cliff in a white froth as it takes the plunge. Observation decks hang beyond the cliff for a bird's-eye view and a potential adrenaline rush. The trail down is steep, but stairs make the trek a little easier. The riparian area around the falls creates wildlife-watching opportunities.

Coyote and Squirrel Loop

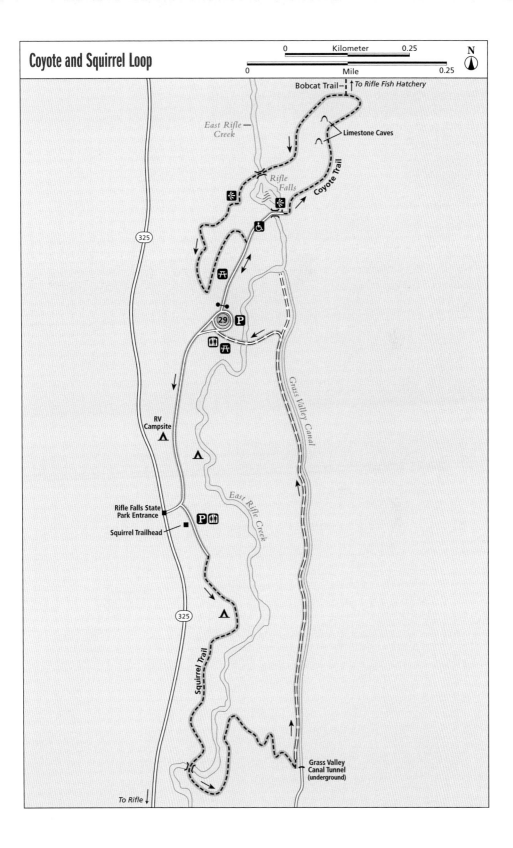

East Rifle Creek

Bobcat Trail — ↑ To Rifle Fish Hatchery

Limestone Caves

Coyote Trail

Rifle Falls

325

29 P

RV Campsite

East Rifle Creek

Grass Valley Canal

Rifle Falls State Park Entrance

Squirrel Trailhead

P

325

Squirrel Trail

Grass Valley Canal Tunnel (underground)

To Rifle ↓

N

0 Kilometer 0.25
0 Mile 0.25

After arriving back at the picnic area, walk through the main campground past the fee kiosk to Squirrel Trail. This trail takes you to the Grass Valley Canal, built between 1891 and 1894. At the same time, a dam was being built about 5 miles away (as the crow flies), across a gap in the Grand Hogback. This tilted ridge is the western Colorado version of the Dakota Hogback west of Denver. The canal brings water from East Rifle Creek to Harvey Gap Reservoir, which stores irrigation water for farms and ranches. The reservoir is in Harvey Gap State Park.

Squirrel Trail follows the creek through the walk-in campground, then crosses it on a swinging bridge. Gambel oaks on the other side create a thick forest, a cool treat on a hot day. The trail twists and climbs up the side of the canyon to the base of the cliff. A T intersection appears after one steep stretch. Turn left and head uphill to where the trail meets the canal before it enters the tunnel. The water is clear and deep. The dirt road along the canal takes you back to the picnic ground by going downhill at the left-hand curve.

Rifle Falls has attracted visitors since the 1880s. Many people consider this area the Hawaii or Costa Rica of Colorado. The swank Zerbe Resort housed tourists for a number of years, starting around 1903 until, unfortunately, it burned down in 1922.

MILES AND DIRECTIONS

0.0 Start at the picnic ground at the closed pipe gate on the paved road. Elevation: 6,500 feet. Head north toward Rifle Falls on the Coyote Trail.

0.1 View the Rifle Falls area and interpretive signs. (**Note:** You might get sprayed by the falling water mist.)

0.2 Reach the start of the limestone caves.

0.3 Come to the intersection with the Bobcat Trail to the fish hatchery. Go straight ahead to the falls overlook. Elevation: 6,600 feet.

0.5 Turn left onto the observation deck for a great view of the falls. Just beyond, the trail drops downhill, sometimes steeply down concrete steps, back to the picnic area.

0.6 Arrive back at the dirt road in the picnic area. Turn right and walk on the road back to the parking lot then through the campground toward the entrance station.

0.8 Reach the Squirrel Trailhead to the left of the entrance station. GPS: N39 40.40' / W107 41.93'

1.1 Stay to the right at campsite 20, drop down, and cross East Rifle Creek on a swinging bridge.

1.35 Squirrel Trail climbs steeply and comes to a T intersection. Turn left and continue uphill on the trail.

1.4 The trail joins the dirt road along the canal at the water tunnel.

1.7 Come to a fork and go left down the road.

1.8 Arrive back at the picnic ground.

30 BLACK MOUNTAIN (WEST SUMMIT) TRAIL

WHY GO?

This hike climbs to the west summit of Black Mountain, a volcanic plateau in the Elkhead Mountains. The trail first winds through an aspen forest with vegetation so thick at times that you might feel the need for a machete. The trail then proceeds into drier lodgepole and spruce-fir forests. Once up on the plateau, a spur trail takes you to a raptor viewing area complete with an interpretive poster and views west toward Dinosaur National Monument and Utah.

THE RUNDOWN

Start: From the Cottonwood Trailhead at the east side of Freeman Reservoir
Distance: 7.4 miles out and back
Approximate hiking time: 3.5 to 5 hours
Difficulty: Difficult due to elevation gain and some rough trail sections
Elevation gain: 2,055 feet
Seasons: Best from mid-June to mid-Oct
Trail surface: Dirt trail with wet areas and some rocky sections
Other trail users: Equestrians, mountain bikers, hunters (in season)
Canine compatibility: Dogs must be on leash

Fees and permits: Day-use fee required for Freeman Recreation Area; America the Beautiful pass accepted
Map: USGS Freeman Reservoir
Trail contacts: Medicine Bow–Routt National Forest, Hahns Peak/Bears Ears Ranger District, Steamboat Springs; (970) 870-2299; www.fs .usda.gov/mbr
Other: The access road is closed by snow about 7.2 miles from the trailhead in winter. The road is used by snowmobiles. The trail is neither maintained nor marked for winter use. Water is sparse on the trail.

FINDING THE TRAILHEAD

From the intersection of US 40 and CO 13 in Craig, head north 13.4 miles on CO 13 to just past mile marker 103. Turn right onto Moffat CR 11 (which becomes FR 112) and drive 9.2 miles to Freeman Recreation Area. Pay the day-use fee at the self-service station. Continue another 0.4 mile to the east end of the reservoir, turn left, and go another 0.1 mile to the parking area at the trailhead near the campground. The hike description starts at the east trailhead. Water and vault toilets are at the campground (fee area). **GPS:** N40 45.83' / W 107 25.37'

THE HIKE

In the Elkhead Mountains of northwestern Colorado, Black Mountain forms a 1.75–mile-long plateau that rises north of Craig. From a distance it does indeed look black. The Elkheads were formed by the same volcanic eruptions that shaped the Flat Tops and White River Plateau between 25 million and 17 million years ago. At the eastern edge of a desert zone, the Elkheads capture enough moisture to feed the Elkhead, Little Snake, and Yampa Rivers. Ute people lived and hunted here. Although very popular in fall with hunters because of large elk, deer, and pronghorn antelope herds, summer finds the area

Black Mountain Trail through aspen

less used than the wilderness areas to the east and south. Aspens flourish in the Freeman Reservoir area and on the lower part of Black Mountain, making this trail a colorful fall hike.

Aspens and willows growing along Little Cottonwood Creek border the first part of the trail. The lush aspen forest provides a home to many animals and plants. Colorado columbine, the state flower, grows in aspen forests. Pink Wood's rose, white geranium, yellow heartleaf arnica (named for its heart-shaped leaves), pinkish-purple fireweed, dandelion, blue harebells, various paintbrushes, pussytoes, white Mariposa lily, and wild strawberries cover the ground. Larkspur, pearly everlasting, and white to pinkish yarrow are common. In moister areas, tall cow parsnip, with its teeny flowers forming a lacy doily, and deep purple monkshood grow in profusion. Cow parsnip is often confused with Queen Anne's lace. Monkshood is aptly named, with its monk's cowl flowers. Listen for the *chick-a-dee-dee-dee* of the mountain chickadee, a small gray and black bird that lives here year-round. Elk and deer find ample food in aspen forests, including grasses and bushes such as serviceberry, snowberry, twinberry, and chokecherry, along with Rocky Mountain maple.

The local elk depend on aspen trees, especially during harsh winters when they cannot uncover buried grasses. Scraping bark off with their lower teeth, they feast on the cambium layer just under the bark. Watch for elk teeth marks as you hike. Black bears enjoy many fruits of the aspen forest, from aspen buds and catkins in spring to berries produced by the numerous shrubs. They sometimes climb aspens, leaving claw marks as testimony to their exploits. Avoid surprising bears that are trying to fatten up before winter, and should you see wildlife of either variety, put your pup on a leash to avoid an encounter.

The hike starts along the east shore of Freeman Reservoir, then heads up the Little Cottonwood Creek drainage. The trail can be very muddy after heavy rains. Farther on, one section is very rocky as it climbs to the Bears Ears Trail (Trail 1144). When you reach Black Mountain Trail (Trail 1185), head north to a big aspen stand. Thick forest undergrowth sometimes obscures the trail. Watch your footing as aspen forests are notorious for hidden roots and fallen trees waiting to twist an ankle. Some large boulders lend a rock-garden atmosphere along trail sections. A few clearings present views to the south and west, including of Freeman Reservoir about 1,000 feet below.

The trail curves up a ridge and enters spruce-fir forest. It climbs steadily to a flat spot below the plateau with views to the north. The big boulders make a nice rest spot. The trail then drops about 60 feet into an open area where a large boulder field on the right lines a thumb of the plateau. After a few tight switchbacks, the trail continues to climb to a saddle on the plateau. After hiking around a boulder field, you'll come to another open area. A spur trail heads north to the raptor viewing area, where an interpretive sign explains why golden and bald eagles enjoy soaring and playing above the edge of Black Mountain. The west summit is a little farther to the northeast. A sign denotes the summit, barely discernible on the fairly flat plateau top. The trail beyond the west summit continues another 1.5 miles to the east summit (10,801 feet), with views of the Yampa Valley.

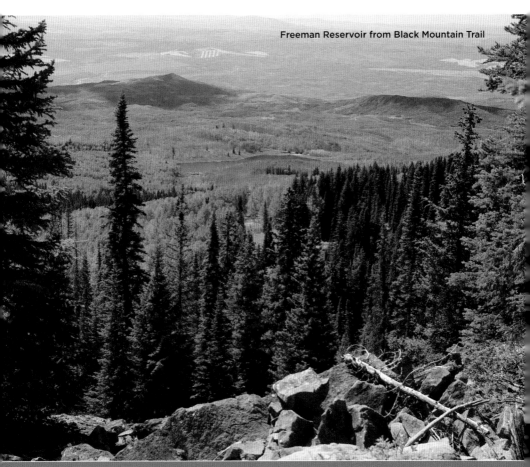

Freeman Reservoir from Black Mountain Trail

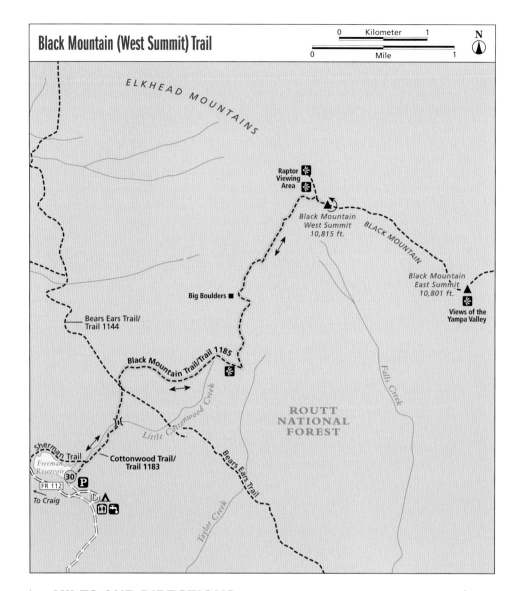

Black Mountain (West Summit) Trail

Raptor
Viewing
Area

Black Mountain
West Summit
10,815 ft.

ELKHEAD MOUNTAINS

BLACK MOUNTAIN

Black Mountain
East Summit
10,801 ft.

Views of the
Yampa Valley

Big Boulders ■

Bears Ears Trail/
Trail 1144

Black Mountain Trail/Trail 1185

Little Cottonwood Creek

Falls Creek

ROUTT
NATIONAL
FOREST

Sherman Trail

Freeman
Reservoir

Cottonwood Trail/
Trail 1183

Bears Ears Trail

FR 112   30 P

To Craig

Taylor Creek

MILES AND DIRECTIONS

0.0 Start at the Cottonwood Trailhead at the east end of Freeman Reservoir. Elevation: 8,760 feet. Follow Cottonwood Trail (Trail 1183).

0.2 Pass the junction with the Sherman Trail (Trail 1010) coming in from the left. Keep hiking straight on Cottonwood Trail.

0.6 Cross Little Cottonwood Creek on a bridge.

0.8 Reach the trail junction of Cottonwood and Bears Ears Trails. Turn left and head uphill on the Bears Ears Trail (Trail 1144).

0.9 Reach the trail junction of Bears Ears Trail and Black Mountain Trail (Trail 1185). Turn right up Black Mountain Trail. GPS: N40 46.41' / W107 24.97'

1.8 Enjoy the views to the south and east as you leave the aspen forest.

2.6 Come to a right switchback and a flat area near big boulders. (**Note:** This is a good rest stop.)

3.3 The trail reaches the edge of a plateau.

3.6 The spur trail to the raptor viewing area. Stay right to go to the summit. (**Side trip:** Taking the out-and-back spur to the raptor viewing area will add a total of 0.5 mile to your hike. Raptors enjoy the thermals in this area. The viewpoint has an interpretive sign explaining the soaring birds of prey you might be lucky enough to see. GPS: N40 47.65' / W107 23.50'. On a clear day you can see west to Dinosaur National Monument and the Uinta Mountains in Utah.)

3.7 Reach the west summit of Black Mountain (10,815 feet). GPS: N40 47.45' / W107 23.30'. Turn around and retrace your tracks back to the start.

7.3 Reach the junction with a trail from the left, but with no sign. Keep going straight ahead or you'll end up back at the campground.

7.4 Arrive back at the trailhead.

I-70 CORRIDOR

I-70 is a major artery in Colorado's mountain traffic. If someone tells you they're headed to the mountains for the weekend, this is likely the route they're taking. Many of the most popular ski resorts are right off I-70, and summer traffic to Summit County, Vail, Glenwood Springs, and other tourist destinations keeps things moving relatively slowly on weekends. (If you're heading west on I-70 on a Friday evening or Saturday morning during the summer—or driving eastbound on a Sunday afternoon—expect to be in the car for an extra hour or more, depending on your final destination.) With that in mind, many of these hikes are best done during the shoulder seasons, particularly in the fall, when you're less likely to be tromping through snow. If you can, make for the high country on a weekday, when you won't be fighting traffic. In any case, hikes in this section are within a close jaunt of I-70, so you can reach them relatively easily after exiting the main thoroughfare.

31 WHEELER TRAIL

WHY GO?

This trail to the top of Wheeler Pass (the unofficial name) is part of both the Wheeler National Recreational Trail and the Colorado Trail. It climbs steadily through spruce-fir and lodgepole forests on the western slope of the Tenmile Range. Views of the Gore Range, Copper Mountain, Breckenridge, French Gulch, and the Front Range are fabulous! Because this trail goes to a ridge above tree line, be sure to get an early start to avoid afternoon thunder and lightning storms.

THE RUNDOWN

Start: From the Wheeler Flats Trailhead
Distance: 8.6 miles out and back (6.6 miles after trailhead is relocated)
Approximate hiking time: 5 to 6 hours
Difficulty: Most difficult due to elevation gain
Elevation gain: 2,730 feet
Seasons: Best from late June to mid-Oct
Trail surface: Dirt trail with some small creek crossings, rocks, and roots
Other trail users: Equestrians, mountain bikers, hunters (in season)

Canine compatibility: Dogs must be under control
Fees and permits: None
Maps: USGS Breckenridge, Copper Mountain, and Vail Pass; Nat Geo Trails Illustrated 109 Breckenridge/Tennessee Pass and 108 Vail/Frisco/Dillon; Latitude 40° Summit County
Trail contacts: White River National Forest, Dillon Ranger District, Silverthorne; (970) 468-5400; www.fs.usda.gov/whiteriver
Other: This trail crosses several avalanche chutes in the winter. It is neither maintained nor marked for winter use.

FINDING THE TRAILHEAD

From Frisco, head west on I-70 to exit 195 (for Copper Mountain and Leadville/CO 91). Exit and take CO 91 over I-70. The entrance to Copper Mountain Resort is on the right; turn left here onto an unnamed road and drive past the gas station (with restrooms, food, and water). It's 0.4 mile to the parking lot at Wheeler Flats Trailhead. **GPS:** N39 30.55' / W106 08.50'

THE HIKE

This area was once a Ute hunting ground rich with bison, deer, elk, antelope, and mountain sheep in the surrounding high open areas. In 1879 Judge John Wheeler purchased 320 acres, now part of Copper Mountain Resort, and started a hay ranch. Silver miners arrived the following year, and the ranch became a town known by various names: Wheeler's Ranch, Wheeler Station, Wheeler's, Wheeler, and Wheeler Junction. Wheeler prospered with a hotel, saloons, and a post office. Several sawmills provided lumber for the numerous mines along Tenmile Creek from Frisco to the top of Fremont Pass.

Despite its status as a mining town, tourists also came to Wheeler for the beautiful scenery and excellent fishing. In 1884 the Colorado & Southern Railroad finished laying tracks to Wheeler on the east side of Tenmile Creek. The railroad station at Wheeler was

View from pass to east down Sawmill Gulch

named Solitude Station. On the other side of the creek, the Denver & Rio Grande Railroad built a line with a station called Wheeler's. The Denver & Rio Grande serviced this area from 1880 to 1911. The Colorado & Southern ended its rail service around 1937.

The trail is mostly flat for the first mile, as it follows part of the old Colorado & Southern Railroad route, now covering a gas pipeline. In one place the trail seems lower than the creek! After 1 mile you reach a junction with a post. Turn left, up the trail, to access Wheeler Pass. After the trailhead is relocated, you will cross a bridge to reach this post, eliminating 2 miles round-trip from your hike. Judge Wheeler used this trail to take his stock from Wheeler to his ranch in South Park. The trail now ends near Hoosier Pass, south of Breckenridge. It was designated a National Recreational Trail in 1979.

In about 3.4 miles the trail exits the forest for a view of Climax Molybdenum Mine's settling ponds. Several prosperous mining towns, including Robinson and Kokomo of Wheeler's era, are buried under the ponds. Watch and listen for marmots. As the trail contours left into another drainage, you can see the ridge of the Tenmile Range and cairns marking the trail. From here the trail winds in and out of forest, meadow, and willows. Colorful wildflowers line the route. Trees become twisted krummholz near tree line, and finally give up. The trail is sometimes smothered by willows, but is passable. Three cairns built of good-size logs mark the way; the second one, however, is not on the trail, so stay alert. Finally, when your breath is short from elevation and the steep trail, the summit cairn comes into view.

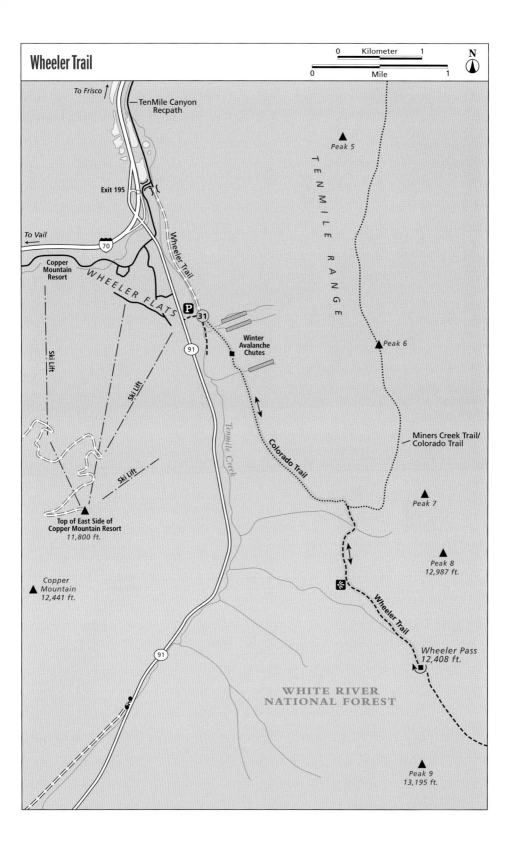

Wheeler Trail

To Frisco

TenMile Canyon
Recpath

Exit 195

To Vail

70

Copper
Mountain
Resort

WHEELER FLATS

Wheeler Trail

P

31

91

Winter
Avalanche
Chutes

TEN MILE RANGE

Peak 5

Peak 6

Peak 7

Ski Lift

Ski Lift

Ski Lift

Tenmile Creek

Colorado Trail

Miners Creek Trail/
Colorado Trail

Top of East Side of
Copper Mountain Resort
11,800 ft.

Copper
Mountain
12,441 ft.

Peak 8
12,987 ft.

Wheeler Trail

91

Wheeler Pass
12,408 ft.

WHITE RIVER
NATIONAL FOREST

Peak 9
13,195 ft.

That is, until you reach it and realize the trail continues farther up. Notice the vegetation along the trail. Willows and little red elephants grow in shallow depressions containing snow and water. The drier areas contain sedges and grasses, old-man-of-the-mountain, paintbrush, American bistort, chickweed, and alpine avens. The tundra is fragile. If you must go off trail, step on rocks as much as possible. When in a group, spread out.

The sign at the top of Wheeler Pass reports an elevation of 12,460 feet, but the topo map clearly indicates it's just under 12,400 feet. Be sure to hike to the little rocky knob on the left (12,408 feet) for the best easterly views. Breckenridge, French Gulch, and part of the Breckenridge ski area are on the east side; Copper Mountain and the Gore Range are to the northwest.

Founded in 1859 by General George E. Spencer, Breckenridge was named after US vice president John Cabell Breckinridge to ensure the new town would receive a post office. During the Civil War, John Breckinridge joined the Confederate Army. Upset Breckinridge residents changed the "i" to "e," spelling the name "Breckenridge." Other stories indicate the town was named after Thomas E. Breckenridge, a member of the original mining party. At one time, men panning gold in the Blue River and French Gulch could earn as much as $12 to $20 a day each! Dredge boats came later to scoop up more gold, and mines were burrowed into the hills. The largest gold nugget ever found in Colorado came from this area. At thirteen pounds it was called "Tom's Baby" (after Tom Groves, its finder).

Today both Breckenridge and Copper Mountain are known for their popular ski areas. Ski lifts at each area can be seen from various points along the trail. Skiing, other forms of outdoor recreation, and vacation homes have replaced mining in a new "gold rush" to the Rockies.

MILES AND DIRECTIONS

0.0 Start in the parking lot. Elevation: 9,680 feet. Cross the wooden bridge over Tenmile Creek, turn right down the paved bike path, and in less than 0.1 mile come to a second bridge over Tenmile Creek. Veer right and walk across the gravel-topped bridge.

1.0 Reach a junction with the Colorado Trail and turn left, heading uphill on the Colorado Trail, marked with a post. GPS: N39 29.83' / W106 08.08' (**Note:** One trail [along the gas pipeline] goes straight along the creek and the other, the Colorado Trail, goes right to CO 91.)

2.8 Reach the trail junction with Miners Creek Trail. GPS: N39 28.63' / W106 06.93'. Go right on Wheeler Trail.

4.3 Arrive at the top of Wheeler Pass and the rocky knob viewpoint. Elevation: 12,408 feet. GPS: N39 27.67' / W106 06.32'. Return the way you came.

8.6 Arrive back at the trailhead.

32 STORM KING FOURTEEN MEMORIAL TRAIL

WHY GO?

This trail, built by volunteers, is a memorial to fourteen firefighters who lost their lives on Storm King Mountain in July 1994. Interpretive signs explain wildland firefighting and this unfortunate disaster. You can stop at the observation point to look across to the ridge where the firefighters died, or hike farther to the memorial sites. The trail is a journey into a burned land, now recovering. The steep trails give you a brief insight into and feeling for the work of those who fight wildland fires.

THE RUNDOWN

Start: From the Storm King Fourteen Memorial Trailhead
Distance: 4.4-miles out and back
Approximate hiking time: 3.5 to 4.5 hours
Difficulty: Moderate to the observation point; most difficult to the memorial sites due to steepness
Elevation gain/loss: 1,280-foot gain / 440-foot loss
Seasons: Best from Apr through Nov
Trail surface: Dirt trail mainly on south- and southwest-facing slopes, fairly steep in spots, slippery when wet, open ridge near observation point
Other trail users: Hunters (in season)
Canine compatibility: Dogs must be on leash
Fees and permits: None
Maps: USGS Storm King Mountain; Nat Geo Trails Illustrated 123 Flat Tops SE/Glenwood Canyon
Trail contacts: Bureau of Land Management, Colorado River Valley Field Office, Silt; (970) 876-9000; www.blm.gov/co/st/en/fo/crvfo.html
Other: No water is available on the trail.

FINDING THE TRAILHEAD

From Glenwood Springs, take I-70 west to exit 109 / Canyon Creek. Turn right, then immediately right again onto the frontage road. Head back east past Canyon Creek Estates for 1 mile to a dead end with a parking lot. The trail starts by several interpretive signs at the east end of the lot. There is a portable toilet but no water at the trailhead. **GPS:** N39 34.43' / W107 26.02'

THE HIKE

On July 2, 1994, a very natural event occurred. A lightning strike started a small fire in a piñon–juniper–Gambel oak forest on Storm King Mountain (8,793 feet). Several large wildland fires were already burning across Colorado, strapping firefighting resources. The small fire received low priority. By July 5 the fire covered 5 acres, and crews arrived to build fire lines. But Mother Nature had other plans. By midafternoon on July 6, a dry cold front passed through the region, causing very strong winds that fanned the fire into a roaring inferno traveling much faster than any human could run, especially uphill. The fire soon consumed over 2,100 acres. Fourteen firefighters could not escape the

Clothes memorial on a ghost tree   Memorial sites

MORE ABOUT STORM KING

Two Rivers Park in Glenwood Springs contains a memorial to the fourteen fire-fighters who died on Storm King Mountain. A bronze sculpture depicting three wildland firefighters is surrounded by a garden, pictures, and information about each of the lost firefighters.

To reach Two Rivers Park from the Storm King Fourteen Memorial Trail, take I-70 eastbound. Exit at West Glenwood and turn left under the highway, then turn right onto US 6 eastbound. Go 1.8 miles to Devereux Drive and turn right. Drive 0.3 mile, crossing over I-70, and look for the park on the left. Turn left into the park. The memorial garden is straight ahead.

The story of the Storm King Mountain Fire (mistakenly reported as being in South Canyon) is captured in the book *Fire on the Mountain* by John N. McLean, published in 1999. The History Channel produced a video, *Fire on the Mountain,* in 2002 (www.historychannel.com). Many interesting articles, including the report of the investigation team, can be found via the Internet.

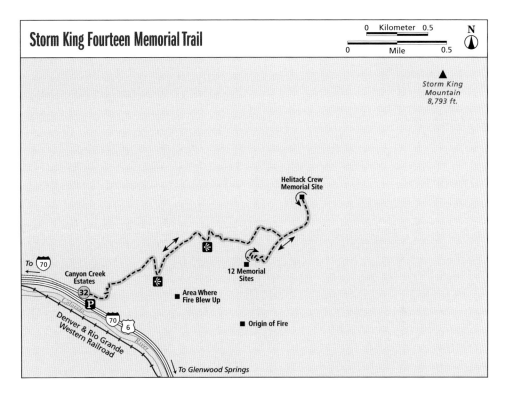

Storm King Fourteen Memorial Trail

0   Kilometer   0.5

0   Mile   0.5

N

Storm King
Mountain
8,793 ft.

Helitack Crew
Memorial Site

To 70
←

Canyon Creek
Estates

32

P

Colorado

12 Memorial
Sites

Area Where
Fire Blew Up

Origin of Fire

Denver & Rio Grande
Western Railroad

70

6

River

To Glenwood Springs

100-foot-high flames racing toward them. Thirty-five others escaped either by hunkering down in their fire shelters or by slipping down an eastern gully to the highway.

Although forest fire is a natural and important process, the fire on Storm King Mountain endangered homes and businesses in West Glenwood to the east and Canyon Creek Estates to the west. The trees on Storm King also provided essential erosion control. Storm King and surrounding mountains are a combination of red sandstone and shale, called the Maroon Formation, deposited over eons by inland seas. When shale gets wet, mudslides often result.

Volunteers built this trail in 1995 to honor wildland firefighters nationwide and to provide an insight into their experiences. The trail begins with several interpretive signs about the July 1994 fire. They invite you to imagine being a firefighter, hiking up steep slopes and carrying thirty to sixty pounds of equipment.

The trail climbs steeply along the south side of a ridge, through rabbitbrush, wild roses, Mormon tea, and cheatgrass, with numerous log steps to hike up. Where the trail turns to follow the west side of a ridge, a small sign describes the camaraderie of firefighters, and gives you a chance to take a few deep breaths. The Colorado River roars below, as does I-70. The trail continues to climb through piñon-juniper forest. The steepness of the trail is tiring even with a light pack. About 0.25 mile up a sign announces entry into Bureau of Land Management (BLM) lands. Switchbacks take you steadily uphill. A bench provides a handy place to check out the western view and catch your breath. Down valley, I-70 twists like a serpent, following the river's contours. The Grand Hogback and Coal Ridge form the horizon to the south.

At 0.6 mile the trail reaches a ridge at 6,280 feet. Storm King Mountain, with scorched sticks and green Gambel oak, comes into view. You can see how the fire raced up gullies to different ridges. The trees to the right of the trail are snags of their former selves. To the left, most trees are green and alive. Narrow-leaved penstemon and blue flax flowers grow among the ghostly trunks. Across the gully Gambel oak once again covers the slopes, although junipers and piñon pines may take forty to one hundred years to reestablish themselves.

The trail follows a mostly flat ridge for 0.4 mile to the observation point. Three large interpretive signs explain the events of that fateful July day. With a pair of binoculars, you can see the slope that twelve firefighters scrambled up trying to reach safety. Look closely for the pair of crossed skis marking one memorial site. You can turn around here or continue to the memorial sites.

To reach the memorial sites on the next ridge, continue on the trail left of the interpretive signs. If you hike this trail, be aware that several sections are very steep with loose footing. Once on that ridge a trail to the left leads to where two helitack crewmembers died, across a steep little gully by a rock outcropping. The trail to the right leads to the slope where nine members of the Prineville, Oregon, Hotshots crew and three smokejumpers died. To reach the twelve sites, walk about 0.1 mile to a trail that switchbacks down the west slope. Memorial sites are noted with the firefighters' names.

The BLM and families request that you stay on the trail and do not walk straight down between the crosses; however, the trail is hidden by bushes and hard to find. The area between crosses is extremely steep and prone to erosion. Look around; see and feel the steepness of the slope. Imagine what it would be like to have a fire chasing you up that hill. Read the poem at trail's end below the memorial sites and reflect for a moment on people who are willing to give their lives to protect the lives and property of others.

MILES AND DIRECTIONS

0.0 Start at the trailhead east of Canyon Creek Estates. Elevation: 5,680 feet. Take a few minutes to read the interpretive signs. (**Note:** The first part of the trail crosses private property, which the BLM has permission to use for this trail. Please respect the owners' property rights.)

0.25 Reach the BLM boundary sign.

0.3 Reach a bench and interpretive sign on the right side of the trail. This is a good place to catch your breath and enjoy the view down the Colorado River.

0.6 Gain a ridge with views of Storm King Mountain and the burned area.

1.0 Arrive at the observation point with interpretive signs. Elevation: 6,360 feet. GPS: N39 34.68' / W107 25.35' (**Option:** You can turn around here for a shorter, moderate hike.)

1.2 Reach the bottom of the first gully, contour around into the second gully, and start climbing up to the next ridge.

1.7 The trail comes to a T intersection. Elevation: 6,680 feet. GPS: N39 34.66' / W107 24.95'. Take the left trail to the helitack crew memorial site.

2.0 Arrive at the helitack crew memorial site. Look across the deep little gully near a rock outcropping to see the crosses. Head back toward the T intersection.

2.3 Arrive back at the T intersection. Proceed ahead to the other twelve memorial sites.

2.4 The trail switchbacks downhill past the memorial sites that are marked with signs along the trail. (**Note:** Please remember to stay on the trail that switchbacks [versus the trail that goes straight downhill]. When you see the Scott Blecha sign, the trail turns right into the bushes. If you walk to Blecha's stone, you'll end up walking straight down an extremely steep slope between the crosses. The area between crosses is prone to erosion.)

2.5 The trail ends below the twelve memorial sites. GPS: N39 34.59' / W107 25.08'. Walk to the end to read the poem. Return the way you came.

2.7 Arrive back at the T intersection. Turn left to head downhill and return to the observation point.

4.4 Arrive back at the trailhead.

33 MOUNT THOMAS TRAIL

WHY GO?

From the summit of Mount Thomas, overwhelming views stretch from the Maroon Bells and Elk Mountains in the southwest, circling northwest to the Flat Tops, then I-70 north of Eagle. The Gore Range rises in the northeast, with the Sawatch Mountains towering in the east and southeast. Cattle still graze on some of the grassy southern slopes. Beautiful alpine wildflowers decorate the upper ridges. The trail traverses an open ridge for about 1.6 miles, so be sure to make the summit and be heading down before thunderstorms hit.

THE RUNDOWN

Start: 0.5 mile from the top of Crooked Creek Pass at the junction with FR 431
Distance: 9.2 miles out and back
Approximate hiking time: 4 to 7 hours
Difficulty: Difficult due to elevation gain and distance
Elevation gain/loss: 1,197-foot gain / 370-foot loss
Seasons: Best from late June to mid-Oct
Trail surface: Dirt road and dirt trail with some steep sections and a boulder field
Other trail users: Equestrians and hunters (in season)
Canine compatibility: Dogs must be on leash

Fees and permits: None
Maps: USGS Crooked Creek Pass; Nat Geo Trails Illustrated 126 Holy Cross/Ruedi Reservoir; Latitude 40° Vail & Eagle
Trail contacts: White River National Forest, Eagle Ranger District, Eagle; (970) 328-6388. White River National Forest, Sopris Ranger District, Aspen; (970) 963-2266; www.fs.usda.gov/whiteriver
Other: In winter the access road is closed by snow just past Sylvan Lake State Park, 5.5 miles from the trailhead. The road is used by snowmobilers and cross-country skiers. The trail is neither maintained nor marked for winter use.

FINDING THE TRAILHEAD

From I-70 (exit 147) in Eagle, head south about 0.3 mile to US 6 and turn right in the traffic circle. Drive 1 mile, following the SYLVAN LAKE signs to a second traffic circle just past mile marker 149. You basically turn left via the traffic circle onto Sylvan Lakes Road. Continue 1.7 miles and turn right onto Brush Creek Road (Eagle CR 307). Drive about 8.8 miles to the fork in the road. Take the right branch, West Brush Creek (smooth dirt road), again to Sylvan Lake. Drive another 10 miles to the top of Crooked Creek Pass. The dirt road narrows and becomes FR 400 past Sylvan Lake State Park. You can park in the dirt area to the right at the top of the pass (add 1 mile round-trip to the hike mileage). Or, at the top of the pass, turn right onto an unmarked dirt road and drive 0.5 mile to the junction with FR 431. Park on the flat grassy area at the junction. **GPS:** N39 26.34' / W106 41.10'. With a 4WD you can drive 0.2 mile from the junction with FR 431 to the actual trailhead and park under the power lines.

THE HIKE

Mount Thomas (11,977 feet) was named after the head of the St. Louis & Colorado Smelting Company. Thomas (the rest of his name apparently lost to history) started a

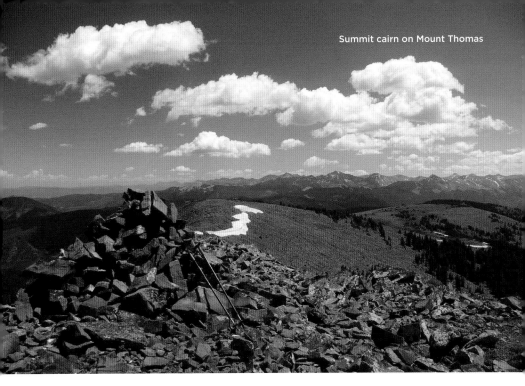

smelter along the Colorado Midland Railroad in the Fryingpan Valley around 1890. The town that grew nearby, Thomasville, also bears his name. He became involved in some mining ventures north of town in the Lime Creek drainage. He did not have much luck; the mines produced little ore, and his unprofitable smelter closed in 1892. A little peak on the ridge between Lime and Brush Creeks commemorates his involvement in the area. The ridge itself is known as Red Table Mountain.

Grassy meadows provide good grazing for cattle in the Lime Creek drainage. When settlers arrived in Colorado in the late 1800s, cattle and sheep grazed freely on public lands. Ranchers and sheepherders ran as much stock as possible, damaging many acres across the West through overgrazing. The Taylor Grazing Act of 1934 created grazing districts to minimize the degradation of public lands. Today the USDA Forest Service grants grazing permits on the lands under its management. A rancher may hold several grazing allotments in an area. With guidance from the Forest Service, the rancher moves his herd at designated times, rotating cattle to different areas. Rotation has several benefits: The cattle continue to have fresh grass to eat; the grass in any given area is not totally consumed and has time to recover and stay healthy; and fences help keep cattle in designated areas. The rancher holding the grazing allotments is responsible for maintaining the fences. In the Lime Creek area, "lay down" fences are common. After the cattle leave the high country in the fall, the rancher lets the fences down. This practice prevents snow damage. In spring trees downed by winter snows and winds are removed from the fence line, the fences are set up again, and cattle are brought back to the grassy slopes. The rancher also helps to maintain the hiking and other trails, which his cattle use.

During the hike you may come across herds of cattle. They will not bother you and will just move up or off the trail as you approach. Here's where you really need to know

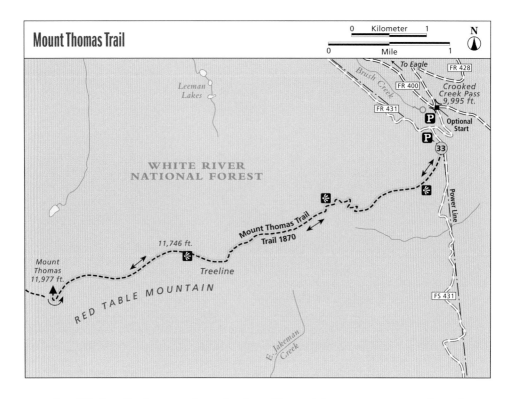

your dog: If he's really the sort of pooch who will stay right next to you regardless of who else is on the trail, by all means, leave him off leash. Otherwise, put your dog on a leash so they don't harass the herd, which is stressful to the cattle and could cause serious injury to your dog.

From the junction with FR 431, the hike follows a rough 4WD road, climbing steadily up to the trailhead located under some power lines. The turnoff to the trailhead is not marked, so follow the cues in the Miles and Directions carefully. A deep, thick, spruce-fir forest surrounds the trail, creating a dark primeval atmosphere where the appearance of elves and gnomes would hardly be surprising. Slip past the forest spirits into an open meadow with an airy view of the Lime Creek drainage. The trail winds between small stands of conifers and open, flower-covered meadows.

The trail continues up to a ridge and follows the north side. Below, the town of Eagle sits in the distance, with Sylvan Lake in the foreground. Catch a breather on a level area in the trees before negotiating an interesting skinny ridge. Red boulder fields drape the ridge to the north and south. The trail is tricky here, with a slippery climb up the next ridge. As the trail enters open meadow at tree line, the views are incredible. The Maroon Bells (Maroon Peak and North Maroon Peak), Pyramid, Snowmass, and Capitol peaks rear their 14,000-foot heads to the southwest.

The trail traverses below the ridge to the south side. After attaining the ridge again, turn right and hike to the red rock Mount Thomas summit. The rocks are the Maroon Formation, the same rocks that comprise the famous Maroon Bells near Aspen. This formation eroded from the Ancestral Rockies in western Colorado. As sediment was buried by streams, a rustlike stain formed, creating the red color. There is no official trail to the top, but it's easy to find the way. Views in every direction include the Gore Range, the Flat Tops, Mount Sopris near Carbondale, the Holy Cross Wilderness, and the peaks mentioned above.

Keep an eye out for thunderstorms. The ridge is no place to be if lightning is flashing, or approaching. Enjoy a picnic lunch and return the way you came.

MILES AND DIRECTIONS

0.0   Start at the junction with FR 431. Walk uphill on the rough 4WD road to the left. Elevation: 10,150 feet.

0.2   A side road heads to the right by some power lines. Turn right here and walk uphill. Follow the road as it curves left. The Mount Thomas (Trail 1870) Trailhead is on the right. GPS: N39 26.18' / W106 41.00'

0.6   The trail enters a meadow. (**Note:** Beautiful views of the Lime Creek drainage.)

1.3   The trail starts to switchback up the ridge.

2.0   The trail crosses some meadows. Cairns mark the route.

2.6   Pass a sign at the boundary of the recommended wilderness area. The trail climbs steeply up the ridge. Red boulder fields lie on both sides of the trail.

3.0   The trail is now above tree line. It is fairly easy to find and is marked by cairns.

3.2   The trail crosses a hump on Red Table Mountain and descends a little from here. (**Note:** Awesome views of the Maroon Bells are to the southwest.)

4.0   The trail leaves the ridge to traverse along the south side through a boulder field.

4.5   At a big cairn, turn right up the ridge to the summit of Mount Thomas. GPS: N39 25.12' / W106 44.59'. There's no trail, but there are some open areas between the krummholz (stunted trees) to walk on. Continue up a boulder field to the top.

4.6   Reach the Mount Thomas summit. Elevation: 11,977 feet. GPS: N39 25.19' / W106 44.58'. Return the way you came.

9.2   Arrive back at the trailhead.

WHY GO?

The Granite Lakes Trail first wanders along the Fryingpan River, meandering up and down through thick forest and around some interesting granitic formations. The first 3.3 miles are fairly gentle. Turning up the Granite Creek drainage, the trail climbs steadily, and often steeply, to Lower Granite Lake, tucked in a bench above Granite Creek. Upper Granite Lake is about 0.75 mile farther along a fairly gentle path. Once in the subalpine zone, the wildflowers and views are beautiful. Backpack in—don't forget supplies for your dog—and take an extra day or two to explore this beautiful and quiet area.

THE RUNDOWN

Start: From the Granite Lakes (Trail 1922) Trailhead
Distance: 13.6-miles out and back
Approximate hiking time: 8 to 12 hours (recommended 2- to 3-day backpack)
Difficulty: Most difficult due to elevation gain, length, and altitude
Elevation gain: 2,930 feet, plus some small undulations
Seasons: Best from late June to mid-Oct
Trail surface: Dirt trail, sometimes steep
Other trail users: Equestrians, anglers, hunters (in season)
Canine compatibility: Dogs must be on leash

Fees and permits: None. Group size limit: No more than 15 people per group with a maximum combination of 25 people and pack or saddle animals in any one group.
Maps: USGS Nast and Mount Champion; Nat Geo Trails Illustrated 126 Holy Cross/Ruedi Reservoir and 127 Aspen/Independence Pass; Latitude 40° Crested Butte, Aspen, Gunnison
Trail contacts: White River National Forest, Sopris Ranger District, Carbondale; (970) 963-2266; www.fs.usda.gov/whiteriver
Other: Water from streams and lakes must be treated.

FINDING THE TRAILHEAD

From Basalt, drive east on Fryingpan River Road (FS 105) about 31 miles (paved all the way) to a sign on the right that says NAST LAKE, GRANITE LAKES TRAIL TRAILHEAD. Turn right and drive down a dirt road about 0.9 mile and cross the Fryingpan River bridge. On the other side of the bridge to the right is a parking area and the trailhead. Be sure to park here and not drive any farther. There are no facilities here. Walk down the road to the Fryingpan River Ranch; the trail continues on the left past the mailboxes. Please stay on the trail and respect private property. **GPS:** N39 17.88' / W106 36.31'

THE HIKE

As early as the 1890s, the Fryingpan valley had earned a reputation as a sportsman's paradise, with large herds of elk and deer and abundant trout in lakes and streams. In the early 1900s Arthur Hanthorn and James Morris built a tourist resort with a large lodge and several other buildings near the Nast railroad siding.

Upper Granite Lake

The mountains in the Fryingpan valley area became part of the Holy Cross Forest Reserve in 1905. Len Shoemaker served as a forest ranger in the area for about twenty years, and in 1958 wrote a book, *Roaring Fork Valley,* in which he relates interesting historical tidbits. In 1918 the last Colorado Midland Railway train ran the Fryingpan route. The sawmills closed soon thereafter, and the Fryingpan River valley returned to a quieter existence.

In 1978 Congress designated the Hunter-Fryingpan Wilderness, named after two of its drainages. When the area around Mount Massive (14,421 feet) was considered for wilderness designation, Congress intended to include it in the Hunter-Fryingpan. An oversight, however, created a separate Mount Massive Wilderness in 1980. The Spruce Creek drainage was added to the Hunter-Fryingpan in 1993, for a total of 82,729 acres.

The first part of the hike crosses Mountain Nast Community, home to the private Fryingpan River Ranch and several summer cabins. Please respect the rights of property owners by staying on the trail. You'll pass through a few meadows, sometimes close to the creek, then enter thick forest. The trail crosses many small creeks while weaving up and down around various granitic formations. The Forest Service has worked on the trail with the help of Colorado Rocky Mountain School and others. Take time to appreciate their work in boggy areas. Part of the task of keeping an area pristine involves maintaining trails to avoid environmental damage. Volunteer and youth groups play an important role by helping the Forest Service with trail projects.

In about 3.3 miles the trail intersects the Fryingpan Lakes Trail. Taking a right turn, the Granite Lakes Trail climbs steeply out of the valley. The trail occasionally levels

Waterslide in Granite Creek

out, giving you a chance for a breather. Granite Creek cascades nearby, forming small waterfalls and interesting waterslides. At 5 miles the trail enters a beautiful meadow with sweeping views up the valley. After crossing Granite Creek twice, you begin climbing again.

Granite Lakes are nestled on a bench above Granite Creek. Trout jump and swim in the clear waters of Lower Granite Lake. The trail to the upper lake crosses flower-filled meadows. If you're backpacking, remember to camp at least 200 feet away from the lakes, streams, and trail. By making yourself less obvious, you and others can fully enjoy the peace and solitude.

MILES AND DIRECTIONS

0.0 Start at the Granite Lakes (Trail 1922) Trailhead by Nast Lake. Elevation: 8,700 feet. Please sign the trailhead register and read up-to-date regulations on the bulletin board.

0.2 Arrive at Fryingpan River Ranch. Walk on the road to the left past the mailboxes for Mountain Nast Community.

0.3 Granite Lakes Trail turns left off the road. Follow the trail to the left along the river. GPS: N39 17.70' / W106 36.15'

1.2 Reach the wilderness area boundary sign.

1.5 The trail comes very close to a U-curve on the Fryingpan River.

2.3 The trail wanders through various granitic boulders and rock formations. Watch out for cairns marking the trail in rocky areas.

Granite Lakes Trail

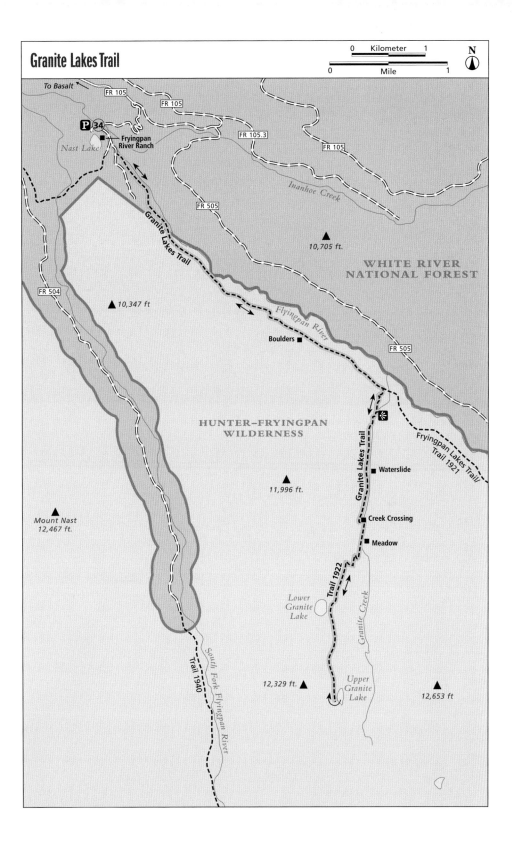

0 — Kilometer — 1
0 — Mile — 1

N

To Basalt

FR 105

FR 105

FR 105.3

FR 105

P 34

Fryingpan
River Ranch

Nast Lake

Inanhoe Creek

Granite Lakes Trail

FR 505

▲ 10,705 ft.

WHITE RIVER
NATIONAL FOREST

FR 504

▲ 10,347 ft

Flyingpan River

Boulders ■

FR 505

HUNTER–FRYINGPAN
WILDERNESS

▲ 11,996 ft.

Granite Lakes Trail

Fryingpan Lakes Trail
Trail 1921

Mount Nast
12,467 ft.

■ Waterslide

■ Creek Crossing

■ Meadow

Trail 1922

Lower
Granite
Lake

Granite Creek

South Fork Flyingpan River

12,329 ft. ▲

Upper
Granite
Lake

▲ 12,653 ft

Trail 1940

3.3 Reach the junction with the Fryingpan Lakes Trail. Elevation: 9,480 feet. GPS: N39 16.05' / W106 33.73'. This is a good place for a break. Turn right onto the Granite Lakes Trail and head uphill. The trail starts to switchback steeply not too far from here.

4.3 To the left is a waterslide down smooth granite.

5.0 The trail comes to a beautiful meadow and goes downstream a little to a Granite Creek crossing over big boulders. (***Note:*** Creek crossing can be tricky.) GPS: N39 15.10' / W106 33.88'. In a few feet you'll cross another little creek. Continue across the meadow, staying right of a big boulder in the meadow. There's a cairn near the trees.

5.1 Cross Granite Creek again. You now leave Granite Creek and climb uphill to a bench above the drainage. The trail switchbacks steeply in spots (again).

5.7 The trail climbs more gently through some wetter areas and more open areas.

6.0 The trail crosses a little creek. Turn right at the cairn. (***Note:*** Remember this spot on the way back as it's easy to miss.) Reach Lower Granite Lake. Elevation: about 11,400 feet. GPS: N39 14.50' / W106 34.22'

6.2 Come to a meadow with a view. Cross a little flat area.

6.4 Come to a creek crossing with lots of tree stumps. The trail is a little hard to find, but there are some cairns. Keep heading across the open area, slightly uphill. (***Note:*** Look behind for a good view of the Sawatch Range.) Come to a little flat area. The trail will drop down to the upper lake.

6.8 Reach Upper Granite Lake. Elevation: 11,600 feet. GPS: N39 13.87' / W106 34.15'. Return the way you came.

13.6 Arrive back at the trailhead.

SOUTH OF I-70

For high elevation and 360-degree views, the mountains just **SOUTH OF I-70**—from the Collegiate Peaks, with their high concentration of Fourteeners, on down to the San Luis Valley and Wolf Creek Pass—are tough to beat. Many of the hikes in this section are accessible either by exiting I-70 just before Copper Mountain onto US 24 or, to avoid heavy weekend traffic on the interstate, by taking Highway 285 from Denver.

35 MOUNT MASSIVE

WHY GO?

Mount Massive is just a stone's throw from Mount Elbert, the highest peak in Colorado, and is just a handful of feet shorter—14,428 feet to Elbert's 14,439, making it the second-highest peak in the state. As its name suggests, however, it's absolutely enormous: Its 3-mile-long summit ridge and numerous satellite summits mean it boasts more terrain over 14,000 feet above sea level than any other peak in the contiguous United States. Despite its lofty summit, though, Massive is an approachable, nontechnical Fourteener route—meaning it's totally possible to bring a fit, well-behaved dog safely to the summit and back.

THE RUNDOWN

Start: From the Mount Massive Trailhead
Distance: 14.5 miles round-trip for the traditional east slopes route
Approximate hiking time: 8+ hours
Difficulty: Very strenuous
Elevation gain: 4,500 feet
Seasons: Summer and fall
Trail surface: Narrow and rocky; there's a trail to the summit, though there are several scree-filled sections
Other trail users: Many other hikers and dogs

Canine compatibility: Dogs must be on leash within the Mount Massive Wilderness area boundary
Map: USGS Mount Massive; National Geographic Trails Illustrated Map #1302: Colorado 14ers North [Sawatch, Mosquito, and Front Ranges]
Trail contacts: Pike and San Isabel National Forests—Leadville Ranger District, 810 Front Street, Leadville; (719) 486-0749; https://www.fs.usda.gov/detail/psicc/about-forest/districts/?cid=fsm9_032740

FINDING THE TRAILHEAD

From Denver, follow I-70 west to exit 195 for CO 91 S toward Copper Mountain. Follow CO 91 S for just over 22 miles; in Leadville, stay on this road, which becomes US 24 E. You'll eventually pass a Subway restaurant where US 24 jogs around to the right, then a stop sign where a left-hand turn puts you onto Harrison Avenue. Follow Harrison, the main drag, through the town of Leadville, then continue as the road becomes Silver Drive, Front Street, and, eventually, US 24 again. Just south of town, turn onto CO 300 and cross a set of railroad tracks. Follow CO 300 for 0.7 mile, then take a left onto CR 11 toward Halfmoon Creek. About 1.2 miles farther down the road, you'll hang a right and go another 5.3 miles to the Mount Massive parking area, which will be on your right. **GPS:** N39 9.10' / W106 25.10'

THE HIKE

Mount Massive lives up to its moniker. Not only is Colorado's second-highest point also home to more above–14,000-foot terrain than anywhere else in the Lower 48, but the hike to its summit is a beast, too. Unlike many of the Fourteeners generally considered to be introductory—such as Mount Bierstadt, which requires only a 6.5-mile round-trip hike to the summit—it's a long day. Still, as Fourteeners go, it's fairly approachable: There's a Class 2 trail, meaning there's mostly maintained trail all the way to the top, and considerably less scree than you'll find on other relatively beginner-friendly Fourteeners like, say, Quandary Peak.

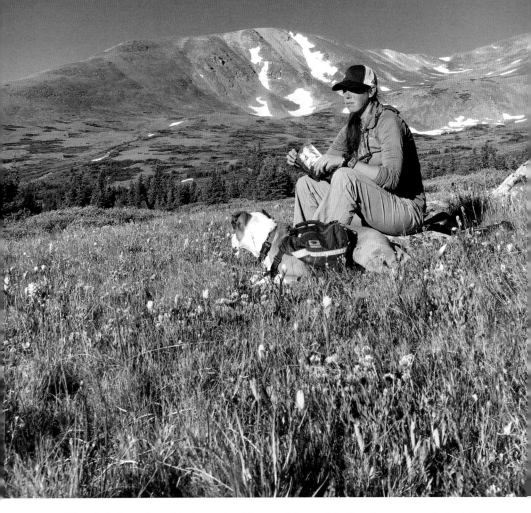

There are some great spots to stop and take a snack break above tree line.

There's little to be said about the hike up Mount Massive that you can't find in a Fourteener-specific guidebook written by someone who's climbed all the Fourteeners and can compare it to its counterparts. Instead, I'll summarize the hike briefly, then present some dog-specific considerations for hiking the Fourteeners.

The hike up Mount Massive begins in earnest almost as soon as you leave the parking area. You'll cross two creeks in the first 3 miles, each of which are fairly straightforward; if you're hiking the trail early or late enough in the season that the creek is at high flow or iced over (often until mid-June, and then ice creeps in again by October in many years), use extra caution. Shortly after the second creek crossing, you'll reach the intersection of the Mount Massive Trail and the 486-mile Colorado Trail, which stretches from Denver to Durango. Take a left to stay on the Mount Massive Trail.

From here, the hiking is straightforward; you'll wind your way through knee-high willows as you begin the real climb. Don't be discouraged by this hike's many false summits:

You'll know when you've really reached the top. The saddle at 13,900 feet is where you'll really start to feel like you're getting close. Take a right from there and ascend the steep, rocky trail. It's well-traveled and obvious, but you may occasionally want to use your hands for added balance.

Finally, after ascending one final false summit, you'll arrive at the Massive summit. Take in the view—it's unbelievable! Keep an eye out for purple sky pilot flowers, which you'll find in abundance on the Mount Massive Trail.

If you're considering hiking a Fourteener, you've no doubt heard all about the special considerations for taking on one of Colorado's giant peaks. Newspapers and local TV stations run stories every season about the things you'll need to pack and the training you'll want to take on before tackling one of the Fourteeners, and, unfortunately, there are often deaths to cover in the news, as well. Certainly, the Fourteeners are more dangerous than many hikes; they're at high altitude, where people's functions can become impaired, and by their very nature, they're largely above tree line, where the risk of lightning strike is increased. But they're also extremely popular, and so the increased rate of accidents on these peaks is due in part to the abundance of people who hit the trail each summer.

That's not to say they're not safe for dogs. Countless Coloradans take their pups up many Fourteeners every summer, and most of the time, both human and dog return to the trailhead no worse for wear! That said, of course, there have been plenty of accidents

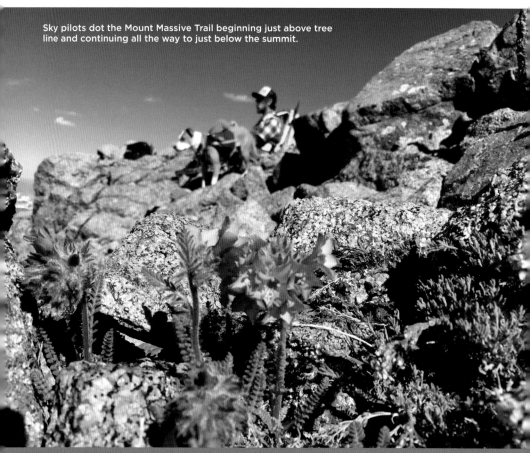

Sky pilots dot the Mount Massive Trail beginning just above tree line and continuing all the way to just below the summit.

The views from the Massive summit are well worth the effort.

involving dogs on the Fourteeners, often when dogs are asked to cross terrain they're not comfortable with. Dogs, like humans, have varying comfort levels with exposure; some dogs will merrily trot down an exposed ridgeline, while others will pump the brakes as soon as they can peer over the edge. The most important thing is to know your dog, and don't force them to do anything they're clearly uncomfortable with; after all, dogs want to please us, so they may go along with something they'd rather not if you ask repeatedly. If your dog's tail is between their legs, or they're repeatedly licking their lips or shivering, that's probably a sign they don't want to go any farther, and you should call it a day.

Dogs must be kept on leash in the Mount Massive Wilderness. In addition to reducing the risk that your dog will find themselves stuck on a cliff band somewhere far away from you, it also means they're less able to harass wildlife, which is crucial in a fragile high-alpine ecosystem. (It's also important for the safety of your dog, who could be seriously injured, or worse, in a scuffle with a critter, especially in exposed areas where a big fall is possible.)

This can make things tricky for the human attached to the other end of the leash, who, without four paws to stabilize, is likelier to trip or tip over. In other words, Mount Massive is a hike best suited for pups that are fairly well-behaved on leash. If your young dog has a tendency to pull you over when they're on a leash, consider working on the "heel" command before tackling this hike. I like to use a hands-free leash, which buckles around my waist or around a belt loop on my backpack, and has a section of stretchy bungee so I'm not yanked over every time my dog catches wind of a new scent. This works well for medium-sized dogs, though if your dog is very large, and you're not, it could make matters worse.

Mount Massive

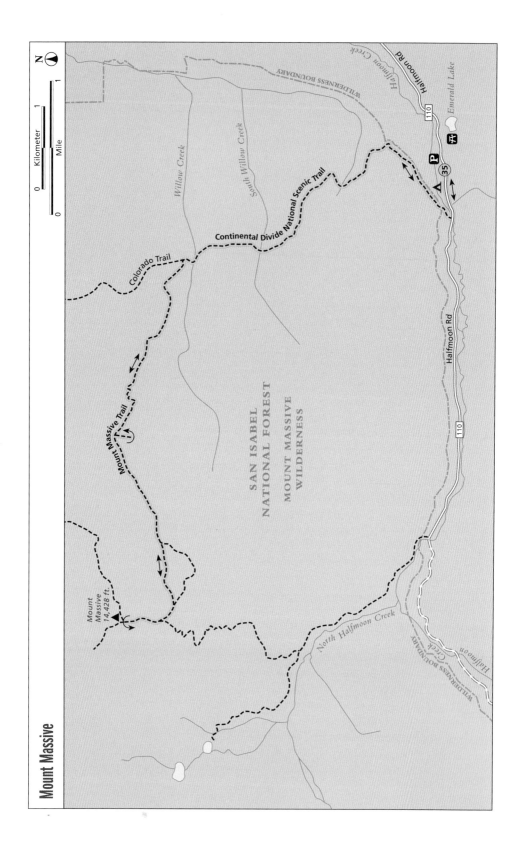

Then there's the matter of a pack. Like humans, dogs can be affected by altitude, and a pack only exacerbates those effects. Again, it's a matter of knowing your dog: If this is your first hike of the season, consider doing Fido a favor and carrying their water in your own pack. If, on the other hand, your dog is young and in excellent health (and is generally fit enough that even a long hike doesn't completely take it out of them), a pack might be a good way to carry enough water and treats for your pup without adding a ton of weight to your own pack.

In terms of water, know that your dog will need to hydrate just as you will. Many Fourteener hikers don't carry nearly enough water; a liter won't cut it. You'll want to carry at least two liters for yourself (preferably more—many hydration bladder systems allow for three liters), plus at least one for your dog. After those two creek crossings, you won't find water along the trail for them to drink, so make sure you've planned accordingly.

The summit ridge is fairly straightforward, but an off-leash dog could easily find themselves cliffed out if they descend too far in pursuit of a little ground squirrel. Take your time at the top to avoid being pulled off your feet, and keep your dog close at hand.

One final warning goes for all hikes above tree line, but especially the Fourteeners, since they leave hikers exposed to the elements for so much of their length: Get an early start—you won't regret it. Not only are you less likely to find the busy trailhead full, especially on a weekend, but you're also less likely to get into trouble with the afternoon storms that roll in like clockwork most summer afternoons in the Rockies. Check the forecast carefully before you leave, and plan to be back below tree line by noon at the latest; it's one thing to knowingly enter a possible lightning storm on your own, but you can't teach your dog the lightning position, so avoid the situation by leaving the trailhead before sunup.

MILES AND DIRECTIONS

0.0   Leave the Mount Massive Trailhead.

2.0   Cross South Willow Creek.

2.9   Cross Willow Creek.

3.0   Reach the junction of the Mount Massive Trail and the Colorado Trail. Take a left to reach the summit.

3.2   A clearing around 11,600 feet gives you your first glimpse of the peak.

4.0   The trail ascends through willows above tree line.

5.2   Reach Point 12,466', from which you can see most of the remaining route.

6.0   Gain the saddle just below 14,000 feet. Take a right to continue toward the summit.

7.1   Ascend a small false summit and continue to the Massive summit.

7.2   Arrive at the Massive summit. Take a quick break and retrace your steps before the clouds roll in!

14.5   Arrive back at the trailhead.

36 HARVARD LAKES

WHY GO?

It's impossible to overstate the beauty of the Upper Arkansas River Valley. The area is known for its high, craggy peaks (the Collegiates), one of which shares a name with these little lakes. A 3-mile section of the 486-mile Colorado Trail, which spans the state from Denver to Durango, deposits hikers at the picturesque Harvard Lakes. The more-northerly lake has a stunning high-altitude backdrop, but either one makes for an excellent picnic (or, if you're doing a longer section, an overnight pit stop). Regular stream crossings mean plenty of water stops for your pooch along the way.

THE RUNDOWN

Start: From the Silver Creek Trailhead
Distance: 6.0 miles (out and back), but easy to add more distance on the Colorado Trail
Approximate hiking time: 2 to 4 hours
Difficulty: Moderate
Elevation gain: About 900 feet
Seasons: Spring through fall
Other trail users: Equestrians, thru-hikers, backpackers

Canine compatibility: Dogs must be under control. There's plenty of water along the way.
Fees and permits: None
Map: USGS Harvard Lakes
Trail contacts: Pike and San Isabel National Forests—Leadville Ranger District, 810 Front Street, Leadville; (719) 486-0749; https://www.fs .usda.gov/detail/psicc/about-forest/ districts/?cid=fsm9_032740

FINDING THE TRAILHEAD

From Buena Vista, head north on US 24. From the stoplight at the intersection of US 24 and Main Street, head north for 0.3 mile. Turn left (west) on Crossman Avenue / CR 350, and continue west for just over 2 miles to CR 361. Take a right (north) on CR 361 and go 1 mile to CR 365. Turn left (west) and drive 3.5 miles to the trailhead. From the junction of CR 361 and CR 365, if the road is dry, a confident driver would be fine in a sedan. Otherwise, you'll want all-wheel drive or better. The trailhead is marked as a Colorado Trail trailhead; there's parking on the left just before the trailhead as well as a quarter-mile down the road at the Silver Creek Trailhead. GPS: N38 51.94' / W106 14.48'

THE HIKE

The nearby town of Buena Vista is one of Colorado's many oddly pronounced townships: say "BYOO-na Vista," and you'll sound like a local. Butchering of its Spanish-language name aside (buena vista translates to "good view"), the town does afford phenomenal views of the high country, including a remarkable concentration of Fourteeners, or peaks above 14,000 feet. The Collegiate Range—many of whose peaks are named for Ivy League universities—is comprised of nine Fourteeners and another ten peaks over 13,000 feet above sea level.

Like most big, easily accessible, nontechnical mountains, the Colorado Fourteeners draw plenty of visitors. More than half a million hikers visit the Colorado Fourteeners on an annual basis, according to the nonprofit Colorado Fourteeners initiative, which works to steward trails up the giants. They're lovely, but they're not the only things to see in the

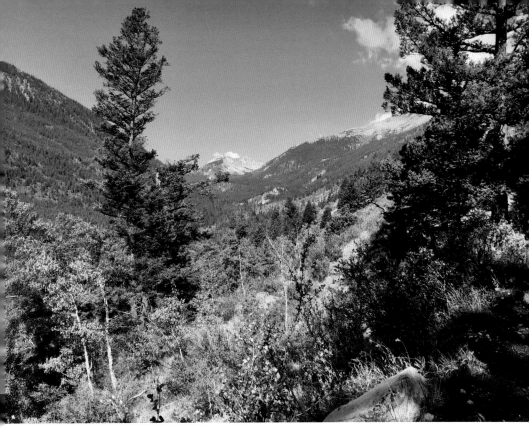
The views begin in earnest almost immediately.

Arkansas Valley. The Collegiate Peaks Wilderness area and surrounding national forest are high-altitude gems in their own right.

The area also provides access to a huge swath of the Colorado Trail. The rugged footpath is largely above 10,000 feet elevation, and parts of it regularly remain under snow until well into June, or even July. A handful of hardy thru-hikers walk all the way from Waterton Canyon in Denver to Durango, in southwestern Colorado, every season, but for most users, it's enjoyed in sections. The Colorado Trail is accessible at several points throughout the Arkansas Valley, and dogs are allowed on all of it. The only thing that changes, based on where you access the trail, is that dogs must be on a six-foot leash in designated, capital-W Wilderness areas, while there's no such regulation in adjacent national forests.

The first 2.5 miles of this hike are in national forest, so while dogs should be under voice command, they're not required to be leashed. Just before Harvard Lakes, the trail toes the wilderness boundary, so use your best judgment (and if the trail is crowded, consider leashing your dog to avoid conflicts). The trail crosses into the wilderness area just north of Harvard Lakes, so if you choose to continue north after you've reached the lakes, you'll need to leash your dog then.

The hike to Harvard Lakes begins a few miles west of Buena Vista proper. Park across from the trailhead—you'll see signs indicating that all vehicles are prohibited on the trail—or a quarter-mile down the road at the Silver Creek Trailhead, where there's a bathroom.

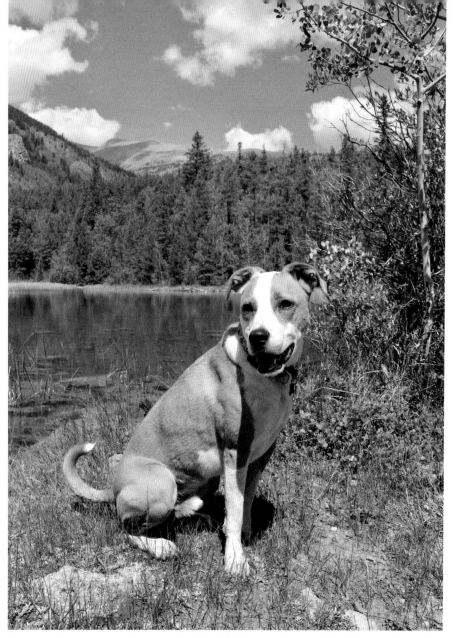

Dogs must be under control in the national forest. If you continue past the lakes, you'll need to use a leash.

Views of the Collegiates begin in earnest almost immediately. The first switchback, just a quarter mile up the trail, affords an excellent view of Mount Harvard, which clocks in at 14,421 feet above sea level. You won't be sorry to stop and take a breath here, as the climbing begins in earnest, too. The first three-quarters of a mile are steep; the trail gains about 600 feet in elevation here before flattening out considerably.

At the 0.75-mile mark, the trail begins undulating, taking a few gentle ups and downs until it reaches the larger of the two Harvard Lakes, at almost exactly 3 miles. Watch for

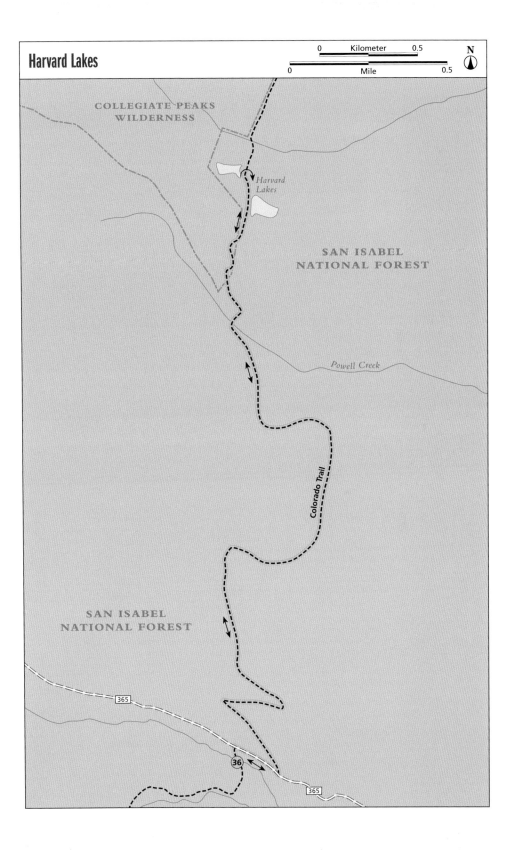

COLLEGIATE PEAKS
WILDERNESS

Harvard
Lakes

SAN ISABEL
NATIONAL FOREST

Powell Creek

Colorado Trail

SAN ISABEL
NATIONAL FOREST

365

36

365

0   Kilometer   0.5

0   Mile   0.5

N

Either of the two small lakes would make a fine picnic spot, but the first offers more shade.

Colorado Trail signage (the distinctive logo is printed on metal plates and nailed into trees just above head level), which will keep you on the right track despite occasional spur trails. The smaller, more northerly lake is just a few hundred yards farther up the trail, and its backdrop is more picturesque than its counterpart. If you're feeling game, you can continue the hike as long as you like; there's no limit until you hit Denver.

MILES AND DIRECTIONS

0.0   Start at the Silver Creek Trailhead, which has the only bathroom in the imme-diate vicinity. Head up the road toward the more-northerly section of the Colorado Trail.

0.2   Meet the Colorado Trail and begin hiking uphill. Stop and sign the register to give the Forest Service data on who's hiking the trail.

0.5   Admire the view of Mount Harvard from the first switchback.

1.1   Having gained something like 600 feet, the trail begins to flatten out. From here it's short ups and downs all the way to the lakes.

2.3   Pass an unmarked spur trail on your right; continue on the Colorado Trail toward Harvard Lakes.

2.6   Cross the small stream on some strategically placed rocks.

3.0   Reach Harvard Lakes. Return the way you came.

6.0   Arrive back at the trailhead.

37 NOTCH MOUNTAIN

WHY GO?

This hike takes you to the historic stone shelter on Notch Mountain for a fantastic view of Mount of the Holy Cross. The trail starts gently, passing through spruce-fir forest with occasional glimpses of the notch in Notch Mountain. Eventually the trail climbs to tree line, then through tundra and boulder fields via switchbacks. Watch for pikas, white-tailed ptarmigans, marmots, and beautiful alpine wildflowers. The switchbacks make the hike easier than most trails up 13,000-foot peaks. Leave early to reach the summit by 11 a.m. so you can head back by noon and avoid thunderstorms.

THE RUNDOWN

Start: From the Fall Creek Trailhead
Distance: 10.8 miles out and back
Approximate hiking time: 5 to 7 hours
Difficulty: Most difficult due to length and elevation gain
Elevation gain: 2,763 feet, plus about 120 feet in undulations
Seasons: Best from late June to mid-Oct
Trail surface: Dirt trail, very rocky in spots
Other trail users: Equestrians (Fall Creek Trail section) and hunters (in season)
Canine compatibility: Technically, dogs must be under control; there's a lot of wildlife and it's a wilderness area, so I recommend leashing your dog.
Fees and permits: None. A free self-issued Wilderness Use Permit is required year-round for all users. One person in each group must carry a permit. Call the Holy Cross Ranger District for details. Group size limit: No more than 15 people per group with a maximum combination of 25 people and pack or saddle animals in any one group.
Maps: USGS Mount of the Holy Cross and Minturn; Nat Geo Trails Illustrated 126 Holy Cross/Ruedi Reservoir; Latitude 40° Vail & Eagle
Trail contacts: White River National Forest, Holy Cross Ranger District, Minturn; (970) 827-5715; www.fs .usda.gov/whiteriver
Other: The dirt access road may be bumpy with rocks and potholes. Most passenger cars can make the trip with care. The road is narrow, so be careful when rounding curves. The parking lot gets crowded early as the trailhead for Mount of the Holy Cross is also here. Half Moon Campground near the trailhead has seven campsites. Bring plenty of water with you.

FINDING THE TRAILHEAD

From Minturn, drive south on US 24 toward Leadville for about 3 miles (5 miles from the junction of I-70 and US 24). Just past mile marker 148, turn right onto Tigiwon Road (FR 707), which provides national forest access. Drive 8.1 miles up this dirt road to the trailhead. **GPS:** N39 30.02' / W106 25.94'

THE HIKE

In the 1800s various stories about a mountain with a "snowy cross" circulated around Colorado. In 1869 William H. Brewer reported seeing Mount of the Holy Cross (14,005 feet) from the summit of Grays Peak (14,269 feet). As part of the Hayden Survey in the 1870s, William Henry Jackson photographed various areas of Colorado. The Hayden Survey was one of four great surveys of the West sponsored by the US government between 1867 and 1878. From 1873 to 1875, expedition leader Ferdinand V. Hayden concentrated on Colorado.

The 1873 survey set a goal to find this mysterious peak. Jackson climbed Grays Peak and also spotted the cross from the summit. By August the survey group arrived near present-day Minturn. For three days they attempted in vain to find a route on Notch Mountain (13,237 feet) from which to view and photograph the "cross." Fallen trees and thick willows made the going too rough for pack animals, and the group ended up carrying Jackson's one hundred pounds of photographic gear on foot. Jackson used a wet glass plate camera. Not only was the "film" made of glass, which had to be handled carefully, but also it needed to be developed soon after exposure. Jackson carried a portable darkroom tent and all necessary chemicals and supplies with him. Finally finding an approach, the still-difficult hike took two days, with little food and no shelter. (The surveyors thought they could do it in one day.) Finally atop Notch Mountain, fog decreased visibility to a few feet. Luckily, the fog broke briefly, giving Jackson a glimpse of the infamous cross across the valley. The next morning dawned clear and still, giving him a

BENEFITS OF LEASHING YOUR DOG

Keeping dogs leashed on the trail benefits you, your pet, other visitors, and wildlife. Dogs will surely come out the losers in a bout with the porcupines and mountain lions that live in these areas. Bears have also been known to chase dogs back to their owners. Freely roaming dogs can cause serious damage to delicate ecosystems. A leashed dog can also help you become more aware of wildlife, as dogs can easily detect smells and movement that would go unnoticed by humans.

WILDLIFE WATCHING ON NOTCH MOUNTAIN

Notch Mountain is a good area to see alpine animals and birds, particularly marmots, pikas, and white-tailed ptarmigan.

In summer ptarmigan blend in perfectly with the mottled rocks, making them hard to see. Members of the grouse family, the males live in the alpine tundra all year. Ptarmigan blend in to the landscape so well, it's possible to almost step on one before noticing it's there.

Ptarmigan mate for life, although after breeding the couple goes their separate ways until the next spring. In summer tiny chicks line up to follow around after their mom. When threatened, the mother will fake a broken wing to draw predators away from her offspring.

In winter ptarmigan plumage turns white, with feet and legs heavily feathered for warmth and flotation on the snow. Willows, which produce next year's buds in the fall, provide food for ptarmigan during long, cold winters. The birds might dive into a snowdrift, especially around willows, to stay warm on cold nights—a ptarmigan version of an igloo. Look for piles of ptarmigan droppings near willows while hiking.

The pika lives in rock piles in the alpine and subalpine zones year-round. The pika alert reverberates through the rocks. Active during winter as well as summer, the pika eats hay piles it busily collects during the summer. The small, mouselike creature with the short tail belongs to the rabbit order. Look closely or you might miss the busy critter as it scurries among the rocks. A mouthful of grass and flowers whizzes by as the pika stores its hay. Researchers have discovered that pikas will steal each other's piles.

Watch for big white splotches on boulders along the trail. The splotches indicate pika restrooms. Bright orange lichen often grows near the splotches, energized by the nitrogen-rich fertilizer.

Please remember to keep your dog on leash to avoid confrontation with or disruption of the wildlife.

---

beautiful shot of the cross. He took several pictures, which caused a sensation across the country, as people believed the snow-filled cross to be a sign from God.

The cross is created by a 1,500-foot vertical gully and a 750-foot horizontal rock bench on the mountain's eastern face. Collected snow causes the formation to stand out against the mountainside. The right arm later deteriorated due to rockslides, and access remained difficult even after the CCC's work. In 1950 President Harry Truman retracted national monument status and returned the land to the Forest Service. Even slightly damaged, a cross of snow still forms today. The Tigiwon Community House, after years of disrepair, has been mostly restored and is occasionally used for weddings. The Forest Service maintains the historic Notch Mountain stone shelter and its lightning rods to provide protection for hikers in case a thunderstorm moves in. Overnight camping is not allowed in the shelter.

Make sure to start on the Fall Creek Trail, not the Half Moon Trail. Just beyond the trailhead and creek crossing, take the right trail and head south, entering the Holy Cross Wilderness. The first mile is fairly gentle, but rocky. The trail then climbs, with occasional small elevation drops. The terrain drops steeply to the left, to Fall Creek below. After 2.4 miles the trail widens, with a scattering of boulders providing a perfect spot for a break before turning right up the Notch Mountain Trail.

From the rest spot it's another 3 miles to the shelter and viewpoint. After a few switchbacks the trail begins to pass through tree line and zigzags across the slope to the summit. More than twenty-seven switchbacks help you ascend the last 780 feet. Avoid

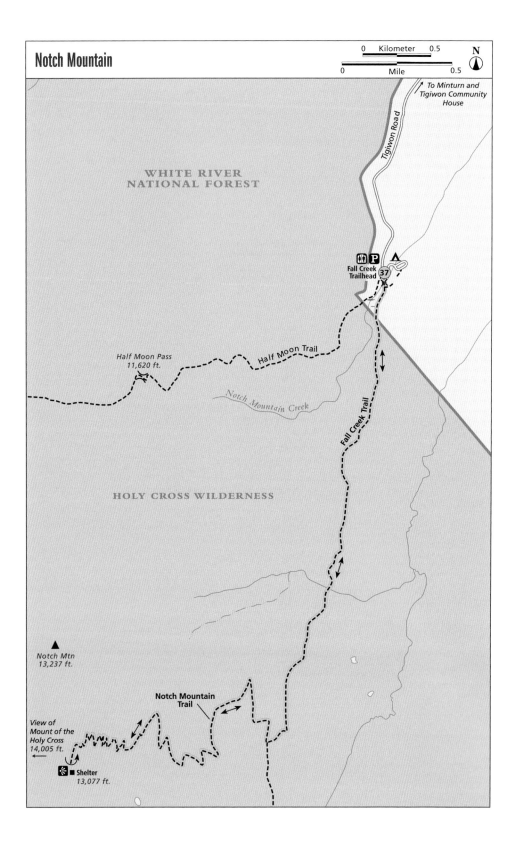

Notch Mountain

0   Kilometer   0.5

0   Mile   0.5

N

To Minturn and
Tigiwon Community
House

Tigiwon Road

WHITE RIVER
NATIONAL FOREST

Fall Creek
Trailhead   37

Half Moon Pass
11,620 ft.

Half Moon Trail

Notch Mountain Creek

Fall Creek Trail

HOLY CROSS WILDERNESS

Notch Mtn
13,237 ft.

Notch Mountain
Trail

View of
Mount of the
Holy Cross
14,005 ft.

Shelter
13,077 ft.

the temptation to shortcut the switchbacks, as they keep the trail at a reasonable grade (which makes for easier hiking in the thinning air) and protect the terrain. Marmots and pikas zip around this area with amusing antics. Watch for white-tailed ptarmigan moms followed by lines of little chicks.

Once you reach the ridge and stone shelter, Mount of the Holy Cross looms large directly ahead. The alpine wildflowers grow thick and beautiful in July and early August. White arctic gentians signal summer's end. Please walk carefully on the fragile tundra, using rocks for steps as much as possible. And if you must camp, do it below tree line.

MILES AND DIRECTIONS

0.0   Start at the Fall Creek Trailhead (versus the Half Moon Trailhead). Elevation: 10,314 feet. Cross a creek on a bridge and take the right fork in the trail (heading south).

1.4   The trail traverses a landslide area.

1.6   Cross a wide creek on boulders. (**Note:** The crossing may be easier or harder depending on water volume. Be careful.)

2.4   Reach the trail intersection with Notch Mountain and Fall Creek Trails. GPS: N39 28.26' / W106 26.52'. This is a good place for a break. Turn right onto Notch Mountain Trail.

3.5   Start to enter the land above the trees. (**Note:** Turn back if thunderstorms are imminent.)

4.2   Switchbacks increase in number up to the ridge. Depending on where you start counting, you'll zigzag up more than twenty switchbacks in 780 feet. (**Note:** Please do not shortcut the switchbacks. Shortcutting causes environmental damage and erosion that does not heal quickly at this elevation. Also, don't attempt this trail during whiteouts or low visibility. If you miss any of four particular switchbacks, you'll be free-falling over a cliff.)

5.4   Reach the stone shelter on Notch Mountain, with a breathtaking view of Mount of the Holy Cross. Elevation: 13,077 feet. GPS: N39 28.17' / W106 27.52' (**Note:** The shelter is meant for protection from lightning. Overnight camping is prohibited.) Return the way you came.

10.8 Arrive back at the trailhead.

WHY GO?

This hike wanders past several volcanic dikes on the south side of West Spanish Peak. The dikes are fascinating, and the views into New Mexico go forever on a clear day. The trail winds through forests of bristlecone, limber, and lodgepole pine, aspen, spruce, subalpine fir, and white fir, with some Gambel oak for good measure. An unmarked overlook by a little dike provides a good view of East Spanish Peak—a good turnaround point for the out-and-back hiker. Beyond the overlook the hike continues descending to the Trujillo cabin, then climbs to the saddle between the two peaks. It descends a final time along the north side of West Spanish Peak to the north trailhead at the upper end of FR 442, then descends to Huerfano CR 360.

THE RUNDOWN

Start: From the Apishapa (a-PISH-a-pa) Trailhead
Distance: 12.9 miles point to point
Approximate hiking time: 6.5 to 8.5 hours
Difficulty: Most difficult due to length and elevation gain and loss
Elevation gain/loss: 2,540-foot gain / 3,860-foot loss
Seasons: Best from June to mid-Oct
Trail surface: Dirt trail with some rocky sections across talus fields, rough dirt road
Other trail users: Equestrians
Canine compatibility: Dogs must be under control
Fees and permits: None. Group size limit: No more than 15 people per group with a maximum combination of 25 people and pack or saddle animals in any one group.
Maps: USGS Spanish Peaks and Herlick Canyon
Trail contacts: Pike/San Isabel National Forest, San Carlos Ranger District, Cañon City; (719) 269-8500; www.fs.usda.gov/psicc
Other: No facilities at the trailhead. There is little to no water on the trail; bring your own. FR 46 is closed by snow 9.3 miles from the trailhead in winter. The trail crosses several avalanche paths on the south side of West Spanish Peak and is neither maintained nor marked for winter use from either trailhead.

FINDING THE TRAILHEAD

For shuttle: Drive to the south end of La Veta on CO 12 to Cuchara Street, next to La Veta Medical Clinic. Turn left onto Cuchara Street. In about 0.3 mile Cuchara Street ends but the road curves right and becomes Huerfano CR 36. Continue on HCR 36. In 1 mile, turn left at the HUAJATOLLA VALLEY sign (HCR 360). In 0.5 mile, turn right where the road lazy Ts onto HCR 360. The road straight ahead is a dead end. In 4.1 miles the road Ys; go right on HCR 360. Drive another mile on this somewhat twisty but maintained dirt road to the WAHATOYA TRAIL (TRAIL 1304), FR 442 sign. **GPS:** N37 25.34' / W104 58.65'. There's a good place to park in about 0.1 mile down the hill. Set up your car shuttle here. With a high-clearance vehicle, you can drive 2 miles up FR 442 to the north Wahatoya Trailhead.

To get to the southern trailhead, where the hike starts, return to La Veta the way you came. Drive south on CO 12 about 17 miles to the top of Cucharas Pass. Turn left onto Cordova Pass Road (FR 46) and drive another 10.8 miles, keeping left at two intersections that are well marked. Pass through the Apishapa Arch, which was cut through a dike by the Civilian Conservation Corps. A little farther down the road, the Apishapa Trailhead will be on your left. **GPS:** N37 20.63' / W104 59.45'

Apishapa Arch on
way to trailhead

THE HIKE

Circumnavigating the peaks is the Scenic Highway of Legends, commemorating the many legends that surround the peaks. One legend tells of a family of giants who once lived around Wahatoya, the ancestral name for the Spanish Peaks. They quarreled among themselves and built rock walls about chest high for protection. They hurled huge boulders at each other. The gods of Wahatoya, angered by the wars, stopped the rains. The giants stopped fighting and left in search of water. One warrior remained behind to guard the valley, but the others never returned. The guard grew tired and sat to rest. The gods turned him to stone for his dedication. The rock is now known as Goemmer's Butte, a volcanic plug south of La Veta.

In pre-Spanish days a saga told of gold being used as offerings to the Aztec deities. One of the Aztec rulers established a dazzling court and "the gods of the Mountain Huajatolla became envious of the magnificence of his court and they placed demons on the double mountain and forbade all men further approach." Years later, in the mid-1500s, when Coronado returned to Mexico after abandoning his search for the fabled cities of gold, three monks remained behind to convert the natives. Legend has it that two were killed, while the third monk, Juan de la Cruz, found the gold mines. He forced Native Americans to extract the precious metal from the mines. Ready to return to Mexico, he killed the tribesmen and left with the gold carried by pack animals. The demons became angry, and the priest and his treasure disappeared. According to some versions, a settler found gold nuggets years later. In any case, the tales of lost treasure drew people to the area in search of the lost gold and mines.

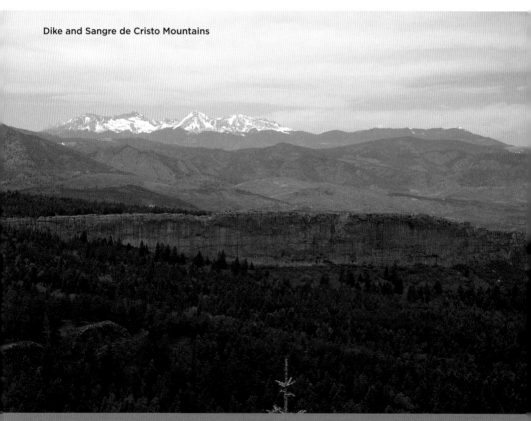

Dike and Sangre de Cristo Mountains

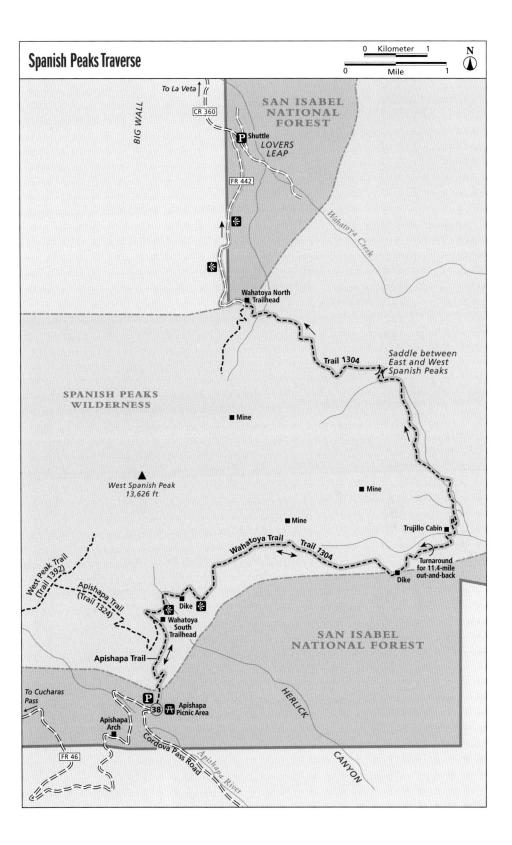

Spanish Peaks Traverse

To La Veta

BIG WALL

CR 360

SAN ISABEL
NATIONAL
FOREST

P Shuttle

LOVERS
LEAP

FR 442

Wahatoya Creek

Wahatoya North
Trailhead

Trail 1304

Saddle between
East and West
Spanish Peaks

SPANISH PEAKS
WILDERNESS

Mine

West Spanish Peak
13,626 ft

Mine

Mine

Trujillo Cabin

Wahatoya Trail

Trail 1304

West Peak Trail
(Trail 1392)

Apishapa Trail
(Trail 1324)

Dike

Turnaround
for 11.4-mile
out-and-back

Dike

Wahatoya South
Trailhead

SAN ISABEL
NATIONAL FOREST

Apishapa Trail

HERLICK

To Cucharas
Pass

P
38

Apishapa
Picnic Area

Apishapa
Arch

Cordova Pass Road

Apishapa River

CANYON

FR 46

The area (not including FR 442) was designated the Spanish Peaks Wilderness area in November 2000. Volunteers for Outdoor Colorado helped the USDA Forest Service build a new 4-mile section of trail higher on the south slope of West Spanish Peak to connect the Wahatoya and Apishapa Trails and avoid private property. Many different types of trees line the trail, including ancient bristlecone pines. You can see west to the Sangre de Cristos, south to the mesas near Trinidad, and farther yet to the volcanoes in northeastern New Mexico. The most interesting parts are the little passages through the volcanic dikes.

The featured hike is a roller-coaster ride, climbing about 1,160 feet in elevation, then losing about 1,920 feet, only to climb another 1,380 feet to the saddle between the two peaks. Finally the trail traverses the north flank of West Spanish Peak, descending 480 feet to the north trailhead at the wilderness boundary, then descending another 1,460 feet to HCR 360. The longer hike between the two peaks gives you an intimate view of the Spanish Peaks Wilderness, but those looking to make an equally enjoyable out-and-back hike can turn around at a little dike with a viewpoint of East Spanish Peak, after dropping only 1,430 feet. The shorter hike allows you to experience the large variety of trees and the area's geology without the roller-coaster effect.

MILES AND DIRECTIONS

0.0 Start at the Apishapa Trailhead, following the Apishapa Trail. Elevation: 9,720 feet.

1.5 Turn right onto the Wahatoya Trail (Trail 1304). GPS: N37 21.42' / W104 59.53' (**Note:** The Apishapa Trail continues to the left and intersects with West Peak Trail [Trail 1392], which in turn heads up West Spanish Peak.)

2.1 Pass through a little dike.

5.3 Cross through a passageway (gap) in a large dike.

5.7 Reach an unmarked overlook at a dike. The trail curves right here and continues downhill. Walk ahead and uphill about 90 feet to a good view of East Spanish Peak. Elevation: 9,450 feet. GPS: N37 21.88' / W104 55.67'. Continue on the trail as it heads downhill. (**Option:** This is an excellent turnaround point for an 11.4-mile out-and-back hike. Simply return the way you came. Approximate hiking time: 6 to 7.5 hours.)

6.3 Reach the Trujillo cabin. Continue on the trail downstream about 0.1 mile to the crossing of South Fork Trujillo Creek.

8.9 Reach the saddle between East Spanish and West Spanish Peaks and the Huerfano and Las Animas county line. Elevation: 10,340 feet. GPS: N37 23.40' / W104 57.05'

10.9 Arrive at the Spanish Peaks Wilderness boundary, the Wahatoya Trailhead, and the upper end of FR 442. GPS: 37 23.91' / W104 58.45'. From here, hike down FR 442 (not in wilderness), which is open to motorized use.

11.6 There's a great view of a big dike to the west from an imbedded dike to the left of the trail.

12.9 Arrive at the trailhead at HCR 360. Elevation: 8,400 feet.

39 MIDDLE FRISCO TRAIL

WHY GO?

The Middle Frisco Trail follows sparkling, gurgling Middle San Francisco Creek and its tributaries up to San Francisco Lakes. Starting among stands of ponderosa pine and Douglas fir, the trail slowly gains elevation, eventually switchbacking up to a nice spruce-fir forest and subalpine meadows. Wildflowers are abundant along the trail in July. Keep an eye open for elk and cattle. Near the upper lake, there is an ancient bristlecone pine forest. The lower part of the trail is fantastic when the aspen are golden yellow and orange. The lakes are snuggled in high basins between Bennett Peak and Pintada Mountain. If you want to sound like a local, pronounce the name of the nearby town "Del NORT"—as if there's no "e" on the end.

THE RUNDOWN

Start: From the Middle Frisco (Trail 801) Trailhead
Distance: 12.9 miles out and back
Approximate hiking time: 6 to 8.5 hours
Difficulty: Most difficult due to length and elevation gain
Elevation gain: 2,520 feet
Seasons: Best from mid-June to mid-Oct
Trail surface: Dirt trail
Other trail users: Equestrians, mountain bikers, hunters (in season)

Canine compatibility: Dogs must be under control
Fees and permits: None
Maps: USGS Jasper and Horseshoe Mountain; Nat Geo Trails Illustrated 142 South San Juan Wilderness/Del Norte (Middle Frisco Creek is on this map, but the trail isn't.)
Trail contacts: Rio Grande National Forest, Divide Ranger District, Del Norte; (719) 657-3321; www.fs.usda .gov/riogrande
Other: Bring your own water or a water treatment system with you.

FINDING THE TRAILHEAD

In Del Norte, head toward the east end of town to find French Street (Rio Grand CR 13). There's a big green-and-white sign stating NATIONAL FOREST ACCESS SAN FRANCISCO CREEK. Turn south onto French Street. In about 1.8 miles the pavement ends and CR 13 becomes a good gravel road. Stop and read the bulletin board on the right side of the road in another 1.9 miles. The trailhead is another 6.1 miles down the dirt road (9.8 miles total from Del Norte). The trail starts on the left after passing the cattle guard/fence where FR 320 starts. There's a large parking area with no facilities. Cattle graze in the area. **GPS:** N37 33.40' / W106 23.75'

THE HIKE

Locals and several signs call these trails, creeks, and lakes by the nickname "Frisco." The official name on topo maps is "San Francisco." So, you're in the correct spot at the Middle Frisco Trailhead. A little farther down the road is West Frisco Trail, open to all-terrain vehicles (ATVs) and dirt bikes.

San Francisco Creek is a tributary of the mighty Rio Grande del Norte (Great River of the North), named by Spanish explorers. On the western edge of the San Luis Valley, the town of Del Norte took its name from the river. Early Native peoples of the Folsom culture lived in the valley more than 10,000 years ago. Starting around 1300 the Moache and Tabeguache bands of Ute called this area home. Juan Bautista de Anza headed north from Santa Fe in 1779 to usurp land from the local Comanche people. He commanded an army of 700 men from Santa Fe and 200 Ute-Apache. They camped about 5 miles downstream from Del Norte.

According to records in Del Norte, in 1932 during the Depression, calves sold for three cents per pound, and two dozen eggs cost fifteen cents.

Gold was discovered in the San Juan Mountains southwest of La Loma in 1870, and Summitville became the major gold camp. Del Norte, founded in 1871, developed into a major mining supply center for Lake City, Silverton, Summitville, and others. Del Norte was so prosperous that one rich mine owner proposed a separate state called San Juan with Del Norte as its capital.

In the 1880s cattlemen and sheepherders disputed over ranges, but actually agreed to boundaries. Sheep grazed between the Rio Grande and San Francisco Creek, while cattle ruled the grasses from San Francisco Creek south to Rock Creek. Today cattle graze near Frisco Lakes.

The trail heads off through aspen groves and meadows and is soon surrounded by forests of limber pine, ponderosa pine, and Douglas fir. Middle Frisco Creek is tiny and lively, a pleasant hiking companion. Aspen becomes the dominant tree species, occasionally alternating with conifers. The trail breaks out of the woods into a meadow area with Pintada Mountain (12,840 feet) to the left, a large ridge delineating the drainage's east side. A few bristlecone pines have stood guard here for centuries. A series of twelve switchbacks soon take you even higher. Colorful wildflowers like cinquefoil,

Lower Frisco Lake

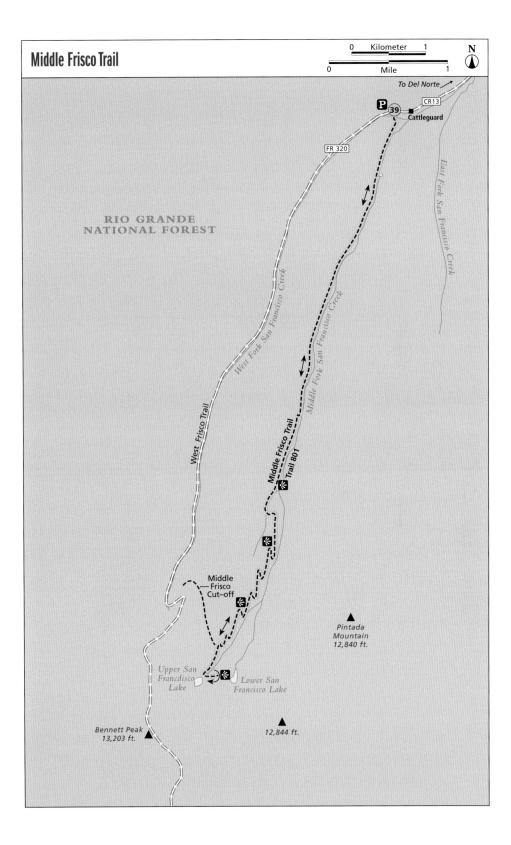

Middle Frisco Trail

0   Kilometer   1

0   Mile   1

N

To Del Norte

P 39
CR13
Cattleguard

FR 320

RIO GRANDE
NATIONAL FOREST

East Fork San Francisco Creek

West Fork San Francisco Creek

Middle Fork San Franciso Creek

West Frisco Trail

Middle Frisco Trail
Trail 801

Middle
Frisco
Cut–off

Pintada
Mountain
12,840 ft.

Upper San
Francdisco
Lake

Lower San
Francisco Lake

Bennett Peak
13,203 ft.

12,844 ft.

death camas, Indian paintbrush, stonecrop, and columbine brighten the climb. As you hike up the ridge, the cliffs above the upper lake resemble the edge of a volcanic crater. The mountains here are part of one of the ancient volcanic calderas that formed the San Juan Mountains. Glaciers carved the upper cirques. A stand of ancient bristlecone pines grows west of the trail.

If you want to hike up the peak above the cliffs, walk back to the junction with the Middle Frisco Cut-off Trail, turn left onto it, and hike about 0.7 mile to the West Frisco Trail. Turn left and head to the summit.

To either overlook the lower lake or hike down to it, cross the creek below the upper lake, wander through a field of old-man-of-the-mountain (alpine sunflowers), then descend a little. There are some good campsites along the hike in and near the lakes. Remember to camp at least 200 feet away from streams, lakes, and trails. The area around the lakes is high subalpine, and trees take years to grow. Wildlife and birds depend on the trees and dead branches. If you camp up high, bring a stove and candles and forgo the campfire to protect the fragile ecosystem.

A little bird you may notice flying overhead near the lakes is the white-crowned sparrow. It indeed looks like a sparrow, but has white around its eyes and a black cap. Watch for a while if you catch sight of one. They pick insects off dead branches. These little sparrows winter as far south as Mexico. When spring arrives, they fly north to mate and nest in the tundra. Their nests are hidden beneath willows, which provide both shelter and the proper temperature to hatch their tiny eggs.

Middle Frisco Trail is an enjoyable hike in a pretty area. The Trail Wise Back Country Horsemen help to maintain the trail. The area shows little sign of human use, so please practice Leave No Trace skills. You'll also be sharing the trail with an increasing number of mountain bikers, especially as the sport becomes more popular in the Del Norte area—so if your dog has even the slightest inclination to chase bikes, you'd be smart to leash them.

MILES AND DIRECTIONS

0.0   Start at the Middle Frisco (Trail 801) Trailhead. Elevation: 9,500 feet. Head toward the creek on Middle Frisco Trail. Reach a brown carsonite post shortly after the trailhead. Go past this post to the left. At the creek's edge, look right. You'll see a little bridge that looks like a flat ladder. Walk across the bridge to find the trail on the other side, which climbs up through aspen and into a meadow. The trail is easy to follow from here.

3.4   The trail enters a large meadow area with a view of Pintada Mountain to the left. GPS: N37 30.77' / W106 24.82' (**Note:** Look for some bristlecone pines here.)

3.6   The trail makes a big U curve. Follow the curve and not a spur trail.

4.1   The trail starts a series of switchbacks. Occasionally a spur trail leads off a switchback, but stick to the main trail unless you're looking for a campsite. (**Note:** Look north occasionally for good views of the San Luis Valley and the Sangre de Cristo Range.)

5.1   The trail crosses a flatter area with a nice view of the cliffs above upper San Francisco Lake. More switchbacks to come!

5.8 The switchbacks are finished, and the trail follows a little creek down to the left. There are many cattle trails in this area. Stay on the trail heading toward the cliffs.

6.1 The Middle Frisco Cut-off Trail (nonmotorized) goes to the right and connects to the West Frisco Trail (Trail 850/motorized). (**Side trip:** You can climb Bennett Peak from the West Frisco Trail [watch out for lightning]. Turn right onto the cut-off trail and hike 0.7 mile to West Frisco Trail, turn left, and follow the ridge about 1.3 miles to the peak.)

6.3 Arrive at the outlet to upper San Francisco Lake. Elevation: 12,000 feet. GPS: N37 29.40' / W106 25.52'. Continue left across the outlet toward the lower lake.

6.45 Enjoy a nice overlook of the lower lake. GPS: N37 29.37' / W106 25.37'. Return the way you came. (**Note:** This area makes a good lunch spot if you don't want to hike down and back up again. Watch for white-crowned sparrows nearby and elk in the high meadows to the east and south.)

12.9 Arrive back at the trailhead.

40 ALBERTA PEAK: CONTINENTAL DIVIDE NATIONAL SCENIC TRAIL

WHY GO?

This hike follows the Continental Divide National Scenic Trail south from Wolf Creek Pass to Alberta Peak. It climbs through a pleasant spruce-fir forest and passes near a ski lift at Wolf Creek Ski Area. Beyond the ski lift the trail winds through the forest, then out onto the edge of a ridge with great views to the south and west. Passing through willows, the trail ascends above tree line with views in all directions and beautiful alpine wildflowers. A short scramble takes you to the top of Alberta Peak (11,870 feet), with its resident pikas.

THE RUNDOWN

Start: From the top of Wolf Creek Pass, on the south side by the interpretive signs

Distance: 6.0 miles out and back

Approximate hiking time: 2.5 to 4 hours

Difficulty: Moderate due to mostly gentle trail and distance

Elevation gain: 1,013 feet, plus about 80 feet in undulations

Seasons: Best from July to Oct

Trail surface: Dirt trail

Other trail users: Equestrians, mountain bikers, hunters (in season)

Canine compatibility: Dogs must be under control

Fees and permits: None

Maps: USGS Wolf Creek Pass; Nat Geo Trails Illustrated 140 Weminuche Wilderness

Trail contacts: Rio Grande National Forest, Divide Ranger District, Del Norte; (719) 657-3321; www.fs.usda .gov/riogrande

Other: No water on the trail; bring your own. Do not hike along the ridge if a thunderstorm and lightning are in the vicinity!

FINDING THE TRAILHEAD

From South Fork, drive west on US 160 for 19.4 miles to the top of Wolf Creek Pass. Park on the south side by the interpretive signs. There are no facilities here. The last part of this trail is above tree line. **GPS:** N37 28.98' / W106 48.09'

THE HIKE

In 1978 Congress designated a National Scenic Trail along the Continental Divide. The trail snakes from the Canadian border across Montana, Wyoming, Colorado, and New Mexico to the Mexican border. Because some ridges on the actual divide might be difficult or dangerous, a 50-mile-wide corridor on either side could be used for the trail. Approximately 1,900 miles of trails and seldom-used roads shaped the initial configuration of the 3,100-mile trail. Ultimately designated the Continental Divide National Scenic Trail (CDNST), most of the trail is closed to motor vehicles.

Benton MacKaye, founder of the Appalachian Trail, first proposed the idea for the CDNST in 1966. Congress authorized a study of his idea under the National Trails System Act of 1968. The study reported that trail users would access great scenery, various ecosystems and life zones, and historical areas while crossing twenty-five national forests and three national parks (Glacier, Yellowstone, and Rocky Mountain). In 1971 Baltimore attorney Jim Wolf finished hiking the Appalachian Trail and looked for another such

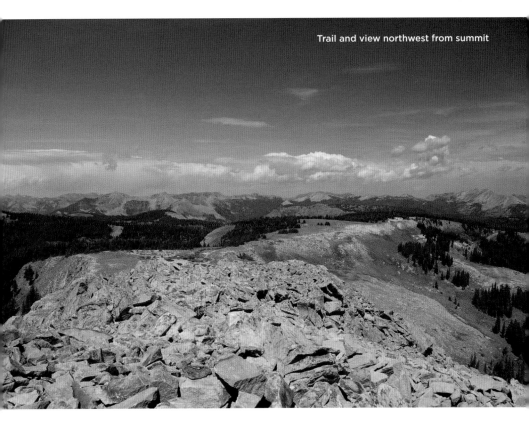

adventure. He started hiking the Divide Trail from the Canadian border and became a strong proponent for the CDNST.

The CDNST legislation gave the USDA Forest Service responsibility for coordinating the completion of the trail. Congress, however, did not appropriate funding to finish it. The corridor crosses National Park Service and Bureau of Land Management lands, and even though existing trails would be used in places, many miles needed maintenance or improvement. Proposed routes also crossed private property in some areas, requiring negotiations with landowners for either purchase or access of the trail corridor.

Two organizations formed to aid the CDNST. First, Jim Wolf founded the Continental Divide Trail Society (CDTS) in 1978. Today the CDTS continues with its mission: "[Dedicated to] the planning, development, and maintenance of the [Continental Divide Trail] as a silent trail." CDTS's efforts focus on the selection and development of the best possible route and on providing reliable information to trail users. Check out www.cdtsociety.org for more information.

The second organization, the Continental Divide Trail Alliance (CDTA), was founded by Bruce and Paula Ward in 1995. CDTA assists federal land managers to complete, manage, and protect the trail. They organize volunteer efforts to build and maintain new and old sections of trail, coordinate an Adopt-a-Trail program, and work with legislators to appropriate funding. Find more information at www.cdtrail.org.

By 2018 about 76 percent of the CDNST had been completed. The remaining 24 percent is mostly on dirt or even occasionally paved roads; only about 3 percent of the

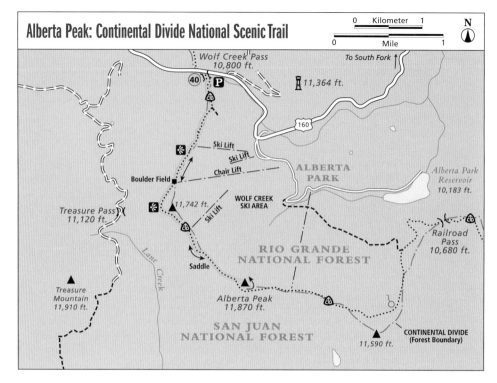

Alberta Peak: Continental Divide National Scenic Trail

Wolf Creek Pass
10,800 ft.

To South Fork

11,364 ft.

Ski Lift

Ski Lift

Chair Lift

Boulder Field

ALBERTA
PARK

Alberta Park
Reservoir
10,183 ft.

Treasure Pass
11,120 ft.

11,742 ft.

WOLF CREEK
SKI AREA

Railroad
Pass
10,680 ft.

Ski Lift

RIO GRANDE
NATIONAL FOREST

Saddle

Treasure
Mountain
11,910 ft.

Alberta Peak
11,870 ft.

Lane Creek

SAN JUAN
NATIONAL FOREST

11,590 ft.

CONTINENTAL DIVIDE
(Forest Boundary)

CDNST is rugged off-trail bushwhacking. However, many miles of existing trail are in need of repair or need to be rerouted from motorized routes or environmentally sensitive areas.

The trail to Alberta Peak travels across a meadow to the south of Wolf Creek Pass. After you cross the bridge and enter the trees, the trail splits in several directions. Turn left to follow the official trail, which then curves right and up. The trail climbs gently along the west side of the ridge. The Wolf Creek Ski Area's ski runs are on the east side. People from the San Luis Valley have skied on Wolf Creek Pass since the 1930s. In 1937 they formed the Wolf Creek Association, and in 1938 installed rope tows on the north side of the highway. In 1956 another corporation formed and built a Poma lift at the existing site. In 1976 the Pitcher family purchased Wolf Creek Ski Area and continues to own and manage it today. You can get a firsthand view of what a ski area looks like without snow at about 1.5 miles, where the top of a ski lift stands silently, waiting for snow to give it life again.

After another patch of forest, you'll arrive at an expansive view of Treasure Mountain (11,910 feet) and points to the southwest. Treasure Mountain earned its name from several legends about a chest full of gold that was buried in the area. Unfortunately, no one has ever found the gold. The trail follows the edge of the ridge, which drops steeply to the west. Curving left, it sneaks between willow bushes and emerges above tree line. The lake to the east is Alberta Park Reservoir. The snowshed to the northeast protects US 160 from frequent avalanches. Wolf Creek Pass typically receives the most snowfall in Colorado, averaging 460 inches of snow annually. Colorful alpine wildflowers bloom along the trail.

From this section, Alberta Peak, the hike's destination, rises meekly to the southeast. It's an easy scramble up the boulder field and grassy slopes to the top. The 360-degree view is worth the extra effort. Resident pikas sun themselves between hasty trips collecting grass and flowers for their winter hay piles. Continue farther along the CDNST if you wish. Watch out for lightning!

MILES AND DIRECTIONS

0.0 Start at the trailhead at the top of Wolf Creek Pass, on the south side. The Continental Divide National Scenic Trail (CDNST) continues south from the left side of the interpretive signs. Elevation: 10,857 feet.

0.1 Cross a bridge and turn left at the T intersection.

0.4 The trail comes to a lazy T intersection. Turn right and continue uphill. (The branch straight ahead takes you to a ski run.)

1.1 The trail makes several switchbacks, with great views to the west and northwest.

1.5 The trail passes near a chairlift to the left and a boulder field to the right. Stay to the right above the boulder field and you'll see the trail. GPS: N37 28.16' / W106 48.34'

1.9 The trail opens up to the right with a view of Treasure Mountain.

2.2 The trail travels the edge of a ridge with a steep drop-off.

2.6 The trail drops slightly to a saddle with good views in most directions. You can readily see Alberta Peak from here. GPS: N37 27.52' / W106 48.00'

2.9 The CDNST continues along the steep south side of Alberta Peak. You can continue on from here for as long as you like. (**Note:** Be aware of any lightning danger!) Turn left by the post and scramble up the gentle northwest side of Alberta Peak.

3.0 Reach the top of Alberta Peak, with wonderful panoramic views. Elevation: 11,870 feet. GPS: N37 27.35' / W106 47.65'. Return the way you came.

6.0 Arrive back at the trailhead.

41 WILLIAMS CREEK TRAIL

WHY GO?

The Williams Creek Trail (Trail 587) in the Weminuche Wilderness reaches the Continental Divide in 10.1 miles. This hike description guides you to the first crossing of Williams Creek. Traveling above the creek, you'll see various volcanic rock shapes from eroded fins to fluted cliffs. The trail progresses through forests of Douglas and white fir, limber pine, Gambel oak, aspen, and some beautiful wildflowers. Watch for deer. At the creek crossing, a little area to the right makes a great lunch stop. You can continue on the trail for a long day hike or a multiday backpack. Crossing Williams Creek can be challenging or unsafe during spring runoff.

THE RUNDOWN

Start: From the Williams Creek (Trail 587) Trailhead
Distance: 6.0 miles out and back
Approximate hiking time: 2.5 to 4 hours
Difficulty: Moderate due to mostly gentle terrain
Elevation gain: 720 feet, plus 340 feet of undulations
Seasons: Best from mid-June to mid-Oct
Trail surface: Dirt trail, sometimes rocky
Other trail users: Equestrians and hunters (in season)
Canine compatibility: Dogs must be under control
Fees and permits: None. Group size limit: No more than 15 people per group with a maximum combination of 25 people and pack or saddle animals in any one group.
Maps: USGS Cimarrona Peak; Nat Geo Trails Illustrated 140 Weminuche Wilderness

Trail contacts: San Juan National Forest, Pagosa Ranger District, Pagosa Springs; (970) 264-2268; www.fs.usda.gov/sanjuan
Other: There is a vault toilet at the trailhead. The Palisades Horse Camp across the parking lot has water, if the pump by the vault toilet doesn't work. The access road is typically closed in the winter beyond the boat ramp at Williams Creek Reservoir, about 3 miles from the trailhead. The trail is neither maintained nor marked for winter use.
Special Considerations: Check with the USDA Forest Service for up-to-date camping restrictions around certain lakes and hot springs, and fire restrictions in certain drainages. Also check on the latest information about bears and protecting food if you're backpacking.

FINDING THE TRAILHEAD

The Williams Creek Trailhead is just past Cimarrona Campground, about 27 miles from Pagosa Springs. The road intersections are well marked. Starting on the west side of Pagosa Springs, turn north onto Piedra Road (Archuleta CR 600) from US 160. In about 6.4 miles the road becomes dirt (FR 631). At about 13 miles the road forks; stay to the left on FR 631 (the right fork is FR 633). The road crosses Piedra Bridge at about 16.1 miles; continue straight ahead on FR 631. The road forks again at about 17.8 miles; take the left fork (right fork is FR 636). At about mile 22 the road forks yet again; this time take the right fork onto FR 640 (Williams Lake Road). In a little over 1 mile, Williams Creek Reservoir is on the right. When the road forks again at about mile 25.6, take the right fork (the left fork goes to Poison Park). Drive about another 1.4 miles to the Williams Creek (Trail 587) Trailhead. **GPS:** N37 32.49' / W107 11.84'

Fluted cliffs

THE HIKE

The Williams Creek Trail is one of many gateways into the Weminuche Wilderness. (I've heard the name of this wilderness area pronounced both "Wem-in-OOCH" and "Wem-in-OOCH-ee" by various knowledgeable locals and land managers. Take your pick.) Multiday loop trips can be designed starting at the Williams Creek Trailhead and returning via Indian Creek Trail or Cimarrona Creek Trail. Hikers can also traverse the wilderness and exit in the Rio Grande Valley to the north.

The Weminuche Wilderness is the largest designated wilderness in Colorado. The process started back in 1927, when the concept of preserving land in its natural state started to become popular. In 1932 the Forest Service established the San Juan Primitive Area, which covered the southern slopes of the San Juans. The Rio Grande Primitive Area was also created on the northern San Juan slopes. In 1964 Congress passed the Wilderness Act; however, the Weminuche was not one of the initial wilderness areas. This area was considered for wilderness status starting in 1968, causing both alarm and enthusiasm among locals. Sheep and cattle had grazed in the area for many years. Ranchers feared they might lose their grazing permits and the predator population would increase. Mining interests in the western part of the San Juans became a hot topic, too. Existing mining claims were not immediately impacted by the Wilderness Act, nor were grazing permits.

According to *Walking in Wildness: A Guide to the Weminuche Wilderness* by B. J. Boucher, during the early efforts for wilderness designation in the 1960s, Ian M. Thompson, then editor of the *Durango Herald*, was an avid wilderness advocate. Thompson wrote in a special wilderness supplement to the newspaper: "The 'Wilderness' effort we are engaged in at this time is, in one respect, a pitifully futile struggle. Earth's total atmosphere is man-changed beyond redemption. Earth's waters would not be recognizable to the Pilgrims. Earth's creatures will never again know what it is to be truly 'wild.' The sonic thunder of man's aircraft will increasingly descend in destructive shock waves upon any 'wilderness area' no matter how remote or how large. We are attempting to save the battered remnants of the original work of a Creator. To engage in this effort is the last hope of religious men."

A proposal to create the Weminuche Wilderness by combining the San Juan and Rio Grande Primitive Areas and adding some additional land was submitted to Congress in 1971. Recreational opportunities were emphasized, as were water quality and quantity. Water is the liquid gold of Colorado, and disputes over water rights and control are a never-ending battle in the state. For three years the proposal suffered through political haggling and boundary adjustments. Finally, in 1975 Colorado senators Peter H. Dominick and Floyd K. Haskell sponsored the bill that created the 405,031-acre Weminuche Wilderness. The name came from the Weminuche band of Utes, who once thrived here.

Congress expanded the Weminuche in 1980 and again in 1993. Today the total area stands at approximately 488,210 acres in both the San Juan National Forest (Pacific drainage) and the Rio Grande National Forest (Atlantic drainage). A wilderness team comprising land managers from both forests provides consistent management for the Weminuche Wilderness. If you're seeking solitude, you won't go wrong with a trip to the Weminuche.

The hike starts along a doubletrack that quickly becomes a trail. After crossing a boulder-filled waterway, which is often dry, you'll enter the Weminuche Wilderness.

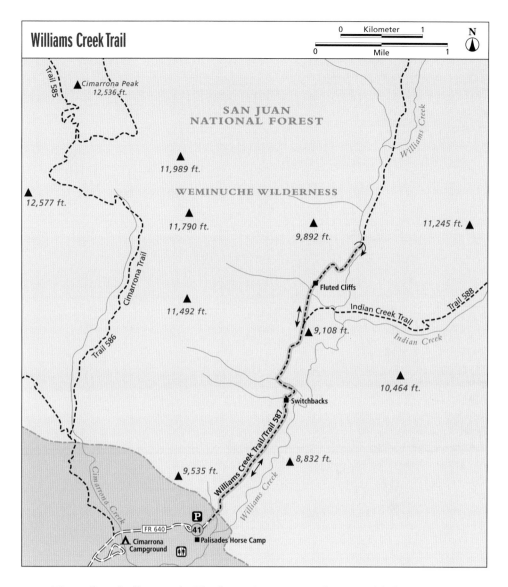

Kilometer

Mile

N

Trail 585

Cimarrona Peak
12,536 ft.

SAN JUAN
NATIONAL FOREST

11,989 ft.

12,577 ft.

WEMINUCHE WILDERNESS

11,790 ft.

9,892 ft.

11,245 ft.

Williams Creek

Cimarrona Trail

Fluted Cliffs

11,492 ft.

Indian Creek Trail

Trail 588

9,108 ft.

Indian Creek

10,464 ft.

Trail 586

Switchbacks

9,535 ft.

Williams Creek Trail/Trail 587

8,832 ft.

Williams Creek

Cimarrona Creek

FR 640

41

P

Cimarrona
Campground

Palisades Horse Camp

The trail gradually ascends. The large pinecones on the ground belong to the limber pine. Limber pines have five needles to a packet on very flexible branches, which give the species its moniker.

As the trail becomes steeper, it narrows considerably, so watch for oncoming horse traffic. If you meet equestrians on the trail, ask the riders for instructions. (Usually the hiker steps off the trail on the downhill side, but this could prove difficult in one stretch.) Along with the first view of Williams Creek, you'll notice an interesting area with eroded volcanic rock to your right.

The trail winds up and down around little creek drainages while slowly gaining elevation. The undergrowth thickens in several places with ferns, geraniums, subalpine larkspur, Wood's rose, and aspen trees. In some areas subalpine larkspur and cow parsnip stand about 5 feet tall. The Spanish called Williams Creek *huerto*, meaning "gardenlike" or "orchard." About 2.5 miles in, you cross a nice meadow with cliffs to the left that appear fluted. Cross over a ridge and drop to the Williams Creek crossing for lunch.

If you are backpacking, please remember to camp at least 200 feet away from streams, lakes, and trails per Forest Service regulations for this area. Do your part in practicing Leave No Trace techniques, and the Weminuche will remain pristine for your next visit, and for future generations.

MILES AND DIRECTIONS

0.0 Start at the Williams Creek (Trail 587) Trailhead. Elevation: 8,360 feet. Please remember to sign the trail register.

0.2 Enter the Weminuche Wilderness area.

1.2 The trail switchbacks above eroded features in the cliff along Williams Creek.

2.1 Reach the junction with Indian Creek Trail. GPS: N37 33.84' / W107 10.98'. Stay left on Williams Creek Trail.

2.6 Enter a large meadow with fluted cliffs to the left.

2.8 Cross a ridge and drop down to Williams Creek.

3.0 Arrive at the creek crossing. Elevation: 8,960 feet. GPS: N37 34.34' / W107 10.51' (**Note:** There's a nice lunch spot to the right along the creek.) Return the way you came.

6.0 Arrive back at the trailhead.

42 DEVILS CREEK AND LAKE

WHY GO?

The hike to Devils Lake is a great warm-up or practice hike for anyone wanting to climb the 14,000-foot peaks near Lake City. The elevation gain is similar, but at lower altitude. For those wishing a shorter hike, the old cow camp at mile 2.6 is a good turnaround point. The Devils Creek Trail into the Powderhorn Wilderness was constructed in 1994. The relatively undisturbed Cannibal and Calf Creek Plateaus contain one of the largest, relatively flat alpine tundra areas in the lower United States. The Cannibal Plateau is named after the area's famous cannibal, Alferd Packer.

THE RUNDOWN

Start: From the Devils Creek Trailhead
Distance: 13.6 miles out and back
Approximate hiking time: 7 to 12 hours (recommended 2- to 3-day backpack)
Difficulty: Strenuous due to elevation gain and altitude
Elevation gain: 3,600 feet
Seasons: Best from mid-June to mid-Oct; closed Apr to mid-June to protect elk-calving areas
Trail surface: Dirt trail and old nonmotorized ranch road, steep in places, through alpine tundra
Other trail users: Equestrians and hunters (in season)
Canine compatibility: Dogs must be under control
Fees and permits: None, except for commercial guides or outfitters
Maps: USGS Alpine Plateau, Cannibal Plateau, and Powderhorn Lakes; Nat Geo Trails Illustrated 141 Telluride/

Silverton/Ouray/Lake City and 139 La Garita Wilderness/Cochetopa Hills; Latitude 40° Southwest Colorado (shows part of the trail)
Trail contacts: Bureau of Land Management, Gunnison Field Office, Gunnison; (970) 641-0471; www.blm .gov/co/st/en/fo/gfo.html. Gunnison National Forest, Gunnison Ranger District, Lake City; (970) 641-0471 or (970) 944-2500; www.fs.usda.gov/ gmug
Other: The road along the creek is mostly one vehicle wide, so be very careful. The bridge over the Lake Fork Gunnison River is closed until June 15 each year to protect elk-calving areas. The area is closed Apr to mid-June. The access road may be closed by snow in winter. The trail is neither maintained nor marked for winter use. There are no facilities at the trailhead, and camping is not allowed. Bring your own water.

FINDING THE TRAILHEAD

From Lake City, drive north on CO 149 for about 7 miles, from the post office to a dirt road heading northeast. The turn is about 0.5 mile north of mile marker 79. Turn right onto the next road, which drops steeply to the river, and follow it 0.5 mile across the Lake Fork Gunnison River and up a hill to a dirt road signed TRAILHEADS. Turn left onto this road and continue about 0.4 mile to the Devils Creek Trailhead. With slow, careful driving, most 2WD cars should be able to reach the trailhead. **GPS:** N38 08.04' / W107 17.07'

THE HIKE

High peaks and high plateaus surround Lake City. The plateaus were formed by both lava and ash flows, estimated to be as thick as 5,000 feet. More recently, ice age glaciers scraped and molded the land, leaving U-shaped valleys, moraines, lakes, and tarns (ponds).

Volcanic activity also deposited gold, silver, and other precious metals in cracks and crevices. In 1871 J. K. Mullen and Henry Henson found the Ute-Ulay veins west of Lake City. This treasure, however, lay in Ute territory guaranteed by the Treaty of 1868.

There's also some disturbing history to this area; it's some of Colorado's most beloved lore. (So much so, in fact, that the cafeteria in the student union of my alma mater, the University of Colorado at Boulder, is called the Alferd Packer Grill. If you don't find this mildly grotesque moniker amusing, you may want to skip the rest of this section.) In the fall of 1873, Alferd Packer was serving a jail sentence in Salt Lake City, Utah Territory, for counterfeiting. Once he heard a rumor of gold discoveries in Colorado Territory, Packer bragged of his knowledge of the area. A group from Provo heard his boasts, paid the fine necessary to release him, and hired him to guide them to the Breckenridge area. The group of twenty-one men left Provo in November 1873. By mid-January they arrived at the winter camp of Ute Spokesman Chief Ouray. Chief Ouray warned them against proceeding, as there was an unusually severe winter coming on. But gold blinds wisdom, and five men plus Packer left Ouray's camp in early February. They headed toward Los Pinos Indian Agency, southeast of Gunnison, via a shortcut across the mountains.

Alferd Packer arrived alone at the agency on April 16, 1874. Apparently healthy, his first request was for a drink of whiskey. He also started spending money on drinks and games in nearby Saguache, although he was known to have had little money when he left Utah. Packer's various stories conflicted, and local Utes reported finding strips of human flesh along his trail. At one point Packer agreed to lead a party to the bodies, but then became disoriented and refused to go farther. Artist J. A. Randolph found five skeletons near Lake City during the summer and sketched the gruesome site. Another story credits

Cow camp

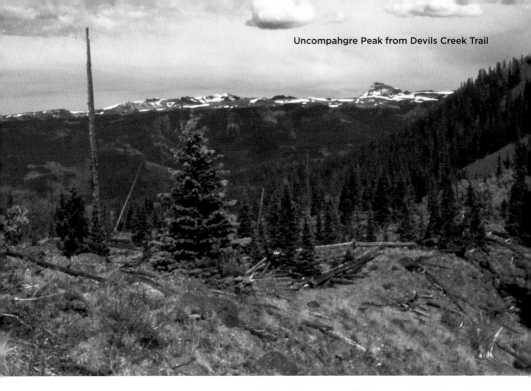

Captain C. H. Graham, a prospector, with the discovery. All five men had been shot, and one body was headless. Packer was jailed in August 1874, but soon escaped. He was recaptured in 1883.

Packer was found guilty of premeditated murder and sentenced to execution on May 19, 1883, in Lake City. The execution was overturned because the murders occurred in Ute territory. Packer was tried again in Gunnison in 1886, found guilty of five counts of murder, and sentenced to forty years in the state penitentiary at Cañon City. In 1900 the owners of the *Denver Post* requested parole for Packer as part of a publicity maneuver for the paper. After several interesting incidents, Governor Charles S. Thomas paroled Packer in 1901. Packer died in 1907 and is buried in a Littleton cemetery. Just south of Lake City, local citizens established a memorial to Packer's victims.

The Devils Creek Trail was completed in 1994 as a western access to the Powderhorn Wilderness. The area sees relatively little use (more during hunting season), so take care to keep it pristine. The trail climbs steadily and fairly steeply through forests of ponderosa pine, Douglas fir, juniper, aspen, and sage to an old cow camp. The trail also crosses a large meadow. Be careful during thunderstorms—this section is very exposed to lightning. The historic cow camp is protected as an antiquity, so please be respectful and leave it untouched. No camping is allowed inside or within 50 feet of the cabins. For a shorter 5.2-mile out-and-back hike, return the way you came from here. To reach Devils Lake in another 4.2 miles, continue hiking up the trail.

The trail winds more gently up along Devils Creek, through aspen groves and into thick spruce-fir forest, finally traveling along the creek at times. Switchbacking away from the creek, the trail enters another open meadow where a forest fire raged more than thirty years ago. Several steep switchbacks through thick forest bring you to a beautiful subalpine meadow, full of colorful wildflowers in July. Cairns mark the trail. Enter

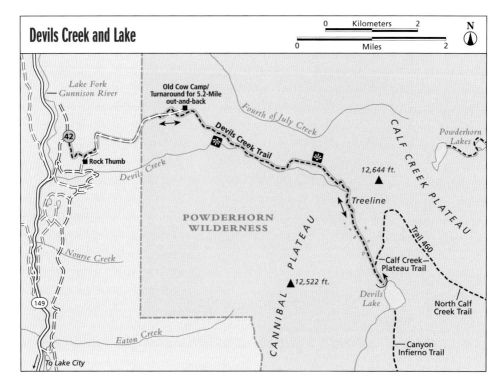

Devils Creek and Lake

a final patch of forest where you need to look closely to find the path. After another flower-filled meadow, the trail reaches tree line at about 12,000 feet. Follow the cairns while climbing through open alpine tundra and rocks. The trail then flattens, crossing more alpine tundra and rocks that reflect the area's volcanic history. Head south across the tundra to Devils Lake.

If you are backpacking, please camp below tree line during thunderstorm season for your own safety. Water is usually available in Devils Creek—be sure to treat it—to about the meadow (created when a forest fire killed the trees). If you camp near the lake, follow BLM regulations and camp at least 200 feet away, out of sight of other visitors, and use only camp stoves, to protect the fragile tundra. Several grassy bluffs above the lake provide excellent camping spots and are more resistant to damage than the alpine tundra near the lake.

MILES AND DIRECTIONS

0.0 Start at the Devils Creek Trailhead. Elevation: 8,480 feet. Remember to sign the trail register.

0.6 The trail makes a left L by a big rock thumb.

0.8 The trail comes to a T intersection with an old road. GPS: N38 07.90' / W107 16.65'. Turn left and continue uphill on the road.

1.0 The road enters a long sagebrush meadow and continues in the open for 0.5 mile. (**Note:** Be careful of lightning.)

1.5 The road curves left above the aspen grove.

1.8 Reach the wilderness boundary sign. GPS: N38 08.22' / W107 15.95'

2.0 The trail turns right and leaves the road. Follow the trail and do not return to the road as the trail crosses it a few more times. (**Note:** The BLM requests visitors stay on the trail when it departs from the old road to avoid creating areas where erosion will occur.)

2.6 The old cow camp appears on the left side of the trail. GPS: N38 08.39' / W107 15.27' (**Note:** There's a big flat rock that's ideal for a break.) (**Option:** For a day hike [three to five hours], return the way you came, arriving back at the trailhead at 5.2 miles.)

3.1 Pass some huge Douglas firs. (**Note:** In an open spot, look back to the west for a view of Uncompahgre Peak, which at 14,309 feet is Colorado's sixth-highest peak. The Cannibal Plateau is above on your right.)

3.4 The trail is finally next to the creek, and you can see it!

4.4 The trees thin as you enter an old burned area. The trail follows a little ridge. (**Note:** Be careful of lightning.)

5.3 The trail leaves the forest and enters a colorful meadow. Follow the cairns along the right side of the meadow until you see some crossing the meadow. Cross and enter another patch of trees (the trail is faint here), cross another meadow, and then follow more cairns.

5.5 The trail is now above tree line. GPS: N38 07.20' / W107 12.78'. Follow the cairns across the alpine tundra and rocks. When cairns no longer exist, keep heading south and downhill to Devils Lake.

6.8 Reach Devils Lake. Elevation: 11,980 feet. GPS: N38 06.33' / W107 12.28'. Return the way you came. (**Option:** You can make a longer trip by connecting with other trails in the area.)

13.6 Arrive back at the trailhead.

43 WASHINGTON GULCH TRAIL

WHY GO?

The Washington Gulch Trail offers several options. The main goal is the ridge at about 11,400 feet, with spectacular views of the Maroon Bells–Snowmass Wilderness and the Raggeds Wilderness. The flowers are sensational during July. The hike starts at the Gothic-side trailhead, climbing through fields of wildflowers and spruce-fir forest to the ridge. The out-and-back option returns from here. The point-to-point option descends to the Washington Gulch side, passing an old mine with relics. A high-clearance vehicle is required to reach the west-side trailhead. Be mindful of mountain bikers the entire way.

THE RUNDOWN

Start: From the Washington Gulch (Trail 403) Trailhead near Gothic Campground
Distance: 3.9 miles point to point
Approximate hiking time: 1.5 to 2.5 hours
Difficulty: Difficult due to elevation gain
Elevation gain/loss: 1,940-foot gain / 410-foot loss
Seasons: Best from mid-June through Sept
Trail surface: Dirt trail with some steep sections
Other trail users: Equestrians, mountain bikers, hunters (in season)

Canine compatibility: Dogs must be on leash. This is a popular mountain bike trail, so keep dogs leashed for their safety as well as bikers' safety.
Fees and permits: None
Maps: USGS Oh-Be-Joyful; Nat Geo Trails Illustrated 133 Kebler Pass/ Paonia Reservoir; Latitude 40° Crested Butte, Taylor Park
Trail contacts: Gunnison National Forest, Gunnison; (970) 641-0471; www.fs.usda.gov/gmug
Other: Gothic Campground is about 0.1 mile south of the Gothic-side trailhead. No facilities at either trailhead.

FINDING THE TRAILHEAD

With shuttle (requires high-clearance vehicle): Drive north and east on Gothic Road from the Crested Butte Chamber of Commerce (located in the old train station at the corner of Elk Avenue and Gothic Road in Crested Butte) toward the town of Mount Crested Butte. Turn left at Washington Gulch Road (GCR 811 / FR 811) in about 1.7 miles. From this intersection, drive about 8 miles up Washington Gulch. The trailhead is on the right side of the road, just up the hill beyond a very sharp and steep left switchback and above the cabins at Elkton by the Painter Boy Mine. Drop one vehicle off here and return to Gothic Road. **GPS:** N38 58.05' / W107 02.53'

To reach the Gothic-side trailhead for the start of the hike, turn right at the intersection of Gothic Road and Washington Gulch Road, continuing north on Gothic Road (GCR 317). The pavement ends at mile 3.7. Drive down the dirt road, which becomes FR 317 just past Gothic and the Rocky Mountain Biological Laboratory. The Washington Gulch Trailhead is located on the left side of the road about 10 miles from Crested Butte, or 6.4 miles from where the pavement ends. **GPS:** N38 58.93' / W107 00.40'

THE HIKE

Gothic Mountain (12,625 feet), south of the Washington Gulch Trail, received its name from the interesting rock formations on its east side that resemble Gothic cathedral spires. In May 1879 John and David Jennings discovered silver at the head of Copper Creek east of Gothic Mountain and named their discovery the Sylvanite. The deposit of silver in wire form was so rich that it often brought in over $15,000 per ton. From 1880 to 1910 the Sylvanite Mine produced over $1 million worth of silver.

Hopeful miners arrived in droves, searching the surrounding hills and valleys for ore, praying to strike it rich. A few months after the deposit was discovered, the town of Gothic was laid out at the confluence of East River and Copper Creek. In one week's time, one hundred tents and cabins reportedly sprang up. Two sawmills were set up and had a hard time keeping up with the demand for lumber. By the end of 1879, more than 200 buildings had been constructed and over 500 people lived in the area. The next summer the town boasted five law firms, four grocery stores, three restaurants, two general mercantile stores, a bank, three doctors, two hotels, and the usual assortment of saloons, gambling halls, and dance halls. A nightly bonfire on Main Street allowed the locals to tell stories and smoke their tobacco. Gothic became the supply center for the area's various small camps and mines.

Transporting ore out of—and goods into—town was a challenge. The East River Toll Road was the main route in 1879. Eventually another road was built around the west side of Crested Butte (12,162 feet), saving several miles. Gothic even supplied Aspen via a road up Copper Creek, over East Maroon Pass, and down Maroon Creek. Gothic

Ruby Range and Raggeds Wilderness

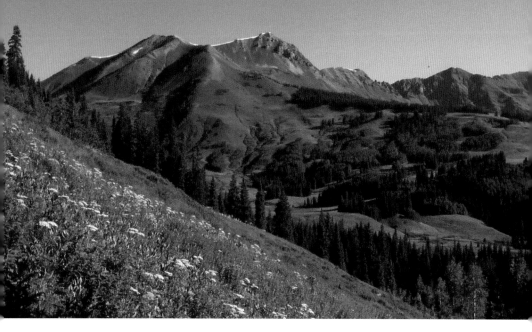

eventually boasted a population of 8,000 people, until the Silver Panic of 1893 signaled the end of the "City of Silver Wires."

In 1928 the Rocky Mountain Biological Laboratory (RMBL) moved into the remaining buildings at Gothic, tearing down some and remodeling others. RMBL was the dream of Dr. John C. Johnson, a biology professor at Western State College at Gunnison. Johnson purchased land and old buildings to create a research and training facility for field biologists. Scientists use the surrounding national forest, wilderness, and Gothic Research Natural Area to hone their investigative and research skills.

The hike starts at the Gothic side of Washington Gulch Trail, as it is more accessible and easier to find. The trail starts by climbing up switchbacks through a field of cornhusk lilies and tall larkspurs. As the trail winds higher, the Elk Mountains expand into view to the east. Columbine, Indian paintbrush, and varieties of sunflowers add color along the trail. Rock Creek rumbles downhill to the left. At times the vegetation is so tall and hanging over the trail that you might feel a machete would be useful. In about 1 mile a cirque on Gothic Mountain comes into view. The mountain will dominate the southern view for most of the hike. Keep an eye out for deer. The trail enters a relatively flat meadow with a red mountain looming just beyond. This is Mount Baldy (12,805 feet).

After crossing Rock Creek the trail meanders a long way through spruce-fir forest and

An amazing toll road was built over Schofield Pass, connecting the towns of Marble and Aspen with Gothic and Crested Butte. The road was only 7 to 8 feet wide in places, instead of the usual 10 feet. Freight traffic normally negotiated an 8 percent grade, with 12 percent being the maximum. Schofield Pass, near the Devil's Punchbowl, however, is a steep 27 percent grade!

Washington Gulch Trail

0 — Kilometer — 1
0 — Mile — 1

N

Mount Baldy
12,805 ft.

GOTHIC
NATURAL AREA

Quigley Creek

MEADOW

Washington Gulch Trail (Trail 403)

Rock Creek

43

Gothic
Campground

Turnaround
for 5.4-mile
out-and-back
11,403 ft.

Painter Boy Mine

Shuttle

GUNNISON
NATIONAL FOREST

Elkton

FR 811

Washington Gulch Road

WASHINGTON GULCH

Gothic Road

East River

FR 317

Gothic

Gothic Mountain
12,625 ft.

To Crested Butte

To Crested Butte

meadows before making a final steep zigzag climb to a fantastic scenic overlook. There's even a "scenic pullout" to the right of the main trail, a great place for lunch. Looking east you can see into the Maroon Bells–Snowmass Wilderness, including the top of one of the Bells. Notice how the rock is folded on one ridge of Avery Peak, across Gothic Road. Tremendous uplifting forces created these mountains. Walk west across the trail to a field of beautiful flowers. Looking west to the Raggeds Wilderness and Ruby Range, you can see Daisy Pass (11,600 feet) snaking upward to the ridge. Washington Gulch lies below.

The overlook area is the turnaround point for the optional out-and-back hike. To continue into Washington Gulch, the trail gently descends about 1 mile to Washington Gulch Road near the Painter Boy Mine, another great ore producer in its day. Remember, old mines can be extremely dangerous—stay out!

As you hike along, enjoying the fabulous views and fantastic wildflower show, visualize miners streaming through the area, searching for the strike that would make them rich.

MILES AND DIRECTIONS

0.0 Start at Washington Gulch (Trail 403) Trailhead north of Gothic. Elevation: 9,460 feet.

1.3 Reach a meadow with a view of Mount Baldy.

1.5 Cross Rock Creek.

1.7 Encounter steep switchbacks.

2.1 Reach a marshy meadow with a view of Gothic Mountain.

2.5 Encounter more steep switchbacks. Views of the Ruby Range are to the left and Elk Mountains to the right.

2.7 Reach a scenic overlook. Elevation: 11,380 feet. GPS: N38 58.22' / W107 01.87'. Great place for lunch! Make sure to check out the spectacular views both east and west, then continue down the trail toward Washington Gulch. (**Option:** For a 5.4-mile out-and-back without a shuttle, turn around here and return the way you came. Approximate hiking time: 2.5 to 3.5 hours.)

3.7 Reach an old mine and relics. GPS: N38 58.18' / W107 02.57'

3.9 Arrive at the Washington Gulch–side trailhead. Elevation: 10,990 feet. (**Note:** This trailhead is an optional starting point. It can also be the turnaround point for a 7.8-mile out-and-back hike.)

44 PTARMIGAN LAKE

WHY GO?

The hike to Ptarmigan Lake winds through spruce-fir forest, gently climbing into an area of beautiful subalpine meadows dotted with tarns and little lakes. For flower aficionados the meadows show off beautiful wildflowers in July. After a little climb up the side of a cirque, you arrive at crystal-clear Ptarmigan Lake. Another 0.3 mile leads to a saddle with a view down into South Cottonwood Creek. This hike travels above tree line, so if the weather is threatening a thunderstorm, stay at the lower lakes.

THE RUNDOWN

Start: From the Ptarmigan Lake Trailhead off the Cottonwood Pass road
Distance: 6.6 miles out and back
Approximate hiking time: 3 to 4 hours
Difficulty: Difficult due to elevation gain and altitude
Elevation gain: 1,490 feet to the lake
Seasons: Best from July through Sept
Trail surface: Dirt trail with some boulders and rocks
Other trail users: Equestrians, anglers, mountain bikers, hunters (in season)

Canine compatibility: Dogs must be under control
Fees and permits: None
Maps: USGS Mount Yale and Tincup; Nat Geo Trails Illustrated 129 Buena Vista/Collegiate Peaks
Trail contacts: San Isabel National Forest, Salida Ranger District, Salida; (719) 539-3591; www.fs.usda.gov/psicc
Other: Vault toilet at the trailhead, but no water. The Cottonwood Pass road is closed by snow from late Nov to May about 4 miles before the trailhead. The trail is neither maintained nor marked for winter use.

FINDING THE TRAILHEAD

From Buena Vista, drive about 14.5 miles west on Chaffee CR 306, which later becomes FR 306, heading to Cottonwood Pass. The trailhead is on the south (left) side of the road about 0.1 mile in. **GPS:** N38 48.22' / W106 22.45'

THE HIKE

Cottonwood Pass was originally a toll road from Buena Vista (if you want to fit in with the locals and don't mind butchering the language, pronounce it "BYOO-na Vista"), connecting with other roads leading to Crested Butte, Gothic, and eventually Aspen in the 1870s. Harvard City, which you pass on the way from Buena Vista to the trailhead, boomed for a couple of years as placer claims were located along Cottonwood Creek. Lode mines were discovered and developed in 1874. Freighters also stopped at Harvard City to repack their loads for the long and difficult climb over the Continental Divide. Times changed, and the road connecting Aspen and Leadville over Independence Pass, opened in 1881, drew traffic away from Cottonwood Pass. The mines in the area couldn't match new mines farther west, and the miners moved on.

Cottonwood Pass, named after the many trees lining the creek alongside the road, fell into disrepair. The USDA Forest Service repaired and improved the road for automobile travel in the late 1950s. Several trailheads and good fishing are all accessible via the road today. The pass is closed during the winter, but is open to various winter sports.

Several lakes in Colorado bear the name Ptarmigan. The white-tailed ptarmigan, *Lagopus leucurus*, is a member of the grouse family that lives year-round above tree line and in the krummholz just below. Krummholz refers to the stunted, twisted tree hedges growing at the edge of tree line. It's usually made up of subalpine fir, Engelmann spruce, or limber pine. Ptarmigans are masters of disguise: During winter they wear snow-white feathers, which turn mottled brown and white in the summer. It's easy to almost step on one because they blend in so well with the rocks. As you hike, look for these birds. Little chicks follow after their moms in the summer. If approached, the mother pretends to have a broken wing to draw predators away from her chicks. Please do not harass ptarmigans to see if they'll pretend an injury, and do not let your dog chase them.

If you head around the lake on the trail to the little saddle, look up to the left and notice the streams of rocks heading down toward the lake. Freezing and thawing, which occurs most of the year, can force rocks buried underground up to the surface. On steep slopes the unearthed rocks roll into depressions. If one rock stops, others may roll into it or along a small water depression, causing a streamlike appearance. In more-level places the rocks may form polygons or garlands. This "patterned ground" is common in Colorado's alpine tundra.

The hike starts in thick spruce-fir forest, opening occasionally as two boulder fields flow over the trail. Watch for raspberry bushes among the boulders. Although you can hear Ptarmigan Creek in the distance, the trail keeps a good distance until you are almost to the lake. The hike continues through spruce-fir forest without much of a view.

Ptarmigan Lake

Turner Peak
13,233 ft.

To Buena Vista →

North Fork

FR 306
Cottonwood Pass Road

Middle Cottonwood Creek

44

FR 346

Boulder Fields

Trail 1444

SAN ISABEL
NATIONAL FOREST

Ptarmigan Lake Trail

Ptarmigan Creek

GLADSTONE RIDGE

JONES MOUNTAIN

13,209 ft.

Ptarmigan Lake
12,132 ft.

12,962 ft.

13,216 ft.

Saddle
(optional
turnaround)

BIG GRASSY

At about mile 1.2, cross a dirt road (FR 346—4WD access to the trail). Go straight and don't turn onto the road. The trail continues to wind and switchback gently through the forest.

About 2.4 miles in, the trees are less dense and more flowers appear. Some possible campsites come into view away from the trail. (Camp at least 200 feet from the trail, lakes, and streams.) Then the world opens, with Jones Mountain on the right and Gladstone Ridge on the left. You can see the edge of the cirque that contains Ptarmigan Lake. Flower-filled meadows dotted with little ponds and a lake line the trail.

Continue hiking through the meadows, jump across Ptarmigan Creek, and two switchbacks later arrive at the lake. Mount Yale (14,196 feet) looms large to the northeast. Two other high peaks rise above other ridges. Those high points are Mount Harvard (14,420 feet) and Mount Columbia (14,073 feet). The pointy peak between you and the Fourteeners is Turner Peak (13,233 feet).

If the weather is good, continue another 0.3 mile to the saddle for views down Grassy Gulch and South Cottonwood Creek. The views to the east and northeast of the Collegiate Peaks are worth the short climb.

MILES AND DIRECTIONS

0.0 Start at the Ptarmigan Lake (Trail 1444) Trailhead. Elevation: 10,650 feet. In 350 feet, cross a bridge over Middle Cottonwood Creek. The trail register is on the other side; please sign in.

0.2 Reach the first boulder field.

0.7 Reach the second boulder field.

1.2 Cross a dirt forest road. GPS: N38 47.53' / W106 22.15'. Go straight on the clearly marked trail. (FR 346 provides access to the trail, but only by 4WD vehicle.)

2.5 Reach the first little kettle pond on the right, and a lake down to the left.

2.9 Cross Ptarmigan Creek.

3.2 Arrive at Ptarmigan Lake. Elevation: 12,132 feet. GPS: N38 46.68' / W106 02.93'. Hike another 0.1 mile to the other side of lake.

3.3 Reach the south side of the lake. Return the way you came. (**Side trip:** Continue another 0.3 mile to the saddle between the Middle Cottonwood and South Cottonwood drainages. This side trip will add 0.6 mile and about 20 minutes to the hike.)

6.6 Arrive back at the trailhead.

WESTERN COLORADO

Colorado's Western Slope and southwestern region are among its least-populated areas. Far from the hustle and bustle of the Front Range and the I-70 corridor, this is where you'll find quieter hikes and fewer distractions. Hiking in this area is generally characterized by fewer and less-strict dog-related regulations, although in the northerly reaches of the Western Slope, you'll want to avoid Colorado National Monument, which doesn't allow canine traffic on its trails. Parts of this area are still very much the Wild West; be prepared to perform first aid if you or someone in your party is injured, as passersby will be fewer and farther between.

45 MARVINE LOOP

WHY GO?

This hike takes you to the top of the White River Plateau in the Flat Tops Wilderness via East Marvine Trail and loops back to the same trailhead via Marvine Trail for a multiday backpacking trip. The public resource and wilderness preservation history in this area is significant. Part of the hike travels through dense spruce-fir forest, conveying a primeval feeling. Once on the plateau, the land rolls along through subalpine meadows and alpine tundra punctuated by clumps of trees and short peaks. Small lakes and ponds abound. Take time to climb Big Marvine Peak or explore the various lakes on your own. Camping is available below the plateau and on top.

THE RUNDOWN

Start: From the East Marvine (Trail 1822) Trailhead
Distance: 23.2-mile loop backpack
Approximate hiking time: 3 days minimum to explore the Flat Tops
Difficulty: Most difficult due to length, elevation gain, and steep sections
Elevation gain/loss: 3,120-foot gain / 290-foot loss
Seasons: Best from late June to mid-Oct
Trail surface: Dirt trail with some muddy sections and several bridgeless creek crossings
Other trail users: Equestrians, anglers, hunters (in season)
Canine compatibility: Dogs must be under control

Fees and permits: None. Group size limit: No more than 15 people per group with a maximum combination of 25 people and pack or saddle animals in any one group.
Maps: USGS Big Marvine Peak, Lost Park, Oyster Lake, and Ripple Creek Pass; Nat Geo Trails Illustrated 122 Flat Tops NE/Trappers Lake
Trail contacts: White River National Forest, Blanco Ranger District, Meeker; (970) 878-4039; www.fs .usda.gov/whiteriver
Other: The access road to the trailhead opens from mid- to late May and remains open through the end of the hunting seasons in Nov. Trails are neither maintained nor marked for winter use.

FINDING THE TRAILHEAD

From Meeker, drive east on CO 13 to where it curves north, and turn right onto Rio Blanco CR 8. Follow the FLAT TOPS TRAIL SCENIC BYWAY sign. In about 28.5 miles (past mile marker 28), turn right onto a dirt road by the MARVINE CREEK sign. In 0.2 mile, turn left by Fritzlans Guest House onto RBCR 12, which later becomes FR 12. Trailhead parking is 5.1 miles down FR 12 on the left. Park away from the corrals reserved for outfitters. There is no water or toilet at the trailhead. Both are available at the two nearby campgrounds (fee areas). **GPS:** N40 00.55' / W107 25.47'

THE HIKE

While hiking up the trail, notice the pockmarked rocks. The White River Plateau is capped with dark basalt from volcanic eruptions that started around 25 million years ago. These eruptions lasted about 17 million years. After cooling off for another 7 million years, an ice age took hold. An ice cap formed over the plateau between 18,000 and 12,000 years ago. Melting glaciers left numerous little lakes and ponds below and on top of the plateau.

Many years later, the Ute people, also called the People of the Shining Mountains, camped in the Flat Tops on the northern end of the White River Plateau during the summer. Deer, elk, bison, and rabbits provided meat. Berries, wild onions, and the root of the yampa rounded out their diet.

As white settlers moved into the area, grazing and timber harvesting ran rampant and forest fires raged. Concerned citizens lobbied to protect Western public resources. In 1891 President Benjamin Harrison set aside the White River Timber Land Reserve. White River is the second-oldest national forest in the United States. The Flat Tops area earned another special place in history in 1919. The USDA Forest Service sent landscape architect Arthur Carhart to Trappers Lake, at the base of the Flat Tops, to survey the area for summer cabins. Instead, Carhart recommended that this beautiful area be set aside and protected from development. He noted: "There are a number of places with scenic values of such great worth that they are rightfully property of all people. They should be preserved for all time for the people of the Nation and the world. Trappers Lake is unquestionably a candidate for that classification."

Carhart later joined Aldo Leopold and began the movement that created the Wilderness Preservation System. The Flat Tops Primitive Area was established in 1932 with special protections. After many years of negotiation, President Lyndon B. Johnson signed the Wilderness Act of 1964. Congress elevated the primitive area to the Flat Tops Wilderness in 1975. The second-largest

> When meeting horses on the trail, step off on the downhill side until the horses pass, keeping your dog under control, preferably on leash next to you. If a horse wants more room, it will move off the trail away from you. It is safer for both the horse and rider if the horse heads uphill. If the trail is narrow, ask the rider for instructions.

wilderness area in Colorado is home to the largest elk herd in the state. Keep an eye open for deer and elk while you're hiking. Other wildlife you might encounter includes black bears, bobcats, pine martens, foxes, coyotes, marmots, and pikas.

The trail follows East Marvine Creek through aspen, Gambel oak, and lodgepole pine forests. Occasional grassy meadows provide views of the Flat Tops escarpment and Little Marvine Peaks. Follow along a small stream, then past the 2-mile mark, where ponds and small lakes start to appear. The trail climbs steadily up through aspen, Engelmann spruce, and subalpine fir. Numerous creeks intersect the trail, and some can be tricky to cross depending on water level. Most creeks have muddy edges and no log bridges, so you'll have to rock-hop.

After contouring around a ridge, Rainbow Lake lies to the left. A few campsites can be found on the ridge above it. Beyond Rainbow Lake the trail levels off and loses some elevation as it runs across meadows and tiny creeks. It finally rejoins East Marvine Creek and passes an energetic cascade before climbing steeply up the side of the Flat Tops. The spruce-fir forest is thick and dark here. Bark beetles infested the forest in the 1940s, and many dead snags make the forest appear ancient. Wood decays slowly in the high, dry Colorado climate. How large animals like elk can maneuver through the tangled dark forest almost defies the imagination.

Two long switchbacks lead to the base of the escarpment. When you find a flat spot, take a breather and enjoy the view. Scan the surrounding cliff bands for silver ribbon

Rainbow Lake

To Meeker

FR 12

— Wild Cow Park Trail

East Marvine Trail

FLAT TOPS
WILDERNESS

THE FLAT TOPS

LITTLE MARVINE PEAKS

Johnson
Lakes

Guthrie
Lake

East Marvine Creek

Rainbow Lake

11,650 ft.

11,751 ft.

East Marvine
Creek Cascades

Marvine Trail

WHITE RIVER
NATIONAL FOREST

East Marvine Trail/Trail 1822

Twin-
Lakes

Big Marvine Peak
11,879 ft.

Marvine Lakes

Oyster Lake Trail
Trail 1825

waterfalls. Six short switchbacks take you even higher, and two final switchbacks bring you close to the edge of the plateau. The climb is still not quite over, but becomes gentler now. You have gained about 1,000 feet in the last mile.

A large cairn holding up a tree trunk greets you at the top edge. A small lake is just beyond, then another and another. Little Marvine Peaks rise to the north, with Big Marvine Peak dominating the southwest view. The subalpine meadows roll along with patches of spruce-fir. After the third little lake, the trail splits. The left branch heads for Twin Lakes and Oyster Lake Trail, while the right branch (an unofficial trail) leads to a good fishing lake and toward Big Marvine Peak. From here you can explore and camp many places. Take a couple of days to enjoy the open high country of the Flat Tops. Then head south on the Oyster Lake Trail to Marvine Trail to make a loop back to the trailhead parking area where you started.

Please remember to camp at least 200 feet away from streams, lakes, and trails. Using a lightweight cookstove instead of a fire will avoid leaving permanent scars on the land. By practicing Leave No Trace techniques, hikers can enjoy a pristine experience and find solitude in the Flat Tops Wilderness for many years.

MILES AND DIRECTIONS

0.0 Start at the East Marvine Trailhead (Trail 1822). Elevation: 8,091 feet.

0.1 Cross the sturdy bridge over East Marvine Creek. At the T intersection, turn right onto the trail and head uphill with the creek on your right.

1.4 The trail leaves East Marvine Creek to follow a small stream.

1.7 The trail splits; stay to the right. (**Note:** The trail can get very muddy in this stretch.)

2.7 Johnson Lake is on the right. GPS: N40 00.27' / W107 23.30'

3.25 Come to the junction with Wild Cow Park Trail (Trail 2244). Stay to the right on East Marvine Trail.

5.0 Reach Rainbow Lake.

7.3 The trail splits. The right spur (nonsystem trail) goes to Ned Wilson Lake. The high point is just past here, at about 11,180 feet.

8.5 Reach the junction with the trail to Big Marvine Peak. Continue on the East Marvine Trail.

10.75 Reach the junction with the Oyster Lake Trail (Trail 1825). Elevation: 10,989 feet. GPS: N39 56.52' / W107 17.75'. Turn right onto Oyster Lake Trail.

12.2 Turn right onto the Marvine Trail (Trail 1823) and drop down the escarpment. GPS: N39 55.83' / W107 18.90'

17.4 Reach Marvine Lakes.

19.2 Reach Slide Lake. Ford Marvine Creek near the lake, being very careful, especially if the creek is high.

23.2 Arrive at the Marvine Trailhead, at the same parking area where you started. GPS: N40 00.53' / W107 25.46'

46 DEVILS CANYON

WHY GO?

This hike takes you into an easily accessible canyon in the Black Ridge Canyons Wilderness area. The trail first crosses open high-desert country of rabbitbrush, junipers, and other thorny plants. It then makes a loop in Devils Canyon, below huge walls of Wingate sandstone and interesting rock formations. Part of the loop follows the creek bottom and should be avoided during thunderstorms. Hiking beneath immense sandstone cliffs and past amphitheaters in a colorful canyon is a real treat! Keep an eye out for desert bighorn sheep and rattlesnakes.

THE RUNDOWN

Start: From the Devils Canyon Trailhead
Distance: 6.9-mile double lollipop
Approximate hiking time: 3 to 5 hours
Difficulty: Moderate due to length and terrain
Elevation gain: 620 feet, plus lots of undulations over gullies and drainages
Seasons: Year-round; avoid hot summer days
Trail surface: Dirt roads (nonmotorized) and trails
Other trail users: Equestrians and hunters (in season)
Canine compatibility: Dogs must be on leash

Fees and permits: None
Maps: USGS Mack and Battleship Rock; Nat Geo Trails Illustrated 502 Grand Junction/Fruita; Latitude 40° Fruita, Grand Junction
Trail contacts: Bureau of Land Management, Grand Junction; (970) 244-3000; www.co.blm.gov/co/st/en/fo/gjfo.html
Other: This area may be closed between Jan 15 and May 15 to protect bighorn sheep lambing areas. There is little to no water on the trail. Bring plenty of water (one gallon per person or dog per day), especially if it's hot.

FINDING THE TRAILHEAD

From I-70, take exit 19 for Fruita. Drive south on CO 340 about 1.3 miles to Kingsview Road. Turn right and drive another 1.2 miles to the turnoff to Devils Canyon. Turn left and drive to the big parking lot 0.2 mile down this dirt road to the left. There are vault toilets at the trailhead. **GPS:** N39 08.39' / W108 45.36'

THE HIKE

The Black Ridge Canyons Wilderness area was designated by Congress on October 5, 2000, and signed into law by President Bill Clinton on October 24, 2000. The wilderness shares its eastern border with the Colorado National Monument. The Black Ridge Canyons area includes the second-largest collection of arches in the country outside of Arches National Park. Access to the arches is via a long trail or a rough 4WD road, then a hike. The grandeur of this area can also be seen on an easier hike into Devils Canyon. If you ask how the canyon got its name, locals will simply state: "It's hotter than Hell!"

Devils Canyon lies on the northeastern edge of the Uncompahgre Plateau. Uncompahgre roughly means "rocks that make the water red" in the Ute language. About 300 million years ago, forces pushed ancient (over 1.7 billion years old) "basement" rock upward to form Uncompahgria, the forerunner of today's Uncompahgre Plateau.

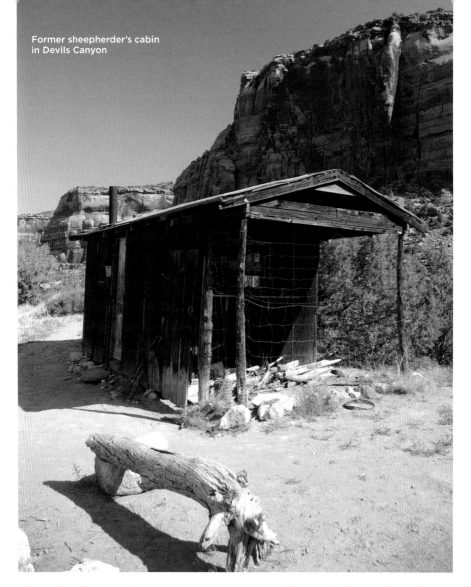
Former sheepherder's cabin in Devils Canyon

About 65 million years later, Uncompahgria had eroded to a plain barely above the level of an inland sea. A delta or floodplain collected red sand on the coastal plain. As the climate changed, the sea receded and windblown sand filled the area. Visualize tall buff- and salmon-colored dunes, like those in Great Sand Dunes National Park and Preserve.

Then the climate changed again, becoming moister, and streams began to flow across the area. Conglomerate comprised of mud and pebbles formed, as did other sand deposits. Over the millennia other seas and dunes covered these sediments, and under great pressure the dunes and conglomerate became rock. The Kayenta Formation of sandstone and conglomerate forms a caprock, or hard-to-erode sandstone, that protects the old dunes, now known as Wingate sandstone. The red floodplain sand changed into the Chinle Formation. Cliffs of Wingate sandstone tower 100 to 200 feet into the sky in Devils Canyon. Look around at the cliffs and try to find the elephant's tail, the coke bottles or ovens, and the tiki head formations eroded by the elements.

This area is harsh and wild. Temperatures soar in the summer, creating an oven effect. In winter, temperatures can drop below freezing. Desert bighorn sheep and mountain lions live here. An interpretive sign near the trailhead explains ways to watch wildlife without disturbing them. Bighorn sheep are especially affected by humans and pets during lambing season, from February through May. Please watch and enjoy from a distance, and keep your dog next to you! The cliffs shelter peregrine falcons—watch for these beautiful birds of prey.

Another area resident that is very fragile is the crypto, a black lumpy growth on the sand. This interesting combination of green algae, bacteria, fungi, lichens, mosses, and cyanobacteria holds the sandy soil together so other plants may grow.

The hike starts out on a road closed to public motorized vehicles. The first part is relatively flat, with sparse vegetation of rabbitbrush, sagebrush, some thorny plants, and a few hardy junipers. After traveling along several roads, the hike turns onto a singletrack trail. A few places require careful observation to find the cairns that mark the route. The cliffs of the canyon loom ahead. Drop into a creek bed and follow it for a little while among cottonwood and ash trees and some tamarisk. Do not hike here if there are thunderstorms anywhere in the area, in case of flash floods.

At the start of the long loop, the trail climbs steeply to the right out of the creek bottom. As you hike along, look back down into the canyon bottom to your left to see black rock walls with shiny mica and lots of lichen. These rocks are the "basement" rocks of Uncompahgria. On the right, sandstone cliffs are a colorful parfait of yellow and pink (think ice cream). Continue climbing through black rocks, mica, and white quartz. The trail traverses the Chinle Formation at the base of the cliffs, undulating across many little creek gullies. Look to the right into each little amphitheater for alcoves or other interesting rock features. The buzz of cicadas and lyrical song of the canyon wren may fill the air.

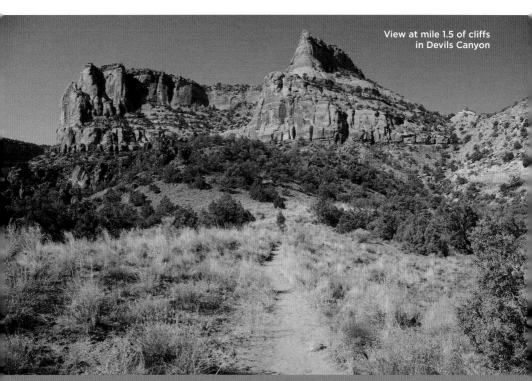

View at mile 1.5 of cliffs in Devils Canyon

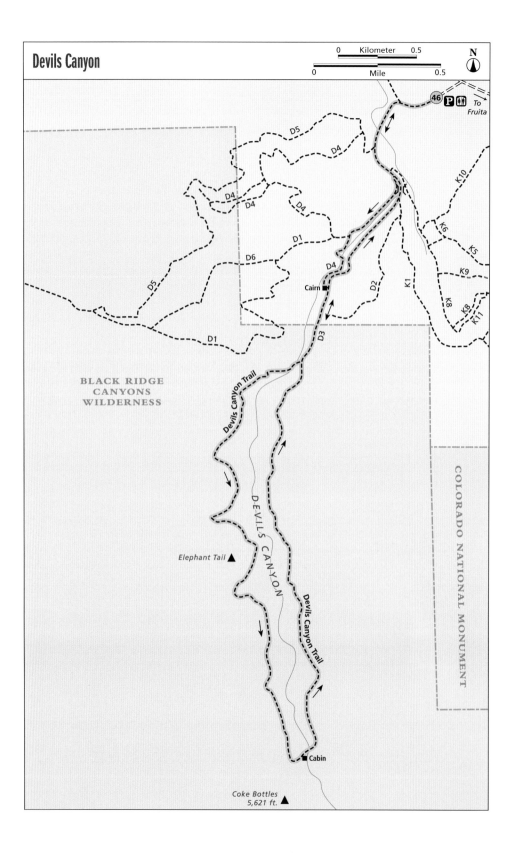

Devils Canyon

0 — Kilometer — 0.5
0 — Mile — 0.5

N

46 🅿 🚻 To
Fruita

D5
D4
D4
D4
D4
D1
D6
D4
Cairn ■
D2
K1
D5
D1
D3
K10
K6
K5
K9
K8
K8
K11

**BLACK RIDGE
CANYONS
WILDERNESS**

Devils Canyon Trail

D E V I L S   C A N Y O N

Elephant Tail ▲

Devils Canyon Trail

COLORADO NATIONAL MONUMENT

■ Cabin

Coke Bottles
5,621 ft. ▲

Domesticated sheep once grazed in Devils Canyon. At the south end of the loop, an old sheepherder's cabin still stands. The cabin provides a little shade and a great place for lunch. To finish the loop the trail drops, crosses the creek, then climbs to the bench above. Again the trail undulates across many little dry creek gullies. Near the close of the loop is a great view of the Grand Valley and the Book Cliffs to the north. A little farther downstream, continue along the creek bed to add variety to your hike and another mini loop back to the trailhead.

MILES AND DIRECTIONS

0.0 Start at the Devils Canyon Trailhead kiosk with bulletin boards. Elevation: 4,580 feet.

0.15 Come to a trail junction. Turn left and continue down the dirt road (Trail D1), which is closed to public motorized vehicles.

0.2 Stop and read the bulletin board, containing interesting area information.

0.4 Come to the trail junction with Trail D5. Turn left onto Trail D1 and follow the dirt road, passing any singletrack trails.

0.5 Reach a junction with multiple trails. Turn right here onto Trail D1 and follow the dirt road. You'll return via the left road. GPS: N39 08.14' / W108 45.54'

0.8 Come to a trail junction. Turn left here onto Trail D4. When you reach a wash, look carefully for rocks and cairns and cross the wash.

1.1 Look carefully for cairns as the trail drops about 60 feet into the canyon to the left. GPS: N39 07.77' / W108 45.84'. When you reach the creek bed, cross the creek, turn right onto Trail D3, and travel upstream. (**Note:** During thunderstorms, do not enter in case of flash floods!)

1.2 Reach the wilderness boundary sign, which is off to your right.

1.4 Reach the start of the loop. Turn right onto Trail D3. Cross the creek and head steeply uphill. The trail meanders past various amphitheaters and cliffs, and up and down little gullies.

3.7 Reach the south end of the loop at the old sheepherder's cabin. Elevation: 5,200 feet. GPS: N39 06.21' / W108 45.93'. This is a great lunch spot. Find the trail on the north side of the cabin to finish the loop. The trail drops into Devils Creek, then follows the bank on the east side.

5.5 The trail drops back down into Devils Creek and starts to retrace the route on which you came (same as mile 1.4).

5.8 Come to a trail junction (same as mile 1.1). You came into the canyon via the left trail. For more variety on the return trip, stay to the right in the creek bed on Trail D3 (unless there's danger of flash flood) and make another mini loop back to the trail junction at mile 0.5 above.

6.2 Arrive at a trail junction. Take the left trail, still D3, which climbs out of the creek bed on a slickrock ledge to avoid a tight spot, then drops back down to the creek.

6.3 At a trail junction with a road, turn left and walk down the road across a little wooden bridge.

6.4 Come to a trail junction (same as 0.5 mile). Go straight on Trail D1 to return to the trailhead. Trail D1 to the left is the way you walked into the canyon. Return on either trail.

6.9 Arrive back at the trailhead.

47 BIG DOMINGUEZ CANYON

WHY GO?

The Big Dominguez Canyon Trail wanders up a beautiful canyon cut in the side of the Uncompahgre Plateau. Desert bighorn sheep were reintroduced here in 1983 and 1985; watch rocky areas and cliff tops for them. Ancient people have traveled through the canyon for at least 1,500 years. Keep your eyes open for (but hands off) petroglyphs pecked in boulders along the trail. Remains of an old mine straddle the trail 6 miles from the parking lot. This red sandstone canyon is part of the Dominguez Canyon Wilderness, designated by Congress in March 2009.

THE RUNDOWN

Start: From the Bridgeport Trailhead
Distance: 13.0 miles out and back (turn around sooner for shorter hikes)
Approximate hiking time: 5.5 to 8.5 hours
Difficulty: Difficult due to distance; shorter, moderate hikes available
Elevation gain: 680 feet, plus some small undulations
Seasons: Best in spring and fall; summer can be very hot
Trail surface: Dirt trail, rocky in a few areas
Other trail users: Equestrians
Canine compatibility: Dogs must be on leash
Fees and permits: None
Map: USGS Triangle Mesa
Trail contacts: Bureau of Land Management, Dominguez-Escalante National Conservation Area, 2465 S. Townsend Ave., Montrose; (970) 240-5367; www.blm.gov/co/st/en/nca/denca.html
Other: Plans have been in the works to reroute the trail from its current location along the railroad tracks to a safer alternative. Check the website or call the BLM office to check current status. Be sure to read the visitor information at the trailhead and follow all safety recommendations regarding hiking near the railroad tracks. (**Note for backpackers:** If you camp along the Gunnison River, please camp in designated campsites. The first part of Big Dominguez Canyon [to about 4 miles from the parking lot] and Little Dominguez Canyon [to the south end of the Rambo property] are day-use only and closed to camping. Please use Leave No Trace techniques and camp at least 200 feet away from small streams. Big Dominguez Creek is dry part of the year, the creek is not always near the trail, and the water, when available, must be treated. Bring your own water—one gallon per person per day is recommended, plus a gallon per day for your dog.)

FINDING THE TRAILHEAD

From the junction of CO 92 and US 50 in Delta, drive 19.2 miles north on US 50 to Bridgeport Road. Turn left onto Bridgeport Road and drive 3.3 miles to the dead end, where there's a parking lot but no facilities. The trailhead is on the left (south) side of the parking lot.

From Grand Junction, drive south on US 50 to Bridgeport Road, near mile marker 52. Turn right onto Bridgeport Road; drive 3.3 miles to the parking lot at the dead end. No facilities. **GPS:** N38 50.95' / W108 22.30'

THE HIKE

On March 30, 2009, President Barack Obama signed legislation designating the Dominguez-Escalante National Conservation Area (NCA) and the Dominguez Canyon Wilderness area. Encompassing 209,610 acres of beautiful canyon country carved out of the eastern edge of the Uncompahgre Plateau, the NCA designation will conserve and protect these lands for wildlife, flora, and future human generations. Public meetings and discussions held over three years set the stage for the legislation. The lands are managed by the Bureau of Land Management, and the agency is tasked with creating a resource management plan to provide for the long-term protection and management of the NCA and wilderness. A citizens' advisory committee has been established to aid in the process. The lands are withdrawn from mining and mineral leasing, but grazing, access to inholdings, control of invasive species, fire prevention, and existing water rights protection are still allowed. The Dominguez Canyon Wilderness consists of 66,280 acres within the NCA.

Long before the Spanish and white settlers arrived, Native Americans wandered these western canyons hunting game and collecting plants, successfully living in the arid climate. These groups arrived perhaps as far back as 6500 BC. Over time, people living around the Uncompahgre Plateau in western Colorado borrowed ideas from their neighbors, the Fremont and the Ancestral Puebloans, and incorporated them into their culture while maintaining a unique way of living. Archaeologists describe their lifestyle as the Uncompahgre Complex, or Gateway Tradition. The petroglyph panel by the BLM's ARCHAEOLOGICAL SITE sign, located along the trail, is categorized as Uncompahgre style, which existed for about 2,000 years, between 1000 BC and AD 1000. The figures on the rock were pecked or carved into it, typically with a bone or an antler. The Uncompahgre style differs from the Fremont style found farther north in Colorado and Utah. Fremont rock art typically uses huge-bodied figures to depict heroes or supernatural beings. The figures in Big Dominguez Canyon tend to be smaller and more humanlike. Bears are common in the Uncompahgre style, and one is apparent on the panel you'll see. Bighorn sheep figures are plentiful. Unfortunately, a few modern folks have defaced parts of the rock art panels in the area—notably with words and a spaceship. Please respect this ancient art and do not touch. Oils from our hands promote deterioration. Ute people, who later occupied these canyons, pecked human-like figures riding horses and other shapes into another rock.

Petroglyph panels throughout western Colorado indicate that these early inhabitants hunted bighorn sheep. Over time, with westward expansion in the 1800s and early 1900s, bighorn were extirpated from this area. The Colorado Division of Wildlife reintroduced the desert bighorn (*Ovis canadensis nelsoni*) to the Big Dominguez area in 1983 and 1985. Slightly smaller and lighter in color than their cousins, the Rocky Mountain bighorn, they live in small groups in arid canyons, using the rocks and cliffs for protection from predators. Ewes (females) and lambs stay together, while the rams create their own herds. They eat sparse desert vegetation, from which they gather water, and drink at water holes or creeks every few days. They even eat cacti, using hooves and horns to remove the spines. During summer's hot days they find shady shelter. At other times they eat during the day and rest at night. Rams grow spiral horns with a new ring emerging each year. Horns can reach 30 inches long with a base circumference of 15 inches. Ewes' horns are 12- to 17-inch spikes. Weighing up to 200 pounds, the rams win mating privileges

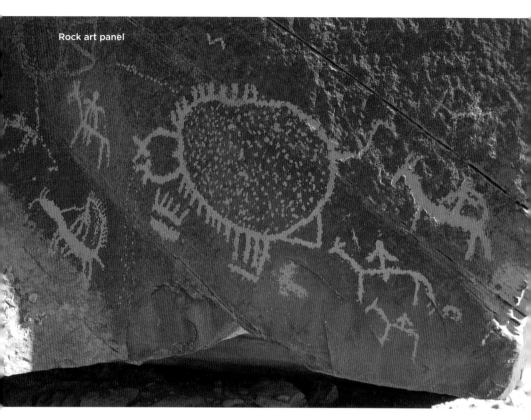
Rock art panel

through head-butting contests with each other. Mating season typically occurs in late fall, with lambs born in April and May.

Watch for bighorn sheep on the canyon rims. If they are down in the canyon, be sure to keep your dog under control. Bighorn sheep have been adversely affected by human activities, from loss of habitat to overhunting to contracting diseases from domestic sheep and cattle.

The trail up Big Dominguez Canyon sometimes looks like a road—it was. Miners built the road to access the uranium mine at mile 6.1. Not much else is known about this mine, although it was probably active during the region's uranium boom between 1940 and the 1960s.

This hike takes you to the junction with the Cactus Park Trail, but turn around sooner if you'd like. The canyon contains many beautiful features, from red rock cliffs with interesting formations to various desert plants to old mining remains. Take keeping your dog on a leash seriously here: Between the possibility of stumbling upon artifacts of the ancestral groups who once lived here and the critters they might encounter, it's a no-brainer.

Water can be in short supply seasonally, so bring more than you think you'll need.

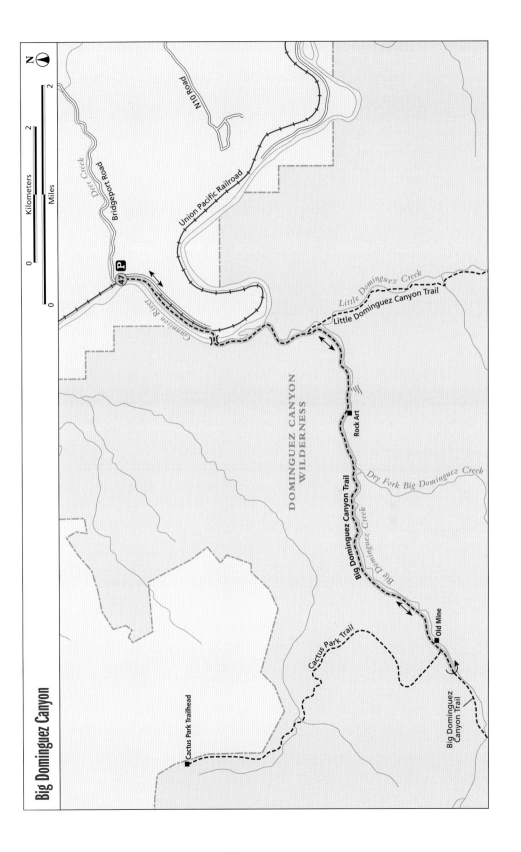

Big Dominguez Canyon

N

Kilometers
0   2

Miles
0   2

Deer Creek

Bridgeport Road

P 47

Gunnison River

Union Pacific Railroad

N10 Road

Little Dominguez Creek

Little Dominguez Canyon Trail

DOMINGUEZ CANYON WILDERNESS

Rock Art

Dry Fork Big Dominguez Creek

Big Dominguez Canyon Trail

Big Dominguez Creek

Cactus Park Trail

Cactus Park Trailhead

Old Mine

Big Dominguez Canyon Trail

MILES AND DIRECTIONS

0.0 Start at the trailhead to the left (south) of the parking lot. Elevation: 4,720 feet. The first 0.3 mile travels along the railroad tracks. If a train is present, wait until it passes. If the train is stopped, wait until the train moves before crossing at the one designated crossing. Delays can be up to 1 hour.

0.3 Cross the tracks at the designated railroad crossing.

1.0 Walk past the trail to the first bridge on the right. This bridge is private. Continue straight ahead, then turn right on the trail to the interpretive signs and the second bridge. GPS: N38 50.19' / W108 22.81'. Cross the Gunnison River and turn left.

1.7 Arrive at the trailhead bulletin board near the wilderness boundary.

2.3 Arrive at a trail junction. Turn right to hike up Big Dominguez Canyon. The two-track trail to the left goes up Little Dominguez Canyon. GPS: N38 49.34' / W108 22.75'

3.1 A side trail marked by cairns heads to the left to a big waterfall (when Big Dominguez Creek has water in it).

3.25 Reach an archaeological site. Please take only pictures; touching, defacing, or tracing any rock art is prohibited. Please leave the petroglyphs intact for others to enjoy. These sites are sacred to Native Americans. (**Option:** For a shorter, moderate hike, turn around here and return the way you came.)

3.7 The trail curves left over rocks—follow the cairns. In another 0.1 mile the trail passes through a tunnel created by two huge rocks leaning against each other.

4.0 Reach the approximate end of the day-use area.

4.6 The trail climbs up black lava rock.

6.1 The trail passes by the remains of a mine. Remember to leave all artifacts for others to enjoy.

6.5 Arrive at the Cactus Park Trail junction. Elevation: 5,400 feet. GPS: N38 48.13' / W108 26.12'. Turn around and return the way you came. Just before this junction is a flat area to the south that is a great lunch spot.

13.0 Arrive back at the parking lot.

48 UPPER ROUBIDEAU AREA LOOP

WHY GO?

This hike explores the upper section of the Roubideau Area, a special part of the Uncompahgre Plateau. First descend on Old Roubideau Trail (Trail 105) from (Gray) Cow Camp to Pool Creek. Aspen trees abound for a beautiful fall hike. After reaching Pool Creek Trail (Trail 113), the trail ascends along tiny Pool Creek through forests of aspen and spruce-fir. The point-to-point hike ends at Pool Creek Trailhead, or you can loop back to Old Roubideau Trailhead via the Parallel Trail (Trail 139). The trail disappears in numerous places, so only attempt this hike if you have the navigation skills necessary to take on some challenging route-finding.

THE RUNDOWN

Start: From the Old Roubideau (Trail 105) Trailhead
Distance: 8.6-mile loop
Approximate hiking time: 3.5 to 5.5 hours
Difficulty: Difficult due to elevation gain on the return and route-finding challenges
Elevation gain/loss: 1,510-foot gain / 1,510-foot loss
Seasons: Best from June through Oct
Trail surface: Dirt trail
Other trail users: Equestrians and hunters (in season)
Canine compatibility: Dogs must be under control. Elk bed and graze along this trail. Cattle also graze in this area. Best to keep dogs leashed to avoid conflicts with wildlife and cattle.

Fees and permits: None. Group size limit: No more than 15 people per group with a maximum combination of 25 people and pack or saddle animals in any one group.
Map: USGS Antone Spring
Trail contacts: Uncompahgre National Forest, Ouray Ranger District, Montrose; (970) 240-5300; www.fs.usda.gov/gmug
Other: No facilities at the trailhead. The cow camp is an active operation and cattle graze in the area. Please respect the range permittee's rights. The access road closes in winter 23.5 miles from the trailhead. The road is used by snowmobiles. The trail is neither maintained nor marked for winter use. Bring your own water or water purification system.

FINDING THE TRAILHEAD

From Montrose, head west on CO 90 from its intersection with US 550. In 2 miles CO 90 turns left. In 1 more mile CO 90 turns right. At Oak Grove Elementary, another 0.9 mile, CO 90 turns left. In another 4.5 miles, stay to the left on CO 90 heading to Nucla, by a sign that reads NO WINTER MAINTENANCE. You are now on CR 90, an all-weather gravel road, but it might be full of washboards. The Uncompahgre National Forest boundary is in another 12 miles, where CR 90 becomes FR 540. There's a T intersection (FR 402) 2.8 miles farther. Go straight ahead, staying on FR 540/FR 402 toward Columbine Pass. At the next fork, 0.7 mile farther up the road, take the right branch (FR 402/Divide Road). (Do *not* go to Nucla.) Continue on FR 402, past several roads coming in from either the right or left, for 7 miles. Turn right onto FR 546 (East Bull). Go right at the fork with FR 547 at mile 0.75. In another 0.25 mile, arrive at the cow camp. Park off the dirt road. **GPS:** N38 22.21' / W108 14.34'

THE HIKE

The Uncompahgre Plateau extends for about 100 miles, running north–south from the San Miguel River to the Colorado River. Rising like a submarine west of Montrose, the plateau is quite rugged. It's a land of multiple uses: hiking trails, 4WD roads, and a long mountain bike route—the Tabeguache Trail. Ute Indians hunted this area, as local names attest. Tabeguache means "place where the snow melts first." As noted in a journal kept by the 1776 Dominquez-Escalante expedition, the Utes called the river to the east the Ancapagari (which, according to our interpreter, means Red Lake), because they say that near its source there is a spring of red-colored water, hot and ill-tasting.

The Roubideau *(ROO-bi-doe)* Area was created by the 1993 Colorado Wilderness Bill. Because the headwaters of its creeks start outside its designated boundaries, Congress denied it full wilderness protection. Water rights in Colorado create many hotly contested arguments and lawsuits. To avoid potential conflicts, the Roubideau Area is managed as wilderness, except its water. Some people call it a baby wilderness. The area is closed to motorized and mechanized use, logging, and mining.

This hike lets you wander in the cool highlands of the Uncompahgre Plateau, away from the bustle of Delta and Montrose. The Old Roubideau Trail switchbacks down to the Goddard Creek drainage, crosses the creek, then climbs up to wander through gently sloping aspen forest. Elk bed and graze in the lush grasses. Some aspens bear scars of carved names and dates; this practice, which exposes aspen to various diseases, should be avoided. Approaching the Pool Creek drainage, the trail drops, with views down into Roubideau Creek. Cattle enjoy the plentiful grasses in this section, and their trails go every which way. Upon reaching Pool Creek, a 0.4-mile jaunt downhill (left) on the Pool Creek Trail brings you to Roubideau Creek, a pleasant place for lunch.

The hike up Pool Creek Trail gains 1,271 feet in 2.7 miles. The trail is overgrown in some areas, but it stays on the north side of the creek. Notice the difference in vegetation. The south side of the creek is sunny and grassy, while the north-facing side is steep, cool, and moist, with dark spruce-fir forest dominating. At Pool Creek Trailhead, return to Old Roubideau Trailhead via the Parallel Trail (Trail 139), which you intersect at the Pool Creek Trailhead. Or you can meet your shuttle vehicle, if you've chosen the point-to-point option (see below).

MILES AND DIRECTIONS

0.0 Start at the cow camp where the dirt road Ys. Elevation: 9,440 feet. Walk straight ahead on the road to the right of the old buildings. (The right fork dead-ends.) About 260 feet down the road, look to your right for the brown carsonite post that indicates the trail is open to hikers and equestrians. The Old Roubideau Trail (Trail 105) starts at this post, which is easy to miss, so be observant.

0.5 Reach the Roubideau Area boundary. The trail switchbacks down into Goddard Creek.

1.25 Cross Goddard Creek.

1.9 Cross another drainage. The trail contours along a hill through pleasant aspen forest.

Facing page: **Old Roubideau Trail through aspen forest**

0　　　Kilometer　　1

0　　　　　Mile　　　　1

N

ROUBIDEAU AREA

Trail 155

FR 546

48

FR 402

FR 547

Cobb Cow Camp

Old Roubideau Trail / Trail 105

Goddard Creek

FR 508

North Divide Road

UNCOMPAHGRE NATIONAL FOREST

Parallel Trail / Trail 139

Pool Creek Trail / Trail 113

Pool Creek

9,021 ft.

Roubideau Creek

To FR 402

FR 402

Tabeguache Creek

Pool Creek Trailhead (end of optional shuttle hike)

To Montrose

2.3　The trail curves left but isn't obvious. Look for blazes on trees to the right to find the faint trail. GPS: N38 21.91' / W108 12.76'

2.8　The trail splits. Turn left and drop to the southeast. It curves to the south, then turns east. Arrive at a tall clump of Gambel oak. GPS: N38 21.88' / W108 12.35'. The trail heads uphill slightly to the left, then disappears. Head east cross-country until you intersect a trail. Turn right. Cross the flatter bench area; with some luck, find a trail and continue downhill to the right. If you lose this trail, find the easiest way to walk down to Pool Creek.

3.3　Reach a T intersection with the Pool Creek Trail (Trail 113). GPS: N38 21.78' / W108 12.30' (*Option:* Turn left here for an 0.8-mile out-and-back spur to Roubideau Creek.) Turn right here to head uphill toward the Pool Creek Trailhead.

3.9　The trail crosses a gooey gully, which can be a little tricky. You might need to walk down the dry creek a few feet to find an easy place to walk across.

5.3　Cross a little water seep coming from under a boulder to the right side of the trail.

5.6　Arrive at the Pool Creek Trailhead. GPS: N38 20.57' / W108 14.07'. Turn right and walk a few steps to the access road, where you go straight ahead onto Parallel Trail (Trail 139), also called the Tabeguache Trail on the sign. This trail is multiple use.

6.0　Cross a road and head straight ahead.

7.75　Arrive at FR 546 (East Bull). Turn right and walk down this road. Turn right when the road forks at FR 547.

8.6　Arrive back at your vehicle and the trailhead near the cow camp.

OPTION

For a shorter point-to-point hike with your dog—5.6 miles—leave a shuttle vehicle at the Pool Creek Trailhead. Turn right off FR 402 at the 5.4-mile mark, where the sign reads POOL CREEK TRAILHEAD. Do not turn right at 3.6 miles at Pool Creek FR 548. The trailhead and shuttle drop-off is 0.2 mile in. GPS: N38 20.58' / W108 14.07'. Park one car here and drive the second back to FR 402 and turn right, resuming with the directions to the Old Roubideau Trailhead at the cow camp, above. Approximate hiking time: 2.5 to 4 hours.

49 JUD WIEBE MEMORIAL TRAIL

WHY GO?

The Jud Wiebe Trail climbs up and across the hill north of Telluride between Butcher and Cornet Creeks. The loop is short, but it has its steep moments in the very precipitous mountains surround Telluride. This trail is a good early-season, south-facing hike, and a great warm-up for longer, more-difficult trails in the area. From various points Bridal Veil and Ingram Falls, the ski area, spectacular craggy peaks, and the town below come into view. The trail was completed in 1987 in memory of Jud Wiebe, a Forest Service employee who designed the trail.

THE RUNDOWN

Start: From the trailhead at the top of Aspen Street
Distance: 2.7-mile loop
Approximate hiking time: 1.5 to 2.5 hours
Difficulty: Difficult due to some steeper sections
Elevation gain: 1,150 feet
Seasons: Best from June to mid-Oct
Trail surface: Dirt road and dirt trail
Other trail users: Equestrians (some trail sections), mountain bikers, hunters (in season)

Canine compatibility: Dogs must be on leash
Fees and permits: None
Maps: USGS Telluride; Nat Geo Trails Illustrated 141 Telluride/Silverton/Ouray/Lake City; Latitude 40° Telluride, Silverton, Ouray
Trail contacts: Uncompahgre National Forest, Norwood Ranger District, Norwood; (970) 327-4261; www.fs.usda.gov/gmug

FINDING THE TRAILHEAD

Find a parking place in Telluride or park in the free parking area across from the visitor center and take the Galloping Goose shuttle into downtown. Walk to Aspen Street (0.4 mile east of the visitor center) and uphill to the top of the street. The west end of the trail starts here. **GPS: N37 56.45' / W107 48.71'**

The other option is to walk to Oak Street and head uphill to the top of the street to the east end of the trail. **GPS: N37 56.42' / W107 48.66'.** Walk along Tomboy Road to the pipe gate and bulletin board and turn left. The hike description starts at the Aspen Street trailhead.

THE HIKE

Telluride, an old mining town snuggled at the mouth of a box canyon, is experiencing a second wave of success. The first came with the mining frenzy in the 1870s, as miners swarmed over the rugged San Juan Mountains looking for gold, silver, and other precious metals. Today the spectacular mountain scenery has attracted writers and artisans, and the ski area (opened in 1972) has created a new building frenzy.

The San Juan Mountains were born of volcanic fire and ash and sculpted by the scraping of glaciers. Eruptions started about 35 million years ago and lasted more than 13 million years. During one phase the volcanoes were so explosive that they often collapsed into themselves, forming calderas. Hot mineralized water oozed up through cracks and faults underground and around the calderas, leaving behind gold, silver, zinc, copper, and lead. Within the last 2 million years, various glaciers covered the area. The San Miguel glacier carved the U-shaped valley floor in which Telluride sits. Spectacular Bridal Veil Falls, at the head of the box canyon, drops 365 feet from a hanging valley.

In 1875 John Fallon discovered ore rich in zinc, lead, copper, iron, silver, and gold. Nearby, the Union Mine also started recovering rich ore. J. B. Ingram discovered that Fallon's claim and the Union were bigger than the legal limit by about 500 feet. He laid claim to the area in between, calling it the Smuggler. The Smuggler's ore contained 800 ounces of silver and 18 ounces of gold per ton. The Union and Smuggler merged and became one of the major producers in Telluride. The Tomboy Mine, about 5 miles up Tomboy Road, started operations in 1880 and continued until 1928. In 1897 it sold for $2 million!

The mountains around Telluride contain over 350 miles of tunnels (think San Francisco to Los Angeles), some going all the way through the mountains to the Million Dollar Highway between Ouray and Silverton. The town itself was established as Columbia in 1878, when 80 acres were laid out and incorporated. It became the county seat of newly established San Miguel County in 1883. The post office, however, had a problem getting mail to Columbia, Colorado, often sending it to Columbia, California, instead. A name change was inevitable. Telluride, the name of a gold-bearing tellurium compound, was chosen for the new moniker in the 1880s.

The rich ore-bearing peaks surrounding Telluride hold a lurking danger—the white death. Three hundred inches of annual snowfall combined with steep terrain result in fairly regular avalanches. In 1902 an avalanche demolished part of the Liberty Bell Mine (farther up the road you'll hike down), killing seven men and injuring several others. While the rescue party was recovering the bodies, a second avalanche swept through. The rescuers escaped without additional injuries or deaths. However, as they made their way back to Telluride, a third avalanche roared down, killing three and injuring five.

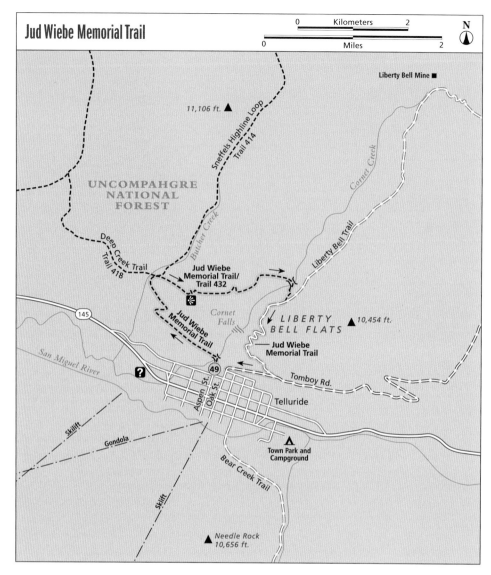

Jud Wiebe Memorial Trail

Liberty Bell Mine ■

11,106 ft. ▲

Sneffels Highline Loop
Trail 414

UNCOMPAHGRE
NATIONAL
FOREST

Cornet Creek

Butcher Creek

Liberty Bell Trail

Deep Creek Trail
Trail 418

Jud Wiebe
Memorial Trail/
Trail 432

*Cornet
Falls*

LIBERTY
BELL FLATS   ▲10,454 ft.

Jud Wiebe
Memorial Trail

Jud Wiebe
Memorial Trail

145

San Miguel River

❓

49

Tomboy Rd.

Telluride

Aspen St.

Oak St.

Skilift

Gondola

Skilift

▲
Town Park and
Campground

Bear Creek Trail

▲ Needle Rock
10,656 ft.

0 Kilometers 2

0 Miles 2

N

In one winter (1905–1906) with unusually heavy snows, one hundred people died in avalanches in the area. Snow isn't the only thing to go sliding around Telluride. In 1914 Cornet Creek overflowed, sending eight feet of mud down Colorado Avenue, Telluride's main street.

The Jud Wiebe Trail (Trail 432) starts at the bulletin board at the top of Aspen Street. Continue uphill to the bridge over Cornet Creek and turn left. The trail climbs steadily and after a couple of switchbacks comes to a junction with the Deep Creek Trail (Trail 418). The Jud Wiebe Trail takes off to the right and continues climbing.

You soon arrive at a viewpoint, locally called Breakfast Rock, with views of Telluride and the surrounding lofty peaks. A few more switchbacks lead to an open area with more fantastic views. To the west is the San Miguel River, heading downstream along a glacial moraine. You might even catch a glimpse of the La Sal Mountains near Moab, Utah. The San Miguel Mountains, home to three 14,000-foot peaks, line up along the horizon. To the south and east, peaks rise dramatically and the gondola climbs the hill from town along ski runs. Ingram and Bridal Veil Falls tumble from cliffs to the east.

The trail meanders down through a lush aspen forest and crosses a bridge over Cornet Creek. Climbing further, the trail then intersects the nonmotorized road to Liberty Bell Mine. This flat area once served as the local playing field for baseball games between miners and town residents. Turn right and follow the steep road down past the town water tank to Tomboy Road. Turn right and walk down the road to the top of Oak Street and back to town.

MILES AND DIRECTIONS

0.0 Start at the trailhead bulletin board at the top of Aspen Street. Elevation: 8,880 feet. In a few feet, turn left and walk across the bridge that crosses Cornet Creek.

0.7 Reach a junction with Deep Creek Trail (Trail 418) and Sneffels Highline Loop (Trail 414). Turn right to continue on the Jud Wiebe Trail (Trail 432).

1.1 Come to an open meadow and slope with fantastic views.

1.6 Cross the bridge over Cornet Creek.

1.7 Reach the junction of Jud Wiebe Trail and a nonmotorized road, which leads to Liberty Bell Mine. GPS: N37 56.70' / W107 48.36'. Turn right and walk down the road.

2.2 The town water tank is on the right.

2.6 Reach the junction of Jud Wiebe Trail and Tomboy Road, which leads to Tomboy Mine. At a pipe gate and bulletin board, turn right and walk down Tomboy Road.

2.7 Arrive at the Oak Street trailhead. Elevation: 8,920 feet. Return to wherever you parked your vehicle.

50 CASCADE AND PORTLAND LOOP

WHY GO?

This pleasant hike loops along Cascade Falls Trail and Portland Trail in Ouray's Amphitheater area. The trail offers nice views of surrounding mountains, jagged cliffs, and mining operations. The hike includes the trail to Upper Cascade Falls. This spur trail switchbacks its way past cliffs for great views of the surrounding mountains. After enjoying the falls, you can walk to the Chief Ouray Mine's bunkhouse.

THE RUNDOWN

Start: From the trailhead at the top of the Amphitheater Campground
Distance: 6.8-mile lollipop (with a moderate 3.6-mile loop option)
Approximate hiking time: 2.5 to 6 hours
Difficulty: Most difficult due to the steep trail to the upper falls and bunkhouse
Elevation gain: 1,920-foot gain (including undulations)
Seasons: Best from May through Oct
Trail surface: Dirt trail, steep and narrow to Upper Cascade Falls
Other trail users: Equestrians, mountain bikers, hunters (in season) on lower parts of the loop

Canine compatibility: Dogs must be on leash. Skip the upper section of the Cascade Falls Trail, which narrows considerably.
Fees and permits: None
Maps: USGS Ouray; Nat Geo Trails Illustrated 141 Telluride/Silverton/Ouray/Lake City; Latitude 40° Telluride, Silverton, Ouray
Trail contacts: Uncompahgre National Forest, Ouray Ranger District, Montrose; (970) 240-5300; www.fs.usda.gov/gmug
Other: There is an outhouse in the campground. Bring your own water.

FINDING THE TRAILHEAD

 From Ouray, drive south out of town on US 550 to the entrance road to the Amphitheater Campground. Turn left onto the campground road and drive 1.1 miles on the paved road to the trailhead at the top of the campground. **GPS:** N38 01.31' / W107 39.59'

THE HIKE

The Ouray area is a jumble of geologic history, from ancient bedrock to glacially carved features. Leadville limestone formed in a sea over 325 million years ago. Reddish rock remains from the erosion of Uncompahgria, part of the Ancestral Rockies. Another sea helped to form Dakota sandstone. Then the explosions of the San Juan volcanoes started, leaving deep deposits of ash and breccia (broken rocks) called San Juan tuff, of which the Amphitheater seen from the Portland Trail is a good example. Hot mineralized water deposited gold, silver, and other metals in the Leadville limestone during the volcanic era. Ice age glaciers carved craggy peaks and scoured the valley north from Ouray, leaving the moraine by Ridgway.

This combination of geologic events produced a gold and silver bonanza for prospectors. On a hunting and fishing expedition in the summer of 1875, A. J. Staley and Logan

Whitlock meandered up the Uncompahgre River to the headwall by the current site of Ouray and discovered veins of ore, which were subsequently named the Trout and the Fisherman lodes. In August of that same year, A. W. Begole and Jack Eckles found the Cedar and Clipper lodes where the hot springs pool is today. As hopeful miners arrived in town, Captain Cline and Judge Long laid out a town site that they called Uncompahgre City.

The following spring, Chief Ouray and his wife, Chipeta, arrived in town to talk with the townspeople. Ouray was chief of the Tabeguache band of Utes, who lived in the Ouray-Montrose area. Half Ute and half Apache, Ouray rose to power thanks to his skill as a negotiator. He was friendly to white interlopers, realizing that fighting could decimate his people. He hoped that through negotiations, his people would survive and perhaps keep some of the land they had called home for hundreds of years. The latter did not happen. The Utes were organized into seven different bands, each with its own leader. Because of his oratorical skill, the US government regarded Ouray as spokesman for all Utes, a status not always acknowledged by other Ute chiefs. Over time Chief Ouray gained much respect among the people who had usurped his ancestral home, and Uncompahgre City was renamed Ouray in his honor.

Ouray continued to grow; its mines mainly produced silver. The transportation of ore and supplies was a struggle for many years. In 1887 the Denver and Rio Grande Railroad finally reached Ouray, adding to its prosperity. The Silver Crash of 1893, which killed many other mining towns, proved a mere burp to Ouray. A gold discovery on Gold Hill northeast of town saved the day.

The Amphitheater

Creek crossing below Upper Cascade Falls

Being surrounded by steep mountains posed occasional problems for Ouray. In July 1909 a downpour filled creek channels with tons of water and debris. Portland Creek, above which part of this hiking loop travels, roared into town, covering the first floor of the Elks Building with mud. It continued into J. J. Mayer's furniture store, carrying carpet rolls and furniture down Main Street.

In wintertime the drive south via Red Mountain Pass is very prone to avalanches, as is witnessed by a marker at one switchback. It commemorates a minister, his two daughters, and three snowplow drivers who met their untimely demise in the "white death."

On the way to the trailhead, stop at the first switchback just south of town. Look to the northeast and you can see the Chief Ouray Mine buildings perched on a shelf in the cliffs. Believe it or not, the trail to Upper Cascade Falls takes you there without the need for ropes.

The hike starts by contouring around a ridge, then above a drainage. The intersection of Upper Cascade Falls Trail (Trail 213) and Portland Trail (Trail 238) is reached in about 0.8 mile. The spur trail to Upper Cascade Falls and the Chief Ouray Mine climbs steeply from the junction, zigzagging its way up a precipitous mountainside. The trail is good, although narrow in a few spots. When you reach a ledge, the walking becomes easier, but it can be dangerous in bad weather. Take time to enjoy the fantastic views. The trail rounds a ridge near some interesting rock outcroppings and drops slightly to Upper Cascade Falls. You can cross Cascade Creek (**Note:** This crossing can be tricky in high water with the falls just downstream) and continue 0.1 mile to explore the old mine bunkhouse and see Ouray far below. The trail past the bunkhouse is not maintained and can be treacherous, so carefully consider whether it's a good fit for you and your dog.

Facing page: Chief Ouray Mine bunkhouse

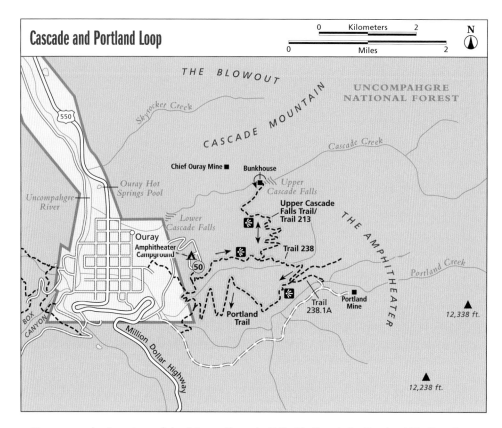

Return to the junction of the Upper Cascade Falls Trail and the Portland Trail and turn left to continue the loop. When crossing the big gully, you can imagine the force of water that races down the steep cliffs. The hike continues through spruce-fir forest and climbs a little ridge to intersect with the Portland Cutoff Trail (Trail 238.1A) to the Portland Mine. Stay to the right on the Portland Trail, enjoy the views into Portland Creek, and continue switchbacking down through a nice forest with aspens. At the next intersection, turn right onto Upper Cascade Falls Trail. After crossing the big gully again, the trail climbs back up to complete the loop and return to the trailhead.

MILES AND DIRECTIONS

0.0   Start at the trailhead at the top of the Amphitheater Campground. Elevation: 8,520 feet.

0.2   Reach a trail junction and trail register. Turn left and head uphill. (You'll return to this junction later.)

0.5   The Lower Cascade Falls Trail (Trail 255) comes in from the left. Continue straight ahead and uphill.

0.8   Reach the junction of the Upper Cascade Falls Trail (Trail 213) and the Portland Trail (Trail 238). GPS: N38 01.35' / W107 39.26'. Turn left onto the Upper Cascade Falls Trail, heading for Upper Cascade Falls and the Chief Ouray Mine bunkhouse. (**Option:** For a shorter, easier hike turn right and follow the Portland Trail. This option will make for a 3.6-mile loop.)

2.0 Round a ridge by some interesting rock formations.

2.2 Reach Upper Cascade Falls. Elevation: 10,000 feet. GPS: N38 01.76' / W107 39.15'

2.4 Arrive at the bunkhouse for the Chief Ouray Mine. Take a look inside, then return the way you came. (***Note:*** The trail beyond is not maintained and can be treacherous.)

2.6 Return to Upper Cascade Falls.

4.0 Arrive back at the junction of the Upper Cascade Falls Trail and the Portland Trail. Turn left onto the Portland Trail to complete the loop.

4.3 Cross a large gully that shows the power of water.

4.6 Reach the junction of the Portland Trail and the Portland Cutoff Trail (Trail 238.1A). GPS: N38 01.24' / W107 38.94'. Turn right to stay on the Portland Trail.

4.7 Enjoy the scenic view.

6.2 Reach a trail junction. The Portland Trail curves right here. The trail to the left goes to the Portland Trailhead. Re-cross the large gully that you crossed higher up.

6.5 Reach a trail junction. Turn right onto the Upper Cascade Falls Trail to return to the trailhead. The trail climbs here.

6.6 Reach the trail junction with the trail register. This junction completes the loop. Turn left; the trailhead is just around the ridge.

6.8 Arrive back at the trailhead.

WHY GO?

This hike makes a loop above Coal Bank Pass via Pass Creek Trail (Trail 500) to the foot of impressive Engineer Mountain, then north on the Engineer Mountain Trail (Trail 508) to return on Coal Creek Trail (Trail 677). The wildflowers are spectacular on many sections of this hike during July and early August. Several places offer great views of the West Needle Mountains in the Weminuche Wilderness to the east and north to the mountains between Silverton and Telluride. The final 1.3 miles of the hike are along US 550 and can be avoided with a car shuttle.

THE RUNDOWN

Start: From the Pass Creek (Trail 500) Trailhead near the top of Coal Bank Pass

Distance: 7.8-mile loop

Approximate hiking time: 3 to 5 hours

Difficulty: Difficult due to elevation gain

Elevation gain: 1,700 feet (including undulations)

Seasons: Best from mid-June through Oct

Trail surface: Dirt trail with some grassy areas, steep in spots

Other trail users: Equestrians, mountain bikers, hunters (in season)

Canine compatibility: Dogs must be under control

Fees and permits: None

Maps: USGS Engineer Mountain; Nat Geo Trails Illustrated 141 Telluride/Silverton/Ouray/Lake City; Latitude 40° Durango and Southwest Colorado

Trail contacts: San Juan National Forest, Columbine Ranger District, Bayfield; (970) 884-2512; www.fs.usda.gov/sanjuan

Other: Bring your own water as not much is easily accessible.

FINDING THE TRAILHEAD

From Silverton, drive south about 13.6 miles on US 550. Turn right just before the top of Coal Bank Pass to enter a gravel parking area where you can access the Pass Creek Trailhead. There is a vault toilet on the east side of the highway at Coal Bank Pass. **GPS:** N37 41.95' / W107 46.71'

THE HIKE

While driving from Silverton to the trailhead, compare the numerous craggy peaks to the south and east with the more-rolling terrain and scattered peaks to the west. Engineer Mountain (12,968 feet) and the area of the hike are readily visible from just south of Molas Pass. Engineer Mountain itself is comprised of sandstone and shale that eroded from part of the Ancestral Rockies called Uncompahgria. These sediments add red color to the peak. The lower slopes are limestone formed from marine sediments in an ancient sea. The rolling hills were lava and ash flows, signs of the volcanic origins of the San Juan Mountains. Glaciers placed the final touches on this area. Engineer Mountain rose above an immense ice cap during more recent ice ages, the last of which only ended about 11,000 years ago.

Across the highway, craggy Twilight Peak is often seen while hiking down the Coal Creek Trail. Although some geologists say coal doesn't exist near Coal Bank Pass, records in Silverton indicate that people found some type of inefficient coal near here and used it for fuel until the coal mines near Durango were discovered.

Engineer Mountain looms large above the surrounding rolling hills. How the mountain was named is not certain, but historians believe the Hayden Survey (1870–1879) coined the name. "Engineer" most likely commemorates a survey engineer versus a railroad engineer. The San Juan region contains two Engineer Mountains, the other located on the Alpine Loop Scenic Byway (4WD) between Ouray and Lake City.

The Pass Creek Trail starts in a field of cornhusk lily, cow parsnip, subalpine larkspur, Indian paintbrush, death camas, geraniums, and columbines. Cornhusk lily (false hellebore) is the large, white-flowered plant with big green leaves resembling cornhusks. Another common name for this member of the lily family is skunk cabbage. The other large plant with clusters of white flowers is cow parsnip, which some people mistakenly call Queen Anne's lace. Both grow in moist areas such as this meadow and are often found with another moisture-loving plant, subalpine larkspur. These three can grow taller than most hikers, forming green walls along the trail. The larkspur is a member of the buttercup family, sporting purple petals with a long spur. Without a close look it can be mistaken for monkshood, which also loves moist areas. Death camas has six joined petals with a yellow band and red stamens. Both death camas and cornhusk lily are poisonous to humans.

The amount and type of flowers change with forest and meadow as you hike along. The trail enters a spruce-fir forest and wanders around little ridges. A little pond surrounded by elephant heads lies in an open meadow at about 1.2 miles. Elephant head, also called little red elephant, is an appropriate name for these pink-to-purple flowers that love boggy areas. The elephant trunk sticks out from the ears as if trumpeting sunny days. Other boggy area plants can be seen along various sections of trail. Globeflowers with their overlapping cream-colored petals, marsh marigolds with their more-separated white petals, king's crowns (ruby flowers), occasional queen's crowns (pink flowers), and Parry's primroses with magenta-to-purple flowers line the trail in wetter areas. After about 2 miles the hills are covered with yellow, rosy, or magenta paintbrush flowers in a profusion of color. As the trees thin, Colorado blue columbine, the state flower, makes a showy appearance. Engineer Mountain towers above the seas of tiny wildflowers like a castle surrounded by its moat.

When you reach the intersection with Engineer Mountain Trail (Trail 508), turn right and follow Engineer Mountain Trail across the open alpine fields. Willows grow here, along with varieties of paintbrush, king's crown, American bistort, Parry's primrose, columbine, elephant head, and alpine avens—all commingled as if a higher power had emptied packages of mixed wildflower seeds.

The trail proceeds north, crossing the head of Coal Creek. Turn right at the marked junction and follow the trail across a little ridge. Just beyond is a trail junction. Turn right, follow the trail through willows, then head down to a saddle. At the saddle the trail disappears in the grasses but is marked by cairns. Turn right and drop down into the Coal Creek drainage, where the trail reappears near a wooden post in the meadow. The flowers aren't as spectacular along Coal Creek, but the occasional views of Twilight Peak are. The trail drops, sometimes steeply, above Coal Creek, then makes several switchbacks down to US 550. If you haven't set up a car shuttle, follow US 550 back to the trailhead. Be sure to put your four-footed friend back on leash.

Flowers and Engineer Mountain

Pass and Coal Creek Loop

SAN JUAN NATIONAL FOREST

MILES AND DIRECTIONS

0.0 Start at the Pass Creek (Trail 500) Trailhead. Elevation: 10,680 feet.

1.2 A little pond is on the left.

1.5 The trail makes a big right switchback.

2.3 Engineer Mountain comes into view, followed by fantastic fields of wildflowers.

2.5 Reach the trail junction with Engineer Mountain Trail (Trail 508). Elevation: 11,660 feet. GPS: N37 42.22' / W107 47.87'. Turn right and follow Engineer Mountain Trail, heading north. (**Note:** A left turn will take you to US 550, south of Coal Bank Pass, in about 4 miles.)

3.3 Reach the top of the Coal Creek drainage. (**Note:** There's a little saddle to the left for a view to the west. Good lunch spot.)

3.5 The trail forks. Turn right onto Coal Creek Trail (Trail 677). (**Note:** You can also go farther north on Engineer Mountain Trail to intersect with the Colorado Trail.)

4.0 The trail rounds a ridge. Just past the top there's a sign on a tree that points to Coal Creek Trail. Just past there is a big cairn. Turn right at the cairn, then go a little downhill and look carefully to the left for the trail through a willow patch. GPS: N37 43.16' / W107 47.53'

4.3 The trail disappears at a saddle in the ridge, but is marked by cairns. Turn right and head downhill in the meadow. Stay to the left along a little gully. Look for a log post in the meadow below. GPS: N37 43.01' / W107 47.29'. If you don't see the trail, stay close to the little gully and you'll come upon the path in about 0.1 mile. Turn left onto the trail, which soon curves to the left.

5.1 Enjoy the view of craggy peaks to the east, including Twilight Peak, the closest.

6.5 Reach the Coal Creek Trailhead along US 550. Elevation: 10,280 feet. GPS: N37 42.51' / W107 46.06'. To complete the entire loop hike, continue walking along the road, being mindful of oncoming traffic.

7.7 Cross the highway and turn right onto the dirt road to the Pass Creek Trailhead.

7.8 Arrive back at the trailhead.

OPTION

If you have two vehicles, you can make this a point-to-point hike of 6.5 miles. From Silverton, drive south about 12.4 miles on US 550. At mile marker 58, leave one car at the dirt parking area on the left side of the road just before a large left switchback. GPS: N37 42.51' / W107 46.06'. Then proceed to the Pass Creek Trailhead for the start of the hike. There is a vault toilet on the east side of the highway at Coal Bank Pass. Turn right just before the top of Coal Bank Pass to enter a gravel parking area where you can access this trailhead. Follow the Miles and Directions to mile 6.5. Turn right, cross the road, and walk about 0.1 mile along the left side up to the parking area, and your shuttle vehicle, back at mile marker 58.

52 FIRST FORK AND RED CREEK LOOP

WHY GO?

The First Fork Trail follows a sparkling little creek up to Missionary Ridge northeast of Durango. Although parts of this forest burned in 2002, the vegetation is lush and trees are growing again. The trail travels through a forest of Douglas fir, ponderosa pine, Gambel oak, and aspen. After joining the Missionary Ridge Trail, head northeast through mixed conifer and aspen forests and several beautiful meadows, with occasional views north to the craggy San Juan Mountains. Return via Red Creek Trail, which drops down several steep switchbacks, then past huge aspens. The trail intersects the road about 0.3 mile above the First Fork Trailhead—a beautiful hike when aspens are golden!

THE RUNDOWN

Start: From the First Fork Trailhead
Distance: 10.0-mile loop
Approximate hiking time: 4.5 to 7 hours
Difficulty: Difficult due to distance and some steep spots
Elevation gain: 2,150 feet (including undulations)
Seasons: Best from May through Oct
Trail surface: Dirt trail, sometimes steep
Other trail users: Equestrians, mountain bikers, hunters (in season)
Canine compatibility: Dogs must be under control
Fees and permits: None
Maps: USGS Durango East, Hermosa, Lemon Reservoir, and Rules Hill (these maps are ancient and the trail is not shown on them); Nat Geo

Trails Illustrated 145 Pagosa Springs/ Bayfield; Latitude 40° Southwest Colorado
Trail contacts: San Juan National Forest, Columbine Ranger District, Bayfield; (970) 884-2512; www.fs .usda.gov/sanjuan
Other: No facilities at the trailhead. Although water may be available in First Fork and Red Creek, cattle graze in this area, so be sure to purify any creek water before drinking, or bring your own water. Because of the Missionary Ridge Fire of 2002, some portions of the access road may be subject to mudslides. The road is closed by snow 0.9 mile from the trailhead. The trail is neither maintained nor marked for winter use.

FINDING THE TRAILHEAD

From the intersection of US 550 and College Drive in Durango (near the train station), drive 0.2 mile into downtown on College Drive to East 3rd Avenue, turn left on East 3rd, and drive 0.7 mile to the intersection of East 3rd and 15th Street and Florida Road. Turn sort of right onto Florida Road / La Plata CR 240 and drive 9.4 miles northeast to the sign COLVIG SILVER CAMPS. Turn left here onto dirt LPCR 246 and drive 1 mile past the camps. The road gets rougher and bumpier. In another 0.3 mile there is a gate, which you may have to open and close. You can park here, off the road. The road beyond is best negotiated with a high-clearance vehicle (4WD not necessary). A parking area is available about 0.25 mile beyond the gate. Park here if the road is getting too rough for your vehicle. The trailhead and a small parking area are another 0.35 mile from this point. The trailhead is marked by a TRAIL sign on the left side of the road. Vehicles are not allowed beyond this point.
GPS: N37 21.31' / W107 44.50'

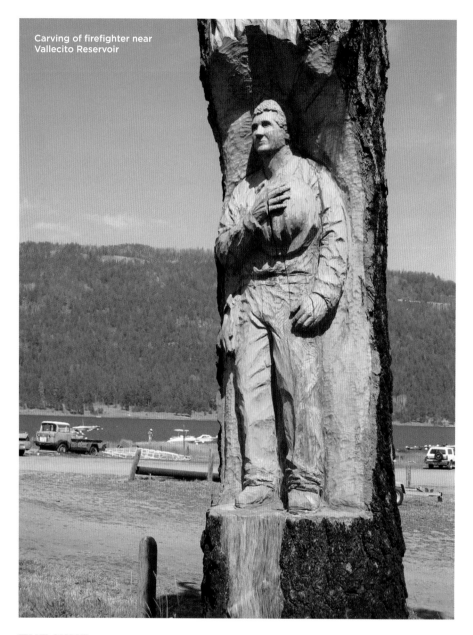

Carving of firefighter near Vallecito Reservoir

THE HIKE

Many early settlers to the Animas Valley were Civil War veterans. Legend has it that one morning, fog cloaked a ridge northeast of Durango. The veterans noticed a similarity with Missionary Ridge, site of a famous Civil War battle near Chattanooga, Tennessee. The ridge has since been known as Missionary Ridge.

On June 9, 2002, a small fire started along the Missionary Ridge Road, allegedly by a discarded cigarette. Little moisture had fallen during winter, and the spring continued to be very dry and hot. Reservoirs were lower than usual and the land was parched.

Scorched ponderosa
pine and aspen

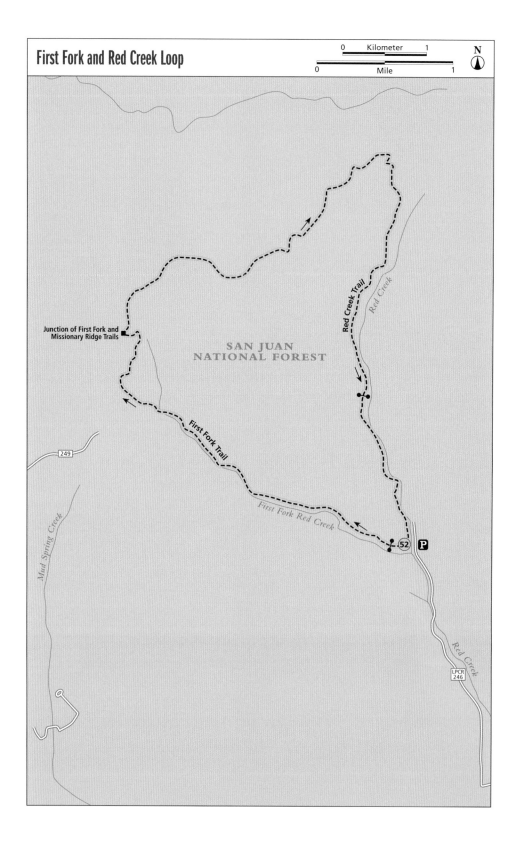

First Fork and Red Creek Loop

0   Kilometer   1

0   Mile   1

N

SAN JUAN
NATIONAL FOREST

Junction of First Fork and
Missionary Ridge Trails

Red Creek Trail

Red Creek

First Fork Trail

First Fork Red Creek

Mud Spring Creek

249

52

P

Red Creek

LPCR
246

The extremely dry trees quickly became torches, and the fire burned 6,500 acres the first day. Helicopters dropped buckets of water on the fire, slurry bombers covered trees with fire retardant, and ground crews created firebreaks and put out spot fires. The fire continued to spread in the dry forest, fanned by typical afternoon winds. Because of dry vegetation the fire even burned downhill, an unusual event. By July 17 officials declared the fire was contained after burning eighty-three buildings and 73,391 acres of forest, and causing some 2,100 people to flee at times. The fire actually continued to burn in small patches until winter snows finally extinguished the stubborn flames.

One firefighter was killed by a falling tree. A tour of tree carvings depicting firefighters and other emergency responders in action can be seen around Vallecito Reservoir, just east of this hike. The carvings were created in dead ponderosa pine trees. One tree with its nearby plaque commemorates the fallen firefighter.

From the smoke and media reports, people envisioned the entire area from Missionary Ridge to Lemon Reservoir to Vallecito Reservoir as being burned to a crisp. Forest fires typically jump around, and this one was no exception. Burned homes were surrounded by unburned forest, while blackened forest encircled unburned homes. This hop-skip-jump phenomenon is readily observed throughout this hike.

In early August a few rainstorms passed over the burned area. In places where trees and ground cover had been destroyed, roots no longer held the soil together. As rain moistened the charred earth, mudslides flowed downhill across roads, into homes and businesses, making a mess of everything in their way. One slide closed the access road to First Fork Trail. Geologists studied one newly created arroyo and discovered that fires and resulting debris flows have occurred in the Vallecito Valley about every 350 years for the last 3,500 years!

By early October 2002, little Gambel oak shoots started to poke through the burned ground. Crop dusters dropped pounds of plant and grass seeds, which sprouted the next spring, along with seeds already in the ground. Within two years grasses, aspen sprouts, and flowers grew knee-high. While you can still see the effects of the fire, nature continues to heal the burned scars.

Starting up First Fork Trail, you'll first cross Red Creek, then come upon a gate. Please close the gate behind you, as cattle graze in this area. The trail follows little First Fork, where flowers sometimes grow waist-high. You'll hike in and out of areas that were burned in the fire. In one place the general area has been burned, except for one tree. In a large open area, the trail climbs steeply, drops, and climbs again.

When you come to a Y intersection, know that you are not at Missionary Ridge. Turn left and continue up to a T intersection with the Missionary Ridge Trail, passing through a burned area. The fire scorched many parts of the ridge, but aspen are once again growing and the vegetation is quite thick among the ghost trees. One advantage of the fire: The view to the north of the craggy San Juan Mountains and the Hermosa Cliffs has improved.

Continue hiking along the ridge, over one saddle to a second saddle. Here the Red Creek Trail drops off the ridge to the right. After switchbacking steeply off Missionary Ridge, Red Creek Trail then wanders through a huge, beautiful aspen forest (making an excellent fall hike) and shoulder-high cow parsnip that sometimes hides the trail. Watch for elk and deer. When you come to a road, turn right to return to your vehicle.

MILES AND DIRECTIONS

0.0 Start at the First Fork Trailhead. Elevation: 7,880 feet. Immediately cross Red Creek and soon arrive at a gate. Remember to close the gate behind you.

2.7 Arrive at an open area filled with bushes. A cliff looms ahead of you. The trail climbs steeply, then drops down and climbs up again.

3.3 The trail arrives at a Y intersection. Turn left here to continue climbing to Missionary Ridge Trail.

3.4 Reach the junction with Missionary Ridge Trail. GPS: N37 22.62' / W107 46.83'. Turn right and proceed north, then east along the ridge.

4.8 Arrive at a large meadow ringed with little aspen and some conifers.

5.2 The trail starts descending, sometimes steeply.

5.5 Pass by an old stile. Before the fire the trail crossed a fence on the stile.

6.0 After dropping and switchbacking down, arrive at a saddle. The trail appears to fork. Take the trail to the left that goes around the hill in front of you. Lots of bushes and flowers grow along the contouring trail.

6.5 Reach the junction with the Red Creek Trail. Elevation: 9,840 feet. GPS: N37 23.74' / W107 44.68'. Turn right, drop down, and follow the steep switch-backs. The trail sign faces east, so look carefully for it.

6.8 The trail mellows out and meanders through a thick aspen forest with lush vegetation.

8.5 Come to a gate. Make sure to close it behind you. Cross the creek to the left. The trail crosses the creek a number of times as you continue down. There are some nice red cliffs along the trail also.

9.7 Arrive at a dirt road (closed to motorized traffic). GPS: N37 21.51' / W107 44.50'. Turn right and walk down the road back to your vehicle.

10.0 Arrive back at the First Fork Trailhead.

APPENDIX A: HIKING GEAR

DAY HIKE GEAR

Certain items are necessary, and desirable, to make your day hikes with your dog safer and more enjoyable. The following list describes gear options that can increase your safety and that of your dog, enhancing your hiking experience. Many of the day hike equipment items are also essential building blocks to a successful backpacking excursion.

COLLARS AND HARNESSES

Either a collar or harness is suitable, but a colorful harness makes your dog more visible and identifies them as domestic. For dogs of intimidating size or appearance, a colorful harness emphasizes their pet status. It is easier to restrain a dog by a harness than a collar when necessary. In addition, a harness is a safer restraint (a collar could slip off or choke your dog) should you need to pull them out of water or hoist them up a hillside. Harnesses are safer than collars off leash because they reduce the risk of neck injury or suffocation from a snag or tangle in brush or with a branch. With an adult dog who insists on pulling you along, the harness will give you more control and prevent damage to his neck and throat.

Material: Although leather is the most durable, nylon collars and harnesses are available in vibrant colors, are usually adjustable, and dry more quickly and without shrinkage. Your dog is less likely to lose a collar or harness with a plastic snap-in clasp than a metal buckle when he's running, swimming, and jostling about.

Fit: You should be able to easily slip your flat hand under the collar and rotate it; however, the collar should not be so loose that it can slip over your dog's head. A puppy will need to be fitted with a new collar a few times as he grows. Harnesses need to fit loosely enough to allow full expansion of the chest and a free stride.

Many trainers now consider choke collars an inhumane training tool, and a choke collar as a permanent collar can be deadly. To mention a few real-life scenarios: One dog was strangled when another dog's jaw got twisted in the choke collar during rambunctious play; another dog snagged his choke collar on a low branch while running through the brush; and another slipped and fell off a boulder, hanging himself at the end of a leash and choke collar.

IDENTIFICATION TAGS

The sight, smell, or sound of another animal could lure your dog away, and thunder or gunshots could startle your dog and cause them to run off. Whatever the reason for the separation, you want to facilitate a reunion. On the trail a tag is the most obvious way to reunite a lost dog and its owner. The information should include the dog's name (and your last name) and a phone number, at the very least. (Some owners put a physical address on the tag; this is up to you.) If another person gets close enough to your dog to see the tag, the first thing he or she will look for is a name. Calling the dog by its name will establish some communication and trust. The phone number allows the finder to leave a message. Along with your dog's nametag, attach an up-to-date rabies tag to their collar. This is required in some areas, and it's never a bad idea to let the humans who find your dog know they're vaccinated.

LEASHES

A leash that will suffer the abuse of the trail (streams, rain, snow, and rocks) must be durable. On the one hand, a colored nylon webbing leash is light, dries quickly, and is easy to spot when you lay it down. You can design your own leash inexpensively by buying nylon webbing by the foot at a mountaineering store and the clasp at a hardware store. (I use a carabiner in place of a traditional clasp, since my dog is stronger than he appears and has broken more than one clasp when in hot pursuit of rabbits.)

On the other hand, leather leashes stay the cleanest and last forever. Place a piece of colored tape or tie a strand of colored fabric to the handle to make finding the leash easier when it is on the ground. Leather leashes are often required in obedience classes.

If you are hiking in a strictly on-leash environment, expandable leashes blend control and freedom. The leashes come in varied lengths and strengths based on dog weight. An expandable leash can also convert into a tie-out line.

REFLECTIVE VEST

If you are going to hike during hunting season, your dog should wear a bright, light-weight reflective vest, specially designed for sporting dogs. This will help distinguish your dog from wildlife.

BOOTIES

If your dog is only an occasional hiker that spends most of his time sauntering across the lawn at home, his pads may get tender after just a couple of miles. Booties can give relief to your dog's sore paws until his pads toughen, as well as prevent cuts from crusty or icy trail conditions. Your dog should practice wearing booties at home before using them on the trail.

Where to buy booties: Booties come in different sizes and materials and are available through pet supply stores, mail-order and online outlets, and mountaineering stores, and are also advertised in dogsledding magazines.

DOG PACKS

Although it is a good idea to introduce young dogs to the idea of packs, loaded packs should be used only on fit, medium-to-large adult dogs (thirty-five pounds or more). Most packs are designed to lie on the dog's back like a saddle with a pouch on each side. The pack weight should not exceed one-quarter to one-third of your dog's weight. (For example, a forty-pound dog should not carry more than ten to thirteen pounds of evenly distributed weight.)

Packs are more appropriate for overnight trips than day hikes. There's significantly more gear when you go overnight, and it's a good use of dog power to train a medium- or large-size dog to assist by carrying her booties, first-aid kit, food and treats, and other accessories related to her needs. (See the introduction for pack-training information.)

Dog pack

Choosing packs: Packs are sold in pet supply stores, outdoor recreation stores, and mail-order and online outlets. They come in different sizes with adjustable straps. Look for the design that best conforms to your dog's body. The pack should feature breathable material, rounded corners, and padding for additional comfort.

Pack fitting: Your dog's comfort depends on a proper fit. The pack should sit on his shoulders between the base of the neck and just short of the hips. There should be one strap that clips on the front of his chest and one or two belly straps to stabilize the pack. Straps should be tight enough to keep the pack in place but loose enough to allow full stride without chafing and comfortable expansion of the chest for breathing.

Loading the pack: Stuff the pack with crumpled newspaper first. Then, once your dog is accustomed to the pack and his endurance has built up, gradually increase the load from 10 percent of his weight not to exceed one-quarter to one-third of his weight. If you use a pack only occasionally, keep the weight on the lighter side. The weight should be equal and evenly distributed to avoid interfering with your dog's balance.

Pack safety: Keep your dog on leash when he is wearing his pack. Packs can make balance awkward when negotiating narrow mountainside trails or crossing fast streams. Give him a break every hour or so by removing the pack so he can enjoy the freedom you both came for by playing, swimming, and rolling around without risking injury to himself and damage to his pack and cargo.

LIFE VEST

A life vest is important to have if you are going to hike near rivers and lakes or if you have to cross high water, especially with dogs that are drawn to water. An elderly or tired dog is more at risk in the water during a hike than she would be at the beach for the day.

FLASHLIGHT AND EXTRA BATTERIES

You will be thankful for a flashlight—especially one that fits in a daypack—if you are still hiking after sunset.

MATCHES AND/OR LIGHTER

Temperatures can drop quickly after the sun goes down. If you are lost or injured, a fire can help keep you warm until daylight or help arrives. Put matches and a strike strip in a pill bottle to protect them from the elements. Gas clicker lighters are lightweight and can be easier to use in inclement weather.

FOOD

It is not necessary to increase your dog's amount of food for a day hike. Instead, supplement his diet at snack breaks. Pack dog biscuits, jerky treats, and a little extra dry kibble. Some dogs like carrots, apples, and melon pieces as much as any canine treat. (Never feed chocolate to dogs. It is toxic.)

In cold weather, bring higher-protein dog snacks. Look for real liver, turkey, chicken, or egg as the first ingredient and avoid products with sugar and fillers.

PLASTIC RESEALABLE BAGS

The airtight, self-sealing invention is in the top five essentials for the trail. These bags are great for carrying food, treats, medication, and first-aid necessities, and they can easily be converted into food and water bowls. Their "sealing" quality also comes in handy for disposing of dog waste.

WATER

Water is as essential to your dog as it is to you. Do not skimp on bringing water or count on finding it along the trail. Dehydration can result in sluggishness, kidney problems, and heat stroke. Both humans and dogs are vulnerable to dehydration in the heat and at high elevations.

Do not let your dog drink from standing water in puddles, ponds, lakes, or swimming holes in slow-moving creeks and rivers. That's where different forms of bacteria and algae breed, and small dogs and puppies have been known to get very ill and in some cases die from drinking contaminated water. Be especially wary of areas where cattle graze.

Both dogs and humans are susceptible to the intestinal parasite *Giardia lamblia*, which can cause cramping and diarrhea, leading to serious dehydration. Giardia can be present in all sources of untreated water.

How Much Water Do I Need?

Carry at least eight ounces of water per dog per hour of hiking. Consider that an average walking pace on level ground is about 3 miles per hour. Fill plastic water bottles three-quarters full and place in the freezer the night before. Your dog will have a source of cool fresh water as the ice melts along the way. Two frozen water bottles can also keep her cooler if you place one in each pouch of her dog pack.

Offer water to your dog frequently (every half-hour, or more frequently on hot days). It is easier to regulate hydration with regular small intakes of water.

Snow may keep your dog cool, but do not believe that a hot, thirsty dog will instinctively know to eat snow to quench her thirst. One hiker reported that her Southern California–born-and-raised dog was almost delirious from dehydration after she took him on a summer hike up a mountain where she thought the abundant snow would make up for the lack of water.

BOWLS

Weight and encumbrances are the main concerns when packing for a hike. There are plenty of ways to create inexpensive doggie dinnerware on the trail. Paper or plastic picnic plates and bowls are lightweight and adequate for food and water. A plastic resealable bag can store the kibble and convert into a food dish or water bowl (you'll need to hold the bag while your dog drinks from it). Pet supply stores and mail-order and online outlets have several doggie gadgets for carrying and serving food and water on the trail, from canteens to collapsible bowls.

FIRST-AID KIT

Although you cannot prepare for all mishaps, it is best to have a few first-aid items. See the First-Aid Kit Checklist in Appendix B.

BACKPACKING GEAR

Maybe it's the thought of retreating deeper into the solitary beauty of the wilderness with your four-legged companion that draws you. Or perhaps you're satisfied with setting up camp a few miles up the trailhead to share an easy, idyllic overnight in the great outdoors with him. Whichever appeals to you, backpacking with your dog requires some extra necessities and additional planning. Your goal is to travel light while considering emergencies, outdoor dining pleasures, and sleeping comforts for both you and your dog. With good planning and careful attention to gear, backpacking can heighten the pleasures of the trail for you and your dog.

Add the following things to your list for a backpacking adventure:

PERMITS

Permits are generally obtained from ranger stations of the government agency that manages the land you wish to hike on (e.g., national or state park and forest, Bureau of Land Management). Permits are usually required for overnights in wilderness areas and in other heavily used recreation areas. In some places, registering or obtaining a permit can be required even for day hiking. In popular areas where use is strictly regulated, you may have to apply for a permit several months ahead of time.

FOOD

Make a list of the number of meals and snacks per hiking day for you and your dog. Package your dog's meals and snacks (preferably dry or semi-moist) individually in resealable bags for convenience and to keep food smells from attracting bears.

You can safely supplement your dog's dry kibbles with most human food you would bring for yourself, except sugar and chocolate (remember, chocolate is toxic to dogs as well as cats). Plan to take one extra cup of human food per day to supplement your dog's dinner in camp. Pasta and rice are lightweight and easy to cook in camp and can be prepared creatively for extra taste and nutrition.

Meat eaters can add canned tuna or chicken, as well as any freeze-dried meat sauce or soup mix. Either way, your dog will appreciate the added flavor to her kibbles and will benefit from the energy fuel. (**Note:** Introduce her to new foods at home gradually before going on an overnight trip.)

Cutting your dog's regular dog food with puppy food will add the extra protein and fat needed for higher-calorie-burning backpacking excursions. Begin mixing in small amounts of puppy food about three days before the hike so your dog's digestive system can adapt gradually.

DAY HIKE GEAR CHECKLIST

- ❏ Flea and tick treatment application prior to hike
- ❏ Bug repellent in sealed plastic bag
- ❏ Collar and bandanna or colorful harness with ID tag and rabies tag
- ❏ Leash
- ❏ Plastic water containers full of water: thirty-two-ounce bottle for half-day hike (under 4 hours) and two-quart bottle for longer hikes
- ❏ Eight ounces of water per dog per hour (or 3 miles) of hiking, in addition to water for you, to be carried with you
- ❏ Water purifier for full-day hikes
- ❏ Snacks for you and your pet
- ❏ Collapsible dish or resealable bag
- ❏ Plastic bags for cleaning up after your dog
- ❏ Sunscreen for tips of ears and nose
- ❏ Booties for pooch and comfortable, sturdy, waterproof boots for you
- ❏ Extra clothing (sweater or coat for thin-coated dog, sweater and windbreaker for you)
- ❏ Pocketknife (Swiss Army–type knife that includes additional tools: fork, scissors, pliers, file)
- ❏ Flashlight and extra batteries
- ❏ Matches or cigarette lighter and emergency fire starter
- ❏ First-aid kit
- ❏ Telephone number and address of closest veterinarian

BACKPACKING GEAR CHECKLIST

Be sure to pack all items on the day hike checklist, plus the following:

Dog Necessities

- ❏ Extra leash or rope
- ❏ Dog pack for your dog and backpack with internal frame for you
- ❏ Doggie bedroll (foam sleeping pad)
- ❏ Dog's favorite chew toy
- ❏ Dog food (number of days on the trail times three meals a day)
- ❏ Additional water in a two-quart bottle
- ❏ Water purifier
- ❏ Dog snacks (enough for six rest stops per hiking day)
- ❏ Nylon tie-out line in camp (expandable leash can be an extra leash and tie-out rope)

Human Necessities

- ❏ Tent with rain fly (large enough for you and your dog to sleep inside)
- ❏ Clothing (raingear, gloves, fleece or knit hat, long pants, wicking top, fleece top, socks)
- ❏ Camp stove and fuel bottle
- ❏ Iodine tablets (backup water purifier)
- ❏ Food (lightweight, nutritious carbs and proteins—instant oatmeal, dried fruits and nuts, pasta, rice, canned tuna, dehydrated backpacking meals, tea bags or cocoa packets)
- ❏ Extra garbage bags
- ❏ Bear-proof food canisters
- ❏ Pepper spray (if hiking in bear country)

THREE REASONS WHY YOUR DOG SHOULD BE ATTENDED IN CAMP AT ALL TIMES

1. He would be vulnerable to wild predators otherwise.
2. It would be unkind to cause him the stress of being separated from you in unfamiliar surroundings.
3. Separation anxiety is often expressed through barking, whining, and howling, which ruins the wilderness experience for other campers. Do not forget that separation anxiety could also bring on a chewing rampage that might leave you with a shredded tent, sleeping bag, or backpack.

SETTING UP CAMP

1. Pick your campsite in daylight, taking into account exposure, water, mosquitoes, and other features that might affect your dog's comfort.
2. Put your dog on her tie-out line, where she can curl up to rest, and give her water while you set up camp (sleeping and cooking quarters). Keep her water bowl full, within easy reach but out of the "step and spill" zone.
3. Get enough water to boil or filter for cooking dinner and breakfast, and enough drinking water for you and your dog for the evening and following trail day (eight ounces per mile per dog).
4. Prepare dinner for you and your dog.
5. Wash the dishes and burn or seal garbage in plastic bags for pack-out, to remove any food smells from camp. Be sure to use the bear-proof metal food storage bins whenever provided, and consider buying your own small bear-proof canisters for your aromatic goods.
6. Walk your dog before bedtime, tidy up camp, and snuggle up for the night.

BREAKING CAMP

1. Walk your dog and clean up any of her waste.
2. Share a hot breakfast with her (instant hot cereal or scrambled eggs over her kibble, with a hot drink for you and warm water for her).
3. Clean up and pack up. Leave your campsite cleaner than you found it.

WATER

You need to take enough water for drinking (for you and your dog) and cooking. If you are sure of the availability of water, consider carrying less and boiling, filtering, or chemically treating the water in camp. Several water purification systems are available at outdoor recreation stores, but be aware that some dogs will not drink chemically treated water.

BEDDING

For yourself, choose a sleeping bag rated to keep you warm in the region and season in which you are backpacking.

For your dog, carry a piece of foam and a towel, which you can roll up with your sleeping bag. Or try a lightweight dog bedroll, designed to be cuddly on one side and durable on the side in contact with the ground; dog bedrolls are available in pet supply stores and through mail-order and online outlets.

If you choose to sleep under the stars, make sure your dog is staked on a line (6-foot radius from a stake or tree) short enough to keep him away from the campfire but long enough to allow him to have physical contact with you. Physical contact gives your dog the security that will help keep him quieter if the sounds of the dark outdoors are new to him. It enables you to hush him at the first hint of a growl, keeps him warmer on cold nights, and lets you know when he's on alert.

APPENDIX B: MEDICAL EMERGENCIES AND TREATMENT

Planning, a common-sense approach, and a leash will help prevent most mishaps on the trail. Keep your dog on leash when:

- Hiking in territory known for its higher concentration of specific hazards (bears, mountain lions, snakes, skunks)
- Crossing fast-moving streams
- Negotiating narrow mountainside trails
- Hiking in wind and snow (dogs can become disoriented and lose their way)

If your dog gets into trouble, here are some basic first-aid treatments you can administer until you can get him to a vet.

BLEEDING FROM CUTS OR WOUNDS

1. Remove any obvious foreign object.
2. Rinse the area with warm water or 3 percent hydrogen peroxide.
3. Cover the wound with clean gauze or cloth and apply firm, direct pressure over the wound for about ten minutes, to allow clotting to occur and bleeding to stop.
4. Place a nonstick pad or gauze over the wound and bandage with gauze wraps (the stretchy, clingy type). For a paw wound, cover the bandaging with a bootie. (An old sock with duct tape on the bottom is a good bootie substitute. Use adhesive tape around the sock to prevent it from slipping off. Be careful not to impede circulation.)

FROSTBITE

Frostbite is the freezing of a body part exposed to extreme cold. The tips of dog's ears and footpads are the most vulnerable. The best thing to do is to remove your dog from the cold and seek medical attention from a veterinarian as soon as possible.

HEATSTROKE

Heatstroke occurs when a dog's body temperature is rising rapidly above 104°F and panting is ineffective to regulate temperature. To treat heatstroke:

1. Get your dog out of the sun and begin reducing body temperature (no lower than 103°F) by applying water-soaked towels on her head (to cool the brain), chest, abdomen, and feet.
2. Let your dog stand in a pond, lake, or stream while you gently pour water over them. Avoid icy water—it can chill them too quickly.

HYPOTHERMIA

Hypothermia occurs when a dog's body temperature drops below 95°F because of over-exposure to cold weather.

1. Bring your dog indoors or into a sheltered area where you can make a fire.
2. Wrap him in a blanket, towel, sleeping bag, your clothing, or whatever you have available, or place warm water bottles in a towel next to him.
3. Hold him close to you for body heat.

INSECT BITES

Bee stings and spider bites may cause itching, swelling, and hives. To treat insect bites:

1. If the stinger is still present, scrape it off with your nail or tweezers at the base, away from the point of entry. (Pressing the stinger or trying to pick it from the top can release more toxin.)
2. Apply a cold compress to the area and spray it with a topical analgesic like Benadryl spray, to relieve the itch and pain.
3. As a precaution, carry an over-the-counter antihistamine (such as Benadryl) and ask your vet about the appropriate dosage before you leave, in case your dog has an extreme allergic reaction with excessive swelling.

FIRST-AID KIT CHECKLIST

- ❏ First-aid book
- ❏ Muzzle: The most loving dogs can snap and bite when in pain. Muzzles come in different styles and sizes to fit all dog nose shapes.
- ❏ Buffered aspirin: Older dogs in particular may be stiff and sore at the end of a hike or a backpacking excursion. Consult your vet on the appropriate dosage.
- ❏ Scissors (rounded tips) to trim hair around a wound
- ❏ Hydrogen peroxide (3 percent) to disinfect surface abrasions and wounds
- ❏ Antiseptic ointment
- ❏ Gauze pads and gauze
- ❏ Clingy gauze wraps and elastic bandages
- ❏ Sock or bootie to protect a wounded foot
- ❏ Duct tape to wrap around a sock used as a bootie
- ❏ Tweezers to remove ticks, needles, or foreign objects in a wound
- ❏ Styptic powder for bleeding
- ❏ Rectal thermometer
- ❏ Hydrocortisone spray to relieve plant rashes and stings
- ❏ Lemon juice for a quick rinse if your dog is skunked; recipe for de-skunking shampoo mix

- ❏ Your veterinarian's telephone number and the telephone number of the veterinary clinic closest to the trailhead
- ❏ National Animal Poison Control Center phone number: (888) 426-4435

SKUNKED

When your dog gets skunked, a potent, smelly cloud of spray burns his eyes and makes his mouth foam. The smell can make you gag, and contact with the spray on your dog's coat can give your skin a tingling, burning sensation. Apply de-skunking shampoo as soon as possible.

De-Skunking Shampoo Mix:

1 quart hydrogen peroxide
¼ cup baking soda
1 tablespoon dishwashing detergent

Put on rubber gloves and thoroughly wet your dog, apply mixture, and let stand for fifteen minutes; rinse and repeat as needed.

SORE MUSCLES

1. Rest your dog.
2. Apply cold-water compresses to tight muscle areas to reduce inflammation.
3. Administer buffered aspirin (check with your vet on dosage for your dog's breed and weight).

VENOMOUS BITES

1. Keep your dog calm (activity stimulates the absorption of venom).
2. Rinse the area with water, and transport your dog to the nearest vet.

CARDIOPULMONARY RESUSCITATION

Check with your veterinarian or local humane society for pet CPR classes.

APPENDIX C: WILDLIFE CONFLICTS

Most hikers with dogs come to the natural world "in peace," to retreat and absorb the beauty. Nevertheless, you are still an uninvited guest at best. Respect the animals whose home you are in, and trespass lightly.

PROTECTING WILDLIFE

Leashes are mandatory in many outdoor recreation areas, primarily to protect the wildlife that lives, breeds, migrates, or nests there. Even in areas where your dog is allowed off leash, do not let him chase wildlife or livestock for sport. It stresses and depletes the animal of survival energy and can cause a serious injury that leads to a cruel, agonizing death.

In the spring nesting birds are very vulnerable to free-roaming dogs in meadows and low brush. Young deer can be separated from their mothers and fall prey to your dog's primal but inappropriate impulses.

Your companion is more likely to chase wildlife at the beginning of the hike, when he is fresh out of the starting gate. Keep him on leash for about thirty minutes while he walks off some of his excess energy and gets used to his surroundings.

If you have any doubts about your dog's behavior, keep him leashed.

PREVENTING ENCOUNTERS

The potential for being injured or killed by a wild animal is extremely low compared with many other natural hazards. Information and preparedness is the safest way for hikers with dogs to enjoy their time on the trail. Although there is no absolute rule to wild animal behavior, there is sufficient knowledge to trust some established guidelines. When given the opportunity, most wild animals are more than happy to avoid humans; unfortunately, people often feed wild animals because they look cute and cuddly. Once a wild animal gets a taste of human food, it becomes habituated to that food and will not forget that humans are a source of food. Wild animals that have grown accustomed to human food and garbage can become brazen, posing a threat to human safety. In bears these bad

BEAR FACTS
- Bears can run, swim, and climb trees.
- Bears have good vision, excellent hearing, and a superior sense of smell.
- Bears are curious and attracted to food smells.
- Bears can be out at any time of day but are most active in the coolness of dawn and dusk and after dark.

  Bears and wild animals in general prefer anonymity. If they know you are out there, they will avoid your path.

"human-engendered" habits identify them as "problem" bears, which sadly leads to their eventual and inevitable destruction. If you love wild animals, respect them, admire them from a safe distance, and please do not feed them.

Be informed about where you plan to hike and what lives there. Contact the region's fish and game, park, or forest headquarters. Keep your eyes open and learn to identify tracks, scat, and concealed kill sites. Keep your dog on a leash in questionable surroundings.

BEARS AND BEAR SAFETY

Development encroaching on habitat and more hikers in remote wilderness areas have increased the bear's exposure to humans, their food, and their garbage. It is more important than ever to know how to minimize the risk of an encounter and what to do if one occurs.

There is no scientific evidence that dogs are "bear bait." But a loose dog in bear country runs more of a chance of surprising a bear and antagonizing it with barking and other antics. Even if your dog gets lucky and runs back to you unharmed, your problems are just beginning if the bear follows.

Stay on the trail, where there are fewer chances of surprising a bear snacking in a berry patch. Make your presence known with noise that is distinctly man-made, such as talking, singing, or humming a tune. The slight jingle of a metal ID tag against the metal rabies tag on your dog's collar or harness acts like a bell and can help notify bears of your presence. A small bell on the dog collar and one your belt, walking stick, or boot lace is an even stronger statement in bear country.

Bear cub

When it comes to odor, in bear country the motto is "less is safer." Pack all food items (human and dog) and any other odorous items in airtight resealable bags. Dispose of all items with food smells in airtight bags or in bear-proof storage containers. Clean your dishes and pet bowls as quickly as possible so food smells do not float through the forest as a dinner invitation to the local bears. Some national forests and wilderness areas require that campers use portable "bear-resistant food canisters." These plastic canisters (some collapsible) are available for sale and rent at sporting goods stores and some ranger stations.

If you see a bear in the distance, stop, stay calm, and don't run. Keep your dog close to your side on leash. You should feel awe rather than panic. Walk a wide upwind detour so the animal can get your scent, and make loud banging or clanging noises as you leave the area. If the bear is at closer range, the same principles apply while you keep your eye on the bear. If the terrain doesn't allow you to negotiate a detour, back down the trail slowly. Avoid sudden movements that could spook or provoke the bear. Be cool, slow, but deliberate as you make your retreat.

MOUNTAIN LIONS

There are fewer mountain lions than bears in the wilderness, and the mountain lion population is concentrated in the western United States and Canada. As with bears, development and human intrusion are at the core of encounter problems.

Know what to do to avoid and manage an encounter:

- Keep your dog on leash on the trail.

- Keep your dog in the tent at night.

- Seeing doesn't mean attacking. If you come across a mountain lion, stay far enough away to give it the opportunity to avoid you.

- Do not approach or provoke the lion.

- Walk away slowly and maintain eye contact. Running will stimulate the lion's predatory instinct to chase and hunt.

- Make yourself big by putting your arms above your head and waving them. Use your jacket or walking stick above your head to appear bigger. Do not bend down or make any motion that will make you look or sound like easy prey.

- Shout and make noise.

- If necessary, walking sticks can be weapons, as can rocks or anything you can get your hands on to fight back with.

MOUNTAIN LION FACTS
- Mountain lions are elusive, and preying on humans is uncharacteristic.
- Mountain lions are most active at dawn and dusk and usually hunt at night.
- They are solitary and secretive and require a vegetated habitat for camouflage while they stalk prey.
- Their meal of choice is big game (deer, bighorn sheep, and elk). In the absence of game, however, they can make a meal of domestic livestock and small mammals.
- They prefer to feed on what they kill. An unattended dog in camp is far more appetizing than his kibble.

OTHER ANIMALS

Bobcats: Smaller than mountain lions, these wild cats are no threat to humans and would prefer climbing a tree over confronting your dog.

Coyotes: In spite of their ability to survive persecution in healthier numbers than their wolf cousins, coyotes are not a threat on the trail. Hikers are more fortunate than some homeowners, though. In some neighborhoods of Southern California and the Southwest, loss of habitat to housing developments has increased the incidence of unattended pets turning into a meal for a coyote.

Skunks and porcupines: Skunks and porcupines are primarily nocturnal and will fend off the curious with a spray or shot of barbed needles, respectively. It's a good idea to carry lemon juice concentrate and a pair of disposable latex gloves (available in hardware store paint departments) in your pack in case your dog gets sprayed by a skunk. A lemon juice rub and stream water rinse will tone down some of the fumes until you can give your pooch a full spa treatment—with a de-skunking shampoo mix—at a pet wash location, groomer, veterinarian, or in your own backyard. Always carry a couple of dog towels or old sheets in your car to wrap your dog and protect your upholstery. In a pinch large plastic trash bags and duct tape come in handy to create a barrier between the seats and a damp, stinky dog.

A dog pierced by a mask of porcupine quills is a pitiful sight. Few dogs can withstand the pain of having barbed needles pulled out of their faces by inexperienced, nervous hands without any anesthetic. Take your dog to a vet as quickly as possible.

Snakes: Snake bites are usually a result of stepping on a snake unknowingly rather than conscious provocation. Most snake bites occur on the nose or front legs and can be lethal to a small or young dog. If taken to the vet quickly, larger adult dogs will survive most bites. Ask your veterinarian if the recently developed rattlesnake vaccine would benefit your dog. Also ask your vet or local dog club about snake avoidance classes in your area. If the dog is bitten, first keep the dog calm (as activity stimulates the absorption of venom). Then rinse the area with water and transport your dog to the nearest vet.

Spiders: Most spider bites cause mild irritation and swelling, but in the case of black widow spiders, their venom can be more lethal than snake venom. Seek veterinary attention if your dog is bitten by a black widow spider.

Bees, wasps, hornets, and yellow jackets: A leash is the best preventive measure to protect your dog from her own curiosity. Insect nests can be in trees or on the ground.

HIKE INDEX